America in the Seventies

CultureAmerica

Karal Ann Marling
Erika Doss

Series Editors

America in the
Seventies

Edited by

Beth Bailey & David Farber

UNIVERSITY PRESS OF KANSAS

Published by the University Press of Kansas (Lawrence, Kansas 66049), which was organized by the Kansas Board of Regents and is operated and funded by Emporia State University, Fort Hays State University, Kansas State University, Pittsburg State University, the University of Kansas, and Wichita State University

Library of Congress Cataloging-in-Publication Data

America in the seventies / edited by Beth Bailey and David Farber.

p.   cm. — (CultureAmerica)

Includes bibliographical references and index.

ISBN 0-7006-1326-9 (cloth : alk. paper) — ISBN 0-7006-1327-7 (pbk. : alk. paper)

1. United States—History—1969–   2. United States—Social conditions—1960–1980.   3. Nineteen seventies.   I. Bailey, Beth L., 1957–   II. Farber, Dave.   III. Culture America

E855.A79   2004

973.924—dc22   2004001998

British Library Cataloguing-in-Publication Data is available.

Printed in the United States of America

10 9 8 7 6 5 4 3 2 1

The paper used in this publication meets the minimum requirements of the American National Standard for Permanence of Paper for Printed Library Materials Z39.48-1984.

Contents

Contents

Introduction

BETH BAILEY AND DAVID FARBER

The best-selling book of the 1970s was Hal Lindsey's *The Late Great Planet Earth*, a novelistic treatment of Biblical prophecy and the coming apocalypse that sold more than thirty million copies. In a time of great uncertainty, this work promised certainty: the end of the world. In the 1970s, it seems, millions found the apocalypse a comforting vision.

The 1970s may be our strangest decade. It was an era of incoherent impulses, contradictory desires, and even a fair amount of self-flagellation. It was the decade that gave us the yellow smiley face, a sadly ironic symbol for a nation on the downswing of postwar prosperity. It was an age of limits and an age of excess: gas lines, pet rocks, and sixteen minutes of orgasmic moaning in Donna Summer's 1975 hit, "Love to Love You Baby." The 1970s were a time when "earth-tone polyester" made sense.

Historians have been slow to put the 1970s into the narrative of American history. In part, it is a generational problem. While the 1960s found a willing legion of historians among those who had invested some of the best years of their lives in the social movements and struggles of the era, the 1970s has few impassioned champions, even among those who quite enjoyed coming of age during the decade. The 1960s tended to overshadow the 1970s, even as people lived them. It was hard not to measure the 1970s against the revolutionary fervor of protest, the black hole of the Vietnam War, the reach of the Great Society, the horrors of martyred leaders, and the grand possibility of a youth culture that hoped to change the world. The Sixties were a decade of passion, grandeur, and tragedy. The Seventies lacked that kind of emotional fire.

But the 1970s offer a different kind of drama. It was during the 1970s that the results of the major social movements of the previous two decades became concrete in American communities and in Americans' daily lives. It was during the 1970s that America struggled through a fundamental economic transformation that dislocated millions of workers and—though few understood it at the time—laid the foundations for a new, successful economy. It was during the 1970s, in the backwash of political and economic crisis, that Americans dealt with a productive uncertainty about the meanings of happiness, success, patriotism, and national identity.

America in the Seventies is not a comprehensive history of America in the 1970s, and it does not focus on the mechanics of policy and politics or the intimacies of private life.[1] Instead, this constellation of essays examines American public culture—the ways and places in which Americans struggled over the meaning of their society during these difficult years. The essays are unified around three major themes: the importance of economic forces in shaping the social and cultural life of 1970s America, the centrality of "identity" and the ways in which identities were reconfigured and contested during the decade, and the pervasive sense of cultural uncertainty that yielded both a culture of freedom and experimentation and a movement toward conservatism. The following sections offer basic information about—and frameworks for understanding—economic transformation, understandings of identity, and cultural uncertainty during the 1970s that should serve as a foundation for the specific arguments of individual essays.

❖ ❖ ❖

ECONOMIC TRANSFORMATION

In the 1970s, the economy betrayed the expectations of the American people. Since shortly after World War II, Americans had counted on a booming job market, low inflation, and steady economic growth. There had been brief recessions and spikes in unemployment, but until the 1970s such downturns had been short lived. In the 1970s, economists had to coin a new term for the economic crisis affecting the nation: stagflation. Inflation (rising prices) and stagnation (low growth or economic decline)—which conventional economic theory held could not happen simultaneously—had a stranglehold on the nation's economy.

The source of the malaise was complicated, but international economic competition, especially from Germany and Japan, was a critical factor. Although America had stood at the pinnacle of the world's economy at the end of World War II, by the 1970s its former enemies had become formidable industrial powers. America's own corporations had failed to invest heavily enough in research and development and in new technologies of production. As a result, the productivity of America's workers grew very slowly, though workers continued to be paid relatively well. As the cost of American-made goods increased even as their quality declined, two things happened. Increasingly, American manufacturers moved their operations outside the United States, where labor was cheap. As a result, by the late 1970s domestic manufacturing was in deep trouble. Throughout the nation, especially in the Northeast and the Midwest, industrial workers lost their jobs. Also, American consumers turned more and more frequently to well-made, relatively inexpensive imported goods. In 1971, for the first time in the twentieth century, the United States imported more goods than it exported. Unemployment rose.

High rates of unemployment had historically been associated with declining prices, as fewer dollars chased goods. But in the 1970s, despite high unemployment and low rates of economic growth, inflation soared. One major cause was federal government policy. By the late 1960s, President Johnson had created large federal budget deficits as he pursued a policy of "guns and butter," funding both the war in Vietnam and the expensive social programs of the Great Society. President Nixon did little to rein in these deficits, and high levels of government spending continued to heat up the economy. Policy makers were in a quandary. When they tried to stimulate the economy and so reduce unemployment, inflation grew. But when they tried to rein in inflation, unemployment skyrocketed. Politically, neither solution was winning.

The oil shocks of the 1970s made a bad situation worse. In 1973, several oil-producing Arab nations instituted an oil embargo to punish the United States and other Western powers for aiding Israel during the October Yom Kippur War. Oil prices in the United States jumped 350 percent. In 1974, the Organization of Petroleum Exporting Countries (OPEC), led by its Arab members, engineered a massive increase in oil prices. And in 1979, the Iranian revolution caused yet another spike in the price of oil. Throughout the decade, Americans wrestled with gasoline shortages and the high cost of petroleum products. With energy costs at record levels, millions of Americans—not usually with enthusiasm—replaced their big, powerful Fords and Chevys with boxy little Toyotas and Datsuns that used less fuel. A nation of people who expected indoor winter temperatures approximating a day at the beach in June had to lower their thermostats and put on sweaters. In 1975, the "misery index"—a combination of the rates of unemployment and inflation—hit 17.5 percent. (It would climax in 1980 at nearly 21 percent.) For the first time since the Great Depression, Americans found themselves confronting a world of limits.

In retrospect, it is clear that the 1970s were a time of economic transition from traditional manufacturing industries to an inchoate service- and technology-driven globalized realm. Although the trajectories of change are clear in hindsight, these large-scale structural transformations were disorienting, frustrating, and frightening. Many American families, communities, and even whole regions faced unexpected challenges to their economic viability and ways of life, even as others gained new opportunities and newly found power on the national stage. Americans during the 1970s commonly described their world and their future in a language of loss, limits, and failure.

RECONFIGURATIONS OF IDENTITY

During the 1970s, Americans wrestled with fundamental questions of identity, particularly those related to gender, race, ethnicity, and sexuality. The social-change movements of the 1960s had broken down many of the legal and political barriers that made people of color and women second-class citizens in the United States. By the end of the 1960s, a gay liberation movement had begun a long campaign to do the same for homosexuals. These efforts continued in the 1970s. The equal rights amendment to the Constitution, which had been stonewalled in congressional committee for more than two decades, was approved by Congress in 1972 and went to the states for ratification. *Roe v. Wade* guaranteed women's choice in abortion; Title IX prompted a massive growth in women's sports. Affirmative action plans, begun in the late 1960s by the Nixon administration, were widely implemented in the 1970s and were upheld by a series of Supreme Court decisions. In the most controversial of these decisions, *Regents of the University of California v. Bakke*, the Supreme Court ruled that universities could craft admissions criteria to guarantee racial "diversity" in their student bodies. Gay rights activists had fewer legal victories, but gay civil rights legislation was introduced in Congress for the first time during the 1970s, and in the 1970s and early 1980s, more than one-third of the nation's states removed antigay laws from the books.

But the struggles over race, gender, and sexuality did not take place in only the political and legal realms. Americans confronted the changes every day during the 1970s—in the workplace, in the media, and in their homes, schools, and places of worship. Many Americans were ambivalent at best about the scale and scope of the changes sweeping the nation. Even for those who supported these movements for equality or who benefited from them, the changes were often disorienting.

As Americans tried to make sense of a new social landscape, larger questions about the meaning of these changes—questions that were not new—came to the center of American public life. People worried not only about race relations but also about the meaning of race, not only about women's *rights* but also about women's and men's roles and the very meaning of gender. What did equality between men and women mean? Were men and women fundamentally different from one another or fundamentally the same? How did African American identity relate to so-called mainstream American identity? How did Hispanics fit the traditional—if historically inaccurate—bipolar construction of race as black and white? This focus on the cultural component of racial identity led some white Americans to question their own racial identities. Did white America have a culture? Was there any such thing as white America? Or did all whites have an ethnic identity, one that might hold the same personal significance as many black Americans found in their racial identity? The gay movement asked many of the same kind of cultural questions. Was the real bipolar division between gay and straight? Was gayness a way of life, a separate culture?

As these kinds of questions took on a new national urgency, other forms of identity were also under scrutiny. What of class identity? Since the 1950s, class had become progressively less clearly delineated in the United States. Did class identity still matter in America? If autoworkers earned more than college professors, what was the meaning of class? If blue-collar workers could buy boats and fancy cars, were they still working class? Was class identity produced at the point of production? Or did consumer choices and leisure-time activities determine class identity? None of these questions found easy answers, but they were fiercely debated during the 1970s, especially as America's unionized blue-collar workers began to lose their economic security and status in the economic turmoil of the era.

In fact, all these questions about identity were negotiated in the context of economic crisis and a belief that America's power and prosperity were no longer bedrock certainties. Thus, women and people of color entered higher education and the job market—with federal protections—just as the economic "pie" stopped growing. Hard economic times, and what President Carter called a "crisis of confidence," gave a sharp edge to debates about identity, diversity, and equality in American society.

❖ ❖ ❖

CULTURAL UNCERTAINTY

A sense of cultural crisis permeated the 1970s. International shocks (from the 1973 oil embargo to the fall of Saigon in 1975 to the Iran hostage crisis of 1979), domestic political debacles (chief among them Watergate and the resignation of the president in 1974), and the travails of stagflation undermined the confidence of the American people. The resulting anxieties and uncertainties combined with the growing freedom from social constraints and the new visibility of marginalized groups, such as gay men and women, to yield a culture of experimentation.

Whatever else might be said about the 1970s, they certainly were not staid. It was during the 1970s, not the 1960s, that sex outside marriage became the norm and illegal drugs became commonplace in middle America. It was during the 1970s that censorship laws were struck down, sex districts in cities flourished, and heterosexual couples flocked to X-rated movies such as the 1972 sensation *Deep Throat.*

In these years, millions of Americans sought spiritual solace, moral certainty, or new avenues to self-fulfillment. Almost 15 percent of best-selling books in the 1970s were self-help books, such as *I'm OK, You're OK.* Radical religious and spiritual alternatives, aimed at the young, found hundreds of thousands of new adherents. As young people joined the Hare Krishnas, the Unification Church (or "Moonies"), or the Children of God (popularly known as "Jesus Freaks"), worried parents sought out "cult deprogrammers." Some of these movements went very wrong, as when the Reverend Jim Jones ordered his followers to commit suicide by drinking cyanide-laced Kool Aid and 973 people died at "Jonestown" in 1978.

Other Americans found answers in therapeutic self-empowerment movements, such as Scientology or EST. Traditional nonwestern religions flourished, and "New Age" spiritual movements moved into the mainstream. More than anything else, millions of Americans responded to the challenges of the 1970s by renewing their Christian faith. But the old, mainline Protestant denominations (such as Episcopalians and Presbyterians) lost congregants to evangelical and fundamentalist churches that emphasized a personal relationship with God. Jimmy Carter was the first American president who was "born again." Although the growth of illegal drug use and born-again Christianity may seem vastly different, both are at least in part responses to a felt sense of crisis and uncertainty. In the 1970s, Americans, even more than usual, felt both the necessity and the freedom to reinvent themselves and form new institutions and new communities.

Social critics at the time accused Americans of rejecting social and familial obligations to embrace a selfish pursuit of individual fulfillment. During the 1970s, the divorce rate rose to new heights, and increasing numbers of young people said they did not plan to have children. With social justice movements no longer rallying in the streets, the interest of many baby boomers in "self-actualization" and "personal growth" was an easy target. Christopher Lasch called it "the Culture of Narcissism"; many "Sixties people" dubbed the 1970s the "Me Decade." There is some truth to these generalizations. But the vibrancy, originality, and hopefulness of the communities that were formed during this era are often overlooked. *America in the Seventies* addresses both the existential despair and the collective creativity of the age.

The essays in this collection explore the themes of economic transformation, reconfiguration of identity, and cultural uncertainty through histories largely cultural in orientation. David Farber, in "The Torch Had Fallen," examines Americans' widespread mistrust of government in the 1970s and the rise of a new conservative hegemony. Christopher Capozzola, writing about the nation's bicentennial, ponders the plight of American patriotism in an age of disappointment. Eric Porter analyzes the ways that race and racial identity are used as political and cultural resources in the 1970s. Jefferson Cowie reflects on the recasting of working-class identity in the face of deindustrialization. In "She 'Can Bring Home the Bacon,'" Beth Bailey traces the tensions between ideological and economic origins of changing gender roles. Peter Braunstein writes about the sexualization of public space and private enterprise in New York City that made it a beacon of liberation for some Americans and the symbol of national depravity for others. William Graebner, in "America's *Poseidon Adventure*," describes the narratives of existential despair that suffuse the era's popular culture. In contrast, Michael Nevin

Willard explores youth subcultures in the 1970s to reveal how some young people confronted diminished economic opportunities and political dead ends by creating a do-it-yourself ethos that allowed them to determine their own codes of behavior and representation. Finally, Timothy Moy tells the story of computer "geeks" who saw the 1970s not as an era of limits but as an age of new possibilities based on technological transformation.

By plotting the lives of Americans caught in the structural transformations of the era and yet freed by the unprecedented liminalities of the post-1960s, post-Movement decade, these essays show the 1970s as a time of high drama in which sexual liberationists and *Gospel Hour* devotees, Mohawk-haired punks and disco dancers, furious displaced steel workers and new women professionals, residents of the Sun Belt and of the Rust Belt, and white ethnics and people of color all struggled to define America and to secure a future on shifting cultural and economic ground.

Note

1. The best overview of the 1970s is Bruce Schulman's *The Seventies: The Great Shift in American Culture, Society, and Politics* (New York: Da Capo Press, 2001). David Frum's *How We Got Here: The 70's, the Decade That Brought You Modern Life (for Better or Worse)* (New York: Basic Books, 2000) offers a conservative critique of 1970s culture. Peter Carroll's *It Seemed Like Nothing Happened: The Tragedy and Promise of America in the 1970s* (New York: Holt, Rinehart & Winston, 1982) is a richly detailed look at the era from an almost-contemporary vantage point.

1

The Torch Had Fallen

DAVID FARBER

We can show through our own example that life in the United States is still
very meaningful and very satisfying and very worthwhile.
—President Gerald R. Ford, *Special Message to the Congress on Drug Abuse,*
April 27, 1976

There they are, the great men of the age martyred on the pyre of national leadership, the fallen heroes of a time not easily forgotten: Martin Luther King Jr. in front of the Lincoln Memorial; Bobby Kennedy reaching out, his boyish grin not yet erased; John Kennedy, coatless at his inaugural. "Let the word go forth," said the young president, "from this time and place, to friend and foe alike, that the torch has been passed to a new generation of Americans—born in this century, tempered by war, disciplined by a hard and bitter peace, proud of our ancient heritage." In truth, these men were far from universally loved—while they were alive—but, ineffably, they offered Americans the sense that the nation was about big things and grand possibilities. "I have a dream," said Martin Luther King Jr., forcing even his implacable foes to ponder what changes his words portended. The chasm separating such iconic figures of the 1960s and the dispiriting stock imagery of the time that followed seems too deep to cross. The first helicopter snapshot: President Nixon on August 9, 1974, about to fly away, his presidency immolated on his own lies and deceptions, an immobile American flag above his head, his arms outstretched, fingers incongruously flashing "V" for victory, a rictus smile, cameras broadcasting the whole sorry affair. The second helicopter snapshot: Saigon, April

30, 1975, Operation Frequent Wind, the last Americans are hauled away from the roof of the U.S. embassy while marines lob gas grenades at desperate Vietnamese allies who had been promised safe passage, defeat marked by betrayal and third-world disorder, a soundless beating of propeller blades against somebody else's skies.[1] And closing out the decade, the third and final helicopter snapshot: the Iranian desert, April 25, 1980, Operation Eagle Claw, the aborted Delta Force plan to rescue the American embassy hostages, an RH-53D helicopter burned beyond recognition, five others left behind to be taken as trophies by the Ayatollah Khomeini's revolutionary forces, eight American fighting men dead without a shot fired against the enemy. Take your pick of presidents: the felonious Nixon; the stolid, unelected Ford; the ineffectual outsider Carter. The torch, it seemed, had fallen.

In the 1970s, the people who were supposed to give national direction were unable to lead. Excepting Mr. Nixon, individual fault had little to do with it. In the post-Watergate 1970s, traditional national leadership did not appeal to large swaths of the population who had lost faith in the types of authorities who had betrayed them. Those in leadership were often enough ridiculed when offering their services, dismissed altogether when partially flawed, endlessly lampooned, held to standards few could meet, and meticulously scrutinized like no earlier generation of leaders had ever been. In part, it was a cleansing, necessary step for a culture so soiled by mewlish presidencies, mendacious generals, crazed political radicals, and a dunderheaded class of big-business executives. For mainstream political liberals, who had made faith in strong national political leadership and an activist government the touchstones of both their electoral strategy and public policy, it would be a most unpleasant era. For conservatives, who had never had anything good to say about Martin Luther King Jr. or either of the Kennedy brothers, the failures of national leadership presented a sweet opportunity to devolve authority from the federal government back to the economic marketplace and, to a lesser extent, to local community decision making.

The failure of national leadership was no secret in the mid-1970s. Ritualistically, one public voice after another intoned that Americans had lost all faith in their leaders and, maybe, in themselves. Missouri congressman William Hungate, who had served on the House Judiciary Committee that brought down Richard Nixon, announced his own retirement soon after: "Politics has gone from the age of 'Camelot' when all things are possible to the age of 'Watergate' when all things are suspect."[2] Arizona congressman Mo Udall, his run at the Democratic presidential nomination dashed on the shoals of anti-

Washington politics, told the 1976 Democratic National Convention, "This is a good country and a good people. But these last years we have lost our confidence and we have lost our way. The fact is that our country hasn't been working very well."[3] *New York Times* editorial page editor John Oakes sighed: "Within the past few years we as a people seem to have lost our way, to be foundering in uncertainty, to be unsure of ourselves in our relations to each other and the world at large. The optimism and moral drive characteristic of Americans throughout the decades have been largely replaced by a deep-seated cynicism and disillusionment."[4] In a 1974 *Time* magazine cover story, "In Quest of Leadership," a journalist mused that if a space alien requested, "take me to your leader," no one would know what to do. A year later, *U.S. News and World Report* concluded that the 1970s would be known as the "age of nonheroes."[5] And, most famously, on July 15, 1979, Jimmy Carter tried to buck up the nation by pointing out its weakness: "I want to talk to you right now about a fundamental threat to American democracy. . . . It is a crisis of confidence. . . . Our people are losing faith, not only in government itself but in the ability as citizens to serve as ultimate rulers and shapers of our democracy. . . . There is a growing disrespect for government and for churches and for schools, the news media, and other institutions. This is not a message of happiness or reassurance, but it is the truth and it is a warning."[6]

At the decade's end, in response to this drumbeat of despair, James Reston, the nation's reigning political pundit, wondered why no stalwart leader had arisen to solve the nation's "political madness." For help and perhaps hope, Reston turned to the distinguished historian, Henry Steele Commager. The seventy-eight-year-old scholar offered him little solace: "Politics and politicians . . . reflect the society they represent." Reston sadly concurred:

> In the 20 years since 1960 we have had five presidents. Kennedy was murdered. Johnson was destroyed by the Vietnam War. Nixon was run out of Washington. Ford held us together but was rejected in the election of 1976. And now we are savaging Jimmy Carter, who has the lowest popularity rating in the history of the polls and mocking his potential successor, Ronald Reagan. It is no wonder, then, that even our allies are asking whether we are really a serious country, and why Commager is suggesting that the crisis of leadership lies not merely in Washington but in the nation as a whole.[7]

No one fared worse in attempting to lead the nation out of the doldrums of despair than the two 1970s presidents: Gerald Ford and Jimmy Carter.

Almost nothing these two men did saved them from mockery and even contempt. Ford, in particular, faced an onslaught of usually unearned disrespect. The president was viciously portrayed, over and over again, in late-night television monologues; newspaper cartoons; and, most indelibly, on the then-new comedy show *Saturday Night Live* as a clumsy clown, an uncoordinated buffoon who wreaked physical havoc on himself and all around him.

As president, Ford did his best to act honorably and to heal the wounds of Watergate (he would later title his presidential memoirs *A Time to Heal*). Memorably, he declared in his short "remarks on taking the oath of office as president" (Ford made no inaugural address), "My fellow Americans, our long national nightmare is over."[8] One of his first major acts as president was to give Richard Nixon a full pardon. With an eloquence few thought he possessed, he carefully explained his decision: "My conscience tells me clearly and certainly that I cannot prolong the bad dreams that continue to reopen a chapter that is closed. My conscience tells me that only I, as President, have the constitutional power to firmly shut and seal this book. My conscience tells me it is my duty, not merely to proclaim domestic tranquility but to use every means that I have to insure it."[9] In retrospect, Ford had acted honorably in seeking to move the country forward. At the time, Americans thought differently. According to a Gallup poll, Ford's public approval rating fell from 71 percent before the pardon to 49 percent after it. The unelected president was pilloried, and many suspected, without an iota of evidence, that he had struck some sordid deal with Nixon.

Ford, perhaps out of his depth in the nation's highest office, was doomed to serve his short term at a time when few Americans were fully prepared to accept his leadership. Ford would be made to embody the failures of the body politic. In an almost medieval gloss on the presidency, the American people seemed to find great humor in mixing the tragedy of the "body political" with the "body natural" of Gerald Ford.[10] The stories and jokes about Ford's physical presence started soon after his ascent to the presidency but at first only in fringe or humor publications. The November 1974 *National Lampoon* cover, for example, featured a moronic-looking Ford with a chocolate ice cream cone that, by missing his mouth, he had stuck onto his broad forehead.[11] The jokes, and the viciousness of the humor, took off in mid-1975 after Ford slipped on the steps exiting *Air Force One* on the tarmac at the Salzburg, Austria, airport.

The entire mass media jumped on this "story." The irony was extraordinary. President Ford had been a star football player for the University of Michigan; he turned down the chance to play in the National Football

League to attend Yale Law School. Throughout his presidency, he was in excellent physical shape; he was a superb skier; and he excelled at that most presidential of sports, golfing. In the early 1960s, the mass media had given the nation images of a graceful and vigorous President John Kennedy playing touch football with family and friends. In fact, Kennedy was a physical wreck with no more than average athletic skills. President Ford was a gifted athlete, easily the best who had ever been president. But as Ford himself recounted, "every time I stumbled or bumped my head or fell in the snow, reporters zeroed in on that to the exclusion of almost everything else. . . . [E]ven more damaging was the fact that Johnny Carson and Chevy Chase used my 'missteps' for their jokes. Their antics—and I'll admit that I laughed at them myself—helped create the public perception of me as a stumbler. And that wasn't funny."[12] As Ford realized, the public—or at least key members of the mass media—deliberately conflated the "king's two bodies" in order to mock the very possibility of Ford's presidential leadership.

In the 1970s, after Watergate, the mass media stopped turning a respectful eye away from the stray presidential slip, awkward moment, or human foible as had been done for decades. (Most famously, polio-stricken President Roosevelt was never pictured being gingerly lifted in and out of his car and John Kennedy's wanton womanizing was never mentioned in the press.) For decades, the president's human condition—literally his bodily needs and failures—had been largely hidden from the public to better maintain the virtue of his role as leader of the body politic.[13] But after the Watergate investigations revealed the president's moral failing, the mass media, with full support of the American people, began instead to highlight every possible instance of the president's human awkwardness or weakness.

This focus on the failings and foibles of presidential behavior and personality was not completely new or solely attributable to post-Watergate cynicism. At the least, it had roots in the emergent consumer society in the 1920s. Fed by a public relations and mass-media juggernaut, Americans had become increasingly obsessed with what social theorist Leo Lowenthal called "the personal lives of consumption idols."[14] Once the personal lives of Hollywood stars were tabloid fodder, it was inevitable that the public would want to know ever more about the personalities of the people who would lead them. Presidential candidates fully participated in the process by which personality would come to matter as much as or more than party, policy, and proven experience. Dwight D. Eisenhower was the first presidential candidate to hire a national advertising firm to package his public persona. And John Kennedy willfully conflated the image of movie star and national leader by selling himself to the American people as a dashing, handsome war hero and charming, happily married family man. The Watergate scandals, to some extent, simply turned the public's attention from the sunny manipulated images their leaders offered them to darker, drearier, and simply more banal images of the men who sought to lead the nation.

Gerald Ford became the nation's fall guy. As Ford historian Yanek Mieczkowski argues, "The image of a klutz stuck to Ford. The pejorative portrayals did more than just convey the unseemly impression that the athletic Ford was clumsy. More seriously, they became translated into the perception of a man who was mentally obtuse, in danger of making policy blunders as well as physical blunders. The image of a genial oaf came to mind. . . ."[15] Ford was the first president to discover that the rules of presidential leadership had changed.

The combined failures of the Vietnam War and Watergate (and by 1975, one could and should enlarge the list of national failures to include economic stagflation and the energy crisis) had led reporters and editors, as well as most Americans, to conclude that an attitude of fierce skepticism, even cynicism, about the honesty, competency, integrity, and even humanity of government officials was a mandatory defense against the knavery and policy failures the nation had endured. The public would not be played again for dupes. With that skepticism and cynicism came a generalized disrespect for politicians that floated freely from person to person, from the amoral Richard Nixon to the ethically sound Gerald Ford. Comedians caricatured Ford as a "genial oaf" not because he was one but because the image fit the public's need for emotional distance from the destruction that presidential power had inflicted on American ideals (Watergate) and American lives (Vietnam War) and from the economic crises of the 1970s (stagflation).

Jimmy Carter fared better than Gerald Ford in the public-mockery department. In part, Carter escaped by virtue of his uncommon good sense about matters of public deportment and his earned reputation for plainspoken honesty. He was a hard man to ridicule. The only real laugh lines used against Carter came shortly before his presidency and then again late in the game, when his presidency was deeply wounded. Still, his attempt to restore pride in the presidency and create a new style of leadership in the White House largely failed.

Carter's remarkable path from an obscure Georgia governor to the president of the United States hit an unlikely rough spot just before the 1976 election when he gave an interview to *Playboy*. He easily held his ground against a hostile interviewer who meant to show the born-again Southern Baptist as some kind of backwoods, Confederate stick-in-the-mud. Carter avoided all the obvious traps, demonstrated his intellect, and ably showed himself to be both religious and tolerant of those who were not. But in an attempt to demonstrate to *Playboy*'s readers that he was no "holier than thou" type, he decided to get down and dirty, in an evangelical-Southern-Baptist manner. Carter admitted that he was a playboy, too: "Christ said, 'I tell you that anyone who looks on a woman with lust in his heart has already committed adultery.' I've looked at a lot of women with lust. I've committed adultery in my heart many times."[16] A good many secular Americans found the "lust in my heart" line, as it became known, humorous (though not in the same league as presidential candidate Bill Clinton's later statement that he had smoked but not inhaled marijuana). Belittling iterations of the line followed Carter around during his presidency.

The very fact that Jimmy Carter chose to do a full-scale interview with *Playboy* revealed the changing character of presidential leadership: the men who would lead the nation had to—and chose to—reveal themselves as individuals unprotected by their status. In part, this position of vulnerability stemmed from Richard Nixon's fall from grace. Nixon had destroyed not only his own presidency but also the aura of respect that had guarded the presidency by limiting the scrutiny placed on the man who held the nation's highest office. The Nixon Oval Office tapes, filled with expletives and ethnic slurs of all kinds, as much as Nixon's specific misdeeds during the Watergate scandals, had shocked the nation into a new understanding of its leaders. Nixon's main defense—that he had done nothing that had not already been done by other presidents—did not help him, the prestige of the presidency, or the American people's views of their leaders. After Watergate, the press and the public would henceforth treat presidents not as holders of the nation's highest office but as men who happened to be president. It was not inherently an unhealthy political attitude (similar, in fact, to the political culture of much of nineteenth-century America), but it would create a new environment for presidential leadership that every president and the public would have to learn how to navigate.

Carter, in submitting to an interview with *Playboy*, had willfully and with full understanding of the new rules regarding public scrutiny of national political leadership sought to turn this new challenge into an opportunity. Running against the incumbent President Ford, Carter recognized that he could use the media's scrutiny of presidential character, rather than policy-making or political ability, to turn his "outsider" status and weak record as a national leader to his own advantage. He chose to reveal himself on the prurient pages of *Playboy* not because he could not find a more high-toned or respectable magazine to introduce him but because the "men's" magazine served perfectly as a contrast to his own higher moral standards. At the same time, his willingness to appear in *Playboy* demonstrated to those suspicious of his strong religious faith that he was not judgmental of those with less biblically oriented lifestyles. Carter did receive some political flak and mockery from appearing close to airbrushed naked Playmates (though the Reverend Martin Luther King Sr., a strong supporter of Jimmy Carter, noted, "they can't kill you for lookin' ").[17] Overall, the interview, and even the "lust in my heart" laugh line pulled from the text, seemed to do him more good than harm with the electorate. More importantly, he solidified a new political campaign style in which candidates vied with one another, informally and with seeming candor, to find new media outlets to display their humanity. (A quick coda: Richard Nixon, long typecast as a ruthless political operator, had made a step in this direction when he had made fun of his uptight reputation by appearing in 1968 on the wacky television show *Laugh-In*.)

Jimmy Carter was elected to the presidency because of his management of the character issue. When he entered the race for the Democratic nomination against far better known politicians, he had no support from party insiders or the party's usual core constituencies. He had no major policy victories or even initiatives to run on. He had not been a general or a movie star; his father had been neither rich nor famous. He presented himself to the people as a good man. He was a peanut farmer from Plains, Georgia, who had served honorably and proudly in the navy. He had been a good governor. His integrity was above reproach. He told the American people, over and over again, with conviction and sincerity, that he would never lie to them. Character was his main (some say only) political platform.

In a way, Carter's campaign was a throwback to the nation's earliest political contests. In the late eighteenth century, historian Joanne Freeman explains, "In a government lacking formal precedent and institutional traditions, reputation was the glue that held the polity together. The fragile new republic was a government of character striving to become a government of rules within its new constitutional framework."[18] Although the post-Watergate political legitimacy crisis did not nearly rival the nation-building challenges faced by Washington, Adams, or Jefferson, Jimmy Carter understood that Americans feared that their "government of rules" had broken down. He was no Jefferson, but he could convincingly claim to be a man of honor. He gambled that in the mid-1970s proof of presidential-caliber experience was less important to voters seeking a trustworthy president than were expressions of character.

Carter won his gamble. Once nominated by the Democrats, he assured Americans of his integrity by emphasizing that he, unlike the incumbent president, was not a Washington "insider" soiled by the dirt of political corruption. Carter staked his claim to national leadership by hammering home how far away from national leadership he had always been until he chose to run for the presidency. Almost every successful presidential candidate since, at least through the candidacy of George W. Bush, has made the same case. (Both Reagan and Clinton managed to make related outsider claims even when running successfully for second terms.)

This "anti-Washington" or, at least, anti–East Coast elite style of politics was not new to the United States in the 1970s. It had been a rhetorical tool in the political kit bag of Andrew Jackson and had been used periodically ever after. But since the crisis-driven presidency of Franklin Roosevelt and the public's post–World War II sense that presidential leadership demanded both a firm grasp of world affairs and an ability to manage the massive federal government, lack of both national political credentials and international policy experience had not been treated by pundits, professional politicians, or most people as an electoral virtue. Jimmy Carter changed that view.

In 1976, and in almost every presidential election year that followed until the end of the twentieth century, a presidential candidate who identified as a political-party insider and member of the Washington political elite carried heavy baggage into the race. The four presidents in office before the 1976 election had all held major national offices (Kennedy had been in the House and Senate; both Nixon and Johnson had been elected to the House, Senate, and vice presidency; and Ford was the long-term House minority leader before his appointment as vice president led to his unexpected "rendezvous with destiny"). The next five presidents, with George Herbert Walker Bush a complicated exception, had not. Carter showed that when it came to the presidency the American people preferred to vote for governors, erstwhile or sitting, preferably from states far away from the nation's capital.

The problem for Carter, and for most of the men who followed in his path, was that the American people had to be introduced to these outsiders quickly and in digestible forms. To become well known, and in Carter's case to fight stereotyping of his Southern Baptist beliefs, outsider candidates courted the mass media, in all its variants, to reach out to the often indifferent and suspicious electorate. Thus, Carter took his case to the revealing pages of *Playboy* to show a key segment of American voters that he had nothing to hide and much to show them.

Presidential aspirants' attention to less-than-respectable media outlets was, in part, just a means to expand their "name recognition" in an age of outsider candidacies and an indifferent or even hostile electorate. In 1992, in a Carteresque attempt to introduce himself to new audiences, Arkansas governor Bill Clinton appeared on MTV, the music television channel. There, he responded to a young person's incisive question—briefs or boxers?—by telling viewers that he wore boxer shorts, a general subject about which the American people would eventually learn far more than most wanted to know. Such off-color media appearances reveal more than candidates' need for public exposure. They are also a piece of the new informality that post-Watergate politics introduced to the presidency.

Carter acted deliberately to craft a new downsized, down-home presidential persona. He wanted Americans to believe that the White House was, once again, the People's house. After the inaugural, he broke precedent and refused to ride in the bulletproof, armored presidential limousine. He and his family walked to the White House like a happy suburban family taking an after-dinner stroll. He directed the White House guards to retire the pompous military uniforms Richard Nixon had insisted they wear and dress less imposingly. He sold the presidential yacht, stopped White House staff car service, limited the number of presidential portraits displayed in government offices, and asked that "Hail to the Chief" not be played at his public appearances.

Carter took more than symbolic acts. In early February 1977, in the midst of a bitter cold spell and a dangerous natural gas shortage that had forced schools to close and factories to shut down, Carter appeared on television to talk directly to the American people about a new era of limits. From the White House library, sitting informally in an unadorned armchair, wearing an unbuttoned cardigan sweater, with few trappings of his high office, Carter gave the first of many "fireside chats." He told the American people what few presidents before or after have dared to say, that the energy crisis that gripped the nation could be solved only with "some sacrifice from you." He promised that in just over two months he would deliver a comprehensive energy policy that would combine conservation measures with deregulation of oil and gas prices.[19] Two weeks earlier, in his inaugural address, he had already warned the American people: "We cannot afford to do everything. . . . We must simply do our best."

At first, many were pleased with Carter's plain-spoken, honest, even humble approach to the presidency. Few, however, maintained their approval as Carter found himself unable to work with the politically minded partisans in Congress or lead the country through the economic reorganization and the energy crisis that brought uncertainty, hard times, and unemployment to millions of American families. The outsider president was by dint of inexperience and temperament not well equipped to govern. His clearly articulated disgust with interest-group bargaining and political deal making ("I owe the special interests nothing. I owe the people everything") made him few friends in his new hometown. Political pundit Chris Mathews, who worked as a Carter speechwriter, summed up the problem: "Carter's decision to 'run against Washington' was a brilliant bit of political positioning. . . . But his mistake was to allow this anti-Washington posture, so formidable out in the country, to hinder his effectiveness once in the capital. . . . 'People don't do their best work while they're being pissed on,' an old Washington hand once remarked to me.'"[20] The American people had been right to trust Carter's honesty; he really meant it when he ran against "politics as usual." Unfortunately, his honesty was no simple substitute for the kind of "hardball" political wheeling and dealing that gets the people's work done in a democratic society.

By 1979, Americans were fast losing faith in their humble president's leadership abilities. One funny result of people's growing certainty that Carter did not have what it takes to lead the nation was seen in the dark pleasure with which Americans greeted reports of their president's aquatic battle with a "killer rabbit." The story broke in that notoriously slow news month of August. The duel, in which a seemingly crazed, swimming rabbit had to be beaten back by an oar-wielding president, had actually taken place months earlier during a Carter fishing trip near his home in Plains. Carter press secretary Jody Powell, showing his own lack of "insider" experience, chose to share the incident with a reporter during the dog days of summer. The reporter, well in tune with the journalistic zeitgeist in which no presidential weirdness was too unimportant to print, wrote up an account of the story, which was picked up by almost every media outlet in America. The *Washington Post*, the paper that had only a few years earlier led the way in taking down the ignoble Nixon, chose to run a cartoon of Carter and the rabbit, titled "Paws" (referencing the contemporary blockbuster movie *Jaws*) on its front page.

The story resonated with the public because Americans by August 1979 had lost faith not in their president's honesty but in his ability to do the job for which they elected him. To many people, the image of an earnest Jimmy Carter squared off in a tough fight against an angry rabbit demonstrated the state of the presidency. Many believed that Carter did not know how to be a president. He could not control the government, and he could not lead the people. Even a rabbit sensed his weakness. When a mob of Iranian students, enthralled by the Ayatollah Khomeini, took over the American embassy in Tehran on November 4, 1979, and kept fifty-two Americans hostage throughout that year and the next, whatever hopes for leadership the American people had in President Carter were squashed.[21]

Well before the embassy takeover and the attack of the swimming bunny, Anthony Lewis, the liberal *New York Times* columnist, feared the cynicism and the moral lethargy that he believed America's leaders had produced in the American people. He was writing in specific response to the failures of Richard Nixon, but his concerns were more general. In a *New York Times* column, he harkened back to Greek tragedy and warned, "It is a classic idea that a whole community may be infected by the sickness of its leadership, by a failure of ideals at the top. . . . We are infected by corruption at the top and most of us know it. . . . In American society, the response to that danger can only come from the citizenry."[22]

Writing in 1974, Lewis pointed out the direction from which political leadership was to come in the years ahead. Rather than have the tone of the nation set by traditional leaders, the United States would enter a short time in which the most dynamic public policies, the most far-reaching cultural agendas, and the most effective social movements would come not from the corrupted "top" but from the far-flung citizenry. Here was a surprising reprise of key elements of the 1960s era during which grassroots civil rights activists and a multifaceted, locally organized antiwar movement, with mixed results, dared to challenge the conventional wisdom of most of the nation's elected leaders.

In the post-Watergate 1970s, many of the new citizen activists had little in common with their 1960s predecessors except for their grassroots approach to political organizing. These activists fit most comfortably on the far right of the political spectrum. Middle aged or older, their grass roots were often enough planted in the nation's suburbs. A polyester faction of Richard

Nixon's proverbial "silent majority" was rebelling against the establishment. Rather than seek new federal protections or expanded social provision programs, these activists wanted to cut back on government spending. Their ideal political leader would not ask them what they could do for their country but would tell them that their government was ripping them off and that they did not have to take it anymore. The new political leadership would honor their distrust of government and commend them for demanding ever less from it.

Howard Jarvis was one of the unexpected champions of popular antigovernment reform in the post-Watergate era. The elderly, retired manufacturer led the tax revolt in California that spread to some thirty states between 1978 and 1983. The political establishment in California had long regarded Jarvis as a political gadfly, to put it most politely. He was a conservative Republican who had been publicly railing against high taxes for years. In 1962, he had run in the Republican Senate primary as a champion of the far right and been badly beaten by the moderate, middle-of-the-road incumbent. Jarvis spent the next sixteen or so years beating the drum against every kind of tax, scoring no successes but much scorn.

Jarvis never gave up. And in 1978, his day at long last arrived. He linked his antigovernment, antitax rhetoric to the new political and economic realities of 1970s America. He cleverly adopted the slogan "I'm mad as hell and I'm not going to take it anymore!" from the 1976 Academy Award–winning anti–media-elite movie *Network* for his antitax campaign. He and his supporters pointed out that in 1978 many California homeowners were seeing their property assessments triple while their incomes remained stagnant or, worse, declined. Free-spending politicians, they said, refused to protect senior citizens, young families, or just plain hardworking Californians from the tidal wave of property-tax increases. The only solution, the antitaxers said, was a statewide policy initiative, Proposition 13, which would roll back the property-assessment increases, severely limit future increases, and restrict local property taxes to 1 percent of market value. Despite almost total opposition from California's political leaders and many of the state's corporate leaders who believed that large-scale public spending was needed in the state, voters rallied to Proposition 13. It passed in a landslide. Jarvis and his allies had successfully turned the tax-cut issue into a middle-class populist crusade against California's political leaders.

Pocketbook politics clearly played a critical part in the passage of Proposition 13 and the other antitax measures that tied the hands of state and local governments in the late 1970s and early 1980s. Americans had watched government revenue collections jump nearly 50 percent in the decade that followed the Great Society programs of Lyndon Johnson. In 1978, state and local taxes alone sucked up 12.7 percent of Americans' stagnating personal incomes. Middle- and upper-income Americans—those most likely to vote, especially in a nonpresidential election year—bore the overwhelming brunt of those taxes. Still, it was more than simple pocketbook politics that motivated voters to rise up in protest against tax increases. Underlying the self-interest was voters' ferocious mistrust of government. This mistrust, according to poll data, reached its post–World War II pathetic nadir in 1978. Taxpayers simply did not trust politicians to use their money wisely.

Howard Jarvis and other grassroots champions of tax-reform measures across the nation used a populist rhetoric to skewer America's democratically elected political leaders. Just as Jimmy Carter promised to clean up a corrupt and mendacious federal government, the tax reformers cried out against "big-government waste," "political fat cats," and "spenders."[23] In 1980, Ronald Reagan (who for years had been seen by the political establishment and mass-media pundits as a right winger out of step with a majority of mainstream Americans) would build on this movement and rhetoric to craft his winning conservative coalition. Historian Michael Kazin astutely observes: "The rage for tax cuts had given Republicans an advantage they had long desired: an economic issue that placed a majority of voters on their side in apparent conflict with an unresponsive elite."[24]

By the end of the 1970s, elected officials at the national, state, and even local level were a ripe target, and a new generation of reformers, grassroots activists, and politicians would rise up by pulling them down. In 1978, Howard Jarvis, who had been seen for nearly two decades by almost everyone professionally involved in California politics as an eccentric right-wing crank, had the last laugh. He had made tax reform the political issue of the late 1970s. In 1980, Ronald Reagan rode that issue—and his antigovernment "citizen-politician" image—into the White House. He would lead the nation by insisting that the people did not need national government leadership. They were better off on their own.

Jarvis and the tax reformers were by no means the only insurgent conservative force in the United States seeking to offer a new kind of leadership. With conventional political leaders under fire at both the state and the national level, a loosely linked network of evangelical Christian religious leaders in the 1970s began to seize the discredited politicians' bully pulpit. When these ministers looked at America, they saw the spectre of Sodom and Gomorrah. These men preached that dark forces of the 1960s—feminists, gay liberationists, liberal judges, morally relativistic intellectuals, and a drug-and-sex-besotted youth culture—had unleashed a godless secular human-ism, championed by the federal government, that threatened to destroy the nation. For many on this nascent "religious right," proof positive of the power of the godless foe came in 1973 when the Supreme Court ruled in *Roe v. Wade* that the Constitution of the United States guaranteed women the right to abort a pregnancy. Feminist lawyers, "legislating" judges, and a cul-ture that no longer automatically vilified sexually active unmarried women had used big-government power to triumph over a core belief of many reli-gious Americans. Religious conservatives were staggered by other secular big-government blows: the fight to pass the equal rights amendment (ERA), the teaching of evolution in the schools, the outlawing of school prayers, IRS attacks on Christian schools' tax-exempt status, and civil rights for homo-sexuals. As the religious conservatives saw it, "traditional family values," the biblically based bedrock of American society, were under attack by the federal government. Many religious conservatives believed with growing fervor that something had to be done to restrict federal power and restore Christian virtue to the nation's institutions and its public policy.

Jerry Falwell, pastor of the Thomas Road Baptist Church in Lynchburg, Virginia, helped lead this new political movement.[25] Among Christian evan-gelicals, Falwell was a figure of national renown long before he turned his attention to national politics. His church, numbering some seventeen thou-sand congregants in the late 1970s, was among the biggest in the nation. He had started preaching on the radio in 1956. By the end of the 1970s, his tele-vision show, *Old Time Gospel Hour,* was seen on over three hundred televi-sion stations all across the country.

For years, Falwell had foresworn politics. During the heyday of the civil rights movement, the reverend had attacked Martin Luther King Jr. for putting politics before his religious duties: "We need to get off the streets and into the pulpits and prayer rooms."[26] Among his fellow white evangelical ministers, his position seemed to be the orthodox one. Throughout the civil rights era, white evangelicals and fundamentalist Christian ministers pub-licly scorned political activism (it was no accident that most of these white clergymen were southerners). A major study of evangelicals concluded in 1971 that "the thrust of evangelical Protestantism is toward a miraculous view of social reform: that if all men are brought to Christ, social evils will disappear. . . . Evangelical Protestant groups largely ignore social and political efforts for reform."[27] Before the mid-1970s, many fundamentalists argued that political activism was a waste of time because the sinful Earth was doomed to imminent, fiery destruction (Armageddon), and God-fearing Christians would be saved by Jesus (the Rapture), anyway. All this was cheerfully outlined in the 1970s bestseller, Hal Lindsey's *The Late Great Planet Earth.*

By the early 1970s, most politicians and pundits took it as a matter of faith that evangelical and fundamentalist Protestants took little interest in public policy, grassroots activism, or electoral politics. Historically, as scholar of American religion Robert Wuthnow points out, this conventional wisdom was inaccurate. Evangelical ministers, with the strong support of their congregants, had been leaders in national and local Prohibition movements; state and local campaigns to honor the Sabbath by regulating work, commerce, and recreation on Sundays; and, going way back, abolitionism.[28] When properly motivated, Christian conservatives had been quite willing to use the political system to turn their religious certainties into legally binding statutes. But it was true that for several decades most white evangelical ministers had been politically quiescent and even vocally opposed to active political participation. Government power and political leadership, most such ministers believed, had little to do with the issues that mattered most to them. In the mid-1970s, Jerry Falwell and a tight network of conservative ministers decided that they had been wrong. American society needed them and it needed the active political participation of every Christian American.

Falwell felt his way into politics slowly. His first overt move came during the 1976 Bicentennial. He understood that in the midst of economic stagflation and foreign policy failings many Americans were not in the mood to listen to the usual politicians giving the usual celebratory speeches. He provided an alternative: "I Love America" rallies. Traveling from state capital to state capital, he and the Liberty Baptist College choir offered spiritually charged revivals that called for a new moral awakening in America. He followed up by joining forces with Florida anti–gay-rights spokesperson Anita Bryant and anti-ERA leader Phyllis Schlafly. Falwell was at the center of what would soon be called the New Right, an uneasy amalgam of religious conservatives, old-line anticommunists, and antitax and anti–big-government activists. Unifying these different, though often overlapping, constituencies was a populist rhetoric that blamed the nation's troubles on a liberal elite that scorned Christian morality and the traditional American values of self-reliance. This liberal elite, Falwell and his allies believed, had captured the federal government and used the federal courts, in particular, to engineer nondemocratic radical social changes.

In 1979, Falwell gave full expression and institutional structure to his vision of a Religious Right by joining with like-minded men to form the Moral Majority. The ministers who led the Moral Majority threw themselves into the 1980 presidential election. They shifted their focus from the coming Rapture to the nuts and bolts of voter registration. By election time, the Moral Majority claimed that they had registered four million new conservative Christian voters (secular social scientists estimated that the combined efforts of the Religious Right had produced around two million new registrants). Christian conservatives had become major players in any politician's electoral calculus. By 1981, Falwell's new force in American politics had chapters in every state, a Washington DC–based office with a budget of about six million dollars, a mailing list of four million people, and a committed membership conservatively estimated at four hundred thousand.[29]

By the end of the 1970s, the major New Left organizations of the 1960s, Students for a Democratic Society and the Student Non-Violent Coordinating Committee, were long gone. The New Right, spearheaded by Jerry Falwell and a host of others, represented political insurgency from the grass roots. Tax revolters, religious fundamentalists, and their allies had captured the political center stage. In Ronald Reagan, these folks and a good many other Americans found a new champion. Reagan would pick up the fallen torch of national leadership by damning the federal government and calling for the return of power to families and communities.

Ronald Reagan—retired actor, retired motivational speaker, and erstwhile California governor—made leadership the centerpiece of his 1980 presidential campaign. He told the American people, "I will not stand by and watch this great country destroy itself under mediocre leadership that drifts from one crisis to the next, eroding our national will and purpose. . . . We need a rebirth of the American tradition of leadership at every level of government and in private life as well. The United States of America is unique in world history because it has a genius for leaders—many leaders—on many levels."[30] For millions of Americans, Reagan would embody that genius for leadership.

Reagan's ability to convince a majority of Americans that it was "morning in America" again stemmed, in part, from his own political gifts, not the least of which was a fine actor's ability to reach people emotionally. But more than personality and a gift for communication were at work. Reagan offered a very different kind of leadership when he ran for office in 1980. He categorically rejected the liberal consensus that had undergirded the presidencies of Franklin Roosevelt, Harry Truman, John Kennedy, Lyndon Johnson, and even Richard Nixon. Each of these presidents had seen the federal government as a unique force in safeguarding critical areas of national life: creating a social safety net, ensuring equal protection under the law, and even supporting American culture and the arts. These presidents had each committed themselves, in different ways, to using government power to improve national life. Jimmy Carter, recognizing Americans' rising concerns that the federal government was not working very well and was not even completely trustworthy, had deliberately lowered peoples' expectations about White House leadership. He had tried to offer Americans a more managerial and less dynamic presidency. His message had worked well enough to get him elected.

Ronald Reagan went much further than did Carter. Rather than downsize the presidency to manage voters' concerns about an out-of-control White House and a profligate and incompetent federal government, Reagan condemned the whole enterprise. He ran for the presidency by denouncing the government he intended to lead. In the simple declarative sentences that so many Americans cherished, he said, "Government is not the solution to our problems. Government is the problem." Liberals and skeptics of all kinds bemoaned what they saw as the Hollywood trickery of the Reagan presidency, but Reagan essentially did what he had promised: he cut taxes to reward wealthy individuals and did his best to starve the federal government of resources it could use for domestic policies. By 1984, a majority of American voters cheered for a new kind of American leader. Rather than propose new government solutions to solve national problems, Reagan would, to paraphrase one of his acolytes, George W. Bush, challenge individual Americans to solve their own problems. The age of uncertainty, for many, was over. A new age of belief—in capitalism, even in the righteous power of greed and selfishness, in God's merciful power to help those who help themselves—had begun, fostered, in part, by grassroots movements, by economic changes, by world events, and by a leader who said he did his best thinking with a "horse between my knees."[31]

Notes

1. Ret. Col. James Kean, "The Last Marines Out of Saigon," MSNBC webpage, http://www.msnbc.com.news/393502.asp?cp1-1.

2. Quoted in Yanek Mieczkowski, "Gerald Ford and America in the Age of Limits" (PhD diss., Columbia University, 1995), 5.

3. Mo Udall, Address, Democratic National Convention, New York, July 14, 1976, http://www.library.arizona.edu/branches/spc/udall/dnc_76.pdf.

4. Mieczkowski, "Gerald Ford and America," 8–9.

5. Both magazine pieces are discussed in Mieczkowski, "Gerald Ford and America," 36.

6. President Jimmy Carter, "Energy and the National Goals—A Crisis of Confidence," http://www.americanrhetoric.com/speeches/jimmycartercrisis of confidence.htm.

7. James Reston, "Where Are We Going?" *New York Times,* August 3, 1980.

8. "Gerald R. Ford's Remarks on Taking the Oath of Office as President," August 9, 1974, http://www.ford.utexas.edu/library/speeches/740001.htm.

9. "President Gerald R. Ford's Remarks on Signing a Proclamation Granting Pardon to Richard Nixon," September 8, 1974, http://www.ford.utexas.edu/library/speeches/740060.htm.

10. I am borrowing from Ernst Kantorowicz, *The King's Two Bodies* (Princeton, NJ: Princeton University Press, 1987), first published in 1957.

11. "The Civics Issue," *National Lampoon,* November 1974.

12. Gerald R. Ford, *A Time to Heal: The Autobiography of Gerald R. Ford* (New York: Harper and Row, 1979), 289.

13. Exceptions, of course, existed, such as President Eisenhower's heart attack and Lyndon Johnson's gall bladder surgery, but the full extent of major health problems was usually hidden and minor concerns often ignored.

14. Quote taken from Lynn Dumenil, *The Modern Temper* (New York: Hill and Wang, 1995), 78.

15. Mieczkowski, "Gerald Ford and America," 86. For more on this portrait of Ford, see Mieczkowski, 83–87.

16. The quoted passages and insights into the Carter interview come from Leo P. Ribuffo, "God and Jimmy Carter," in *Transforming Faith: The Sacred and Secular in Modern American History,* ed. M.L Bradbury and James Gilbert (New York: Greenwood Press, 1989), 145–146.

17. Ibid., 146.

18. Joanne Freeman, "Explaining the Unexplainable: The Cultural Context of the Sedition Act," in *The Democratic Experiment,* ed. Julian Zelizer, Meg Jacobs, and William Novak (Princeton, NJ: Princeton University Press: 2003), 23.

19. The February 2, 1977, "Fireside Chat" is viewable at the C-Span site on the American presidency: http://www.americanpresidents.org/presidents/president.asp?PresidentNumber=38. My discussion of the Carter energy policy draws on John C. Barrow, "An Age of Limits: Jimmy Carter and the Quest for a National Energy Policy," in *The Carter Presidency,* ed. Gary Fink and Hugh Davis Graham (Lawrence: University Press of Kansas, 1998), 158–159.

20. Christopher Mathews, *Hardball* (New York: Free Press, 1989), 33–34. The

"special interest" quote is from a Carter campaign speech; William Leuchtenburg, "Jimmy Carter and the Post-New Deal Presidency," in *Carter Presidency*, 11.

21. Burton Kauffman, *The Presidency of James Earl Carter, Jr.* (Lawrence: University Press of Kansas, 1993), 138–149.

22. Anthony Lewis, " 'Then Enterprise Is Sick,' " *New York Times*, February 25, 1974.

23. The quoted passages come directly from Lisa McGirr, *Suburban Warriors: The Origins of the New American Right* (Princeton, NJ: Princeton University Press, 2001), 238. She is quoting the *California Journal*; see her endnote 103 for chapter 6. Throughout this section I am relying on the evidence and insights of Ballard Campbell, "Tax Revolts and Political Change," *Journal of Policy History* 10, no. 1 (1998): 153–178. He discusses the antigovernment poll data on pages 164–165. I have also consulted McGirr, *Suburban Warriors*, 114, 238–239; Bruce Schulman, *The Seventies* (New York: De Capo, 2001), 212–215; and Michael Kazin, *The Populist Persuasion* (Ithaca, NY: Cornell University Press, 1998), 263.

24. Kazin, *Populist Persuasion*, 263.

25. I am closely following the chapter on Jerry Falwell by Robert C. Liebman, "Mobilizing the Moral Majority in the New Christian Right: Mobilization and Legitimation," in *The New Christian Right*, ed. Robert C. Liebman and Robert Wuthnow (New York: Aldine Publishing, 1983), 49–73.

26. David Bennet, *The Party of Fear* (New York: Vintage, 1990), 384.

27. Quoted in the excellent essay by Robert Wuthnow, "Political Rebirth of American Evangelicals," in *New Christian Right*, 168.

28. Ibid., 167. Several Christian preachers had been outspoken anticommunists in the 1950s and early 1960s, but they were relatively few.

29. For the statistics, see Liebman, "Mobilizing the Moral Majority," 54–59. For background, see also Paul Gottfried, *The Conservative Movement* (New York: Twayne Publishers, 1993), 102–117; and Bennet, *Party of Fear*, 375–392.

30. Ronald Reagan, "Acceptance of the Republican Nomination for President," July 17, 1980, Detroit Michigan, http://www.tamu.edu/scom/pres/speeches/rraccept.html.

31. Michael Schaller, *Reckoning with Reagan* (New York: Oxford University Press, 1992), 4.

2

"It Makes You Want to Believe in the Country"

Celebrating the Bicentennial in an Age of Limits

CHRISTOPHER CAPOZZOLA

"I must say to you that the state of our Union is not good." This blunt assessment, delivered to the American people by President Gerald R. Ford in his first State of the Union address on the evening of January 15, 1975, expressed the sense of doubt that permeated American political culture in the 1970s. Yet this was supposed to be a time of celebration: the two-hundredth anniversary of the signing of the Declaration of Independence was just a year and a half away. Would Americans come together to celebrate on that day, after the tumult of the 1960s, after Watergate and the Vietnam War?[1]

On July 4, 1976, of course, Americans did mark their bicentennial, with events ranging from the profound to the trivial, in what one commentator accurately summed up as "an odd mixture of silliness, greed, irony and excellence." But Bicentennial celebrations, although festive, were sometimes marked by an ambivalent tone—especially when compared with the festivities that had accompanied the Centennial one hundred years earlier. In 1876, President Ulysses S. Grant marched behind four thousand troops at the opening of the Centennial Exhibition in Philadelphia's Fairmount Park. That military pomp and circumstance would be muted a century later, and across the political spectrum, some preferred it that way. Writing in March 1975, an essayist for the *New Yorker* argued that recent political events had dealt such a severe blow to the nation's grand principles that a bombastic celebration of American greatness would be inappropriate. "Our noble commitments, our firm stands, our global responsibilities—how frequently, in recent years, have they served as a cover for self-interest and greed, then as sunglasses against the flames?" Instead, a quiet celebration was in order. Festivities in Philadelphia in 1876 had included a "Centennial Inauguration March" specially composed by Richard Wagner and Handel's "Hallelujah Chorus" sung by a choir of eight hundred. On the eve of the Bicentennial, people had something else in mind: "What we must do, when the time comes, is sing 'Happy Birthday' with feeling, but softly—very softly."[2]

National ambivalence could be found not only in the pages of elite magazines, but also on the sidewalks of places like Peoria, Illinois. "It makes you want to believe in the country," said one woman who was watching Peoria's Bicentennial parade. There, along the parade route, she articulated a central contradiction of 1970s political culture. Her statement showed a desire to express her patriotism, but also her sense, at some level, that she could not—or should not. Why not? Maybe she felt overwhelmed. In the wake of the Vietnam War and a host of political scandals, many Americans—even those who had supported the war—found the language of national greatness distasteful. Or maybe she felt alienated. Plenty of Americans—on both the Left and the Right—were skeptical of unitary visions of the American past conveyed to them from Washington, believing themselves to be victims rather than members of the federal government. Maybe she was uneasy about who was going to pay for this party. In the midst of an economic downturn, the confidence of the postwar boom had been replaced by a sense of uncertainty so widespread that some had begun to call the decade the Age of Limits. Or maybe, after the yearlong buildup to the Bicentennial that had permeated television, newspapers, and consumer culture, she was simply bored.[3]

The political culture of the 1970s shaped the Bicentennial. There were significant political divisions, cultural conflicts, and economic realities that determined how Americans would celebrate their two-hundredth anniversary as a nation. But although the language of limits and doubts was an important political vocabulary that Americans used in the 1970s to talk about their country, it was only one of many competing notions in the arena of political culture. Not all Americans were as ambivalent as the Peoria paradegoer. Some had passionate opinions, demonstrating that the conflicts of the 1960s were alive and well in the new decade. Struggles over the meaning of the American experiment played out across the country on July 4, 1976, in local communities from Philadelphia to Montana. Our ambivalent Bicentennial revealed a nation engaged in a vigorous battle over the terrain of political meaning but strikingly unaware that the ground was then shifting under its feet.

PLANNING THE FOURTH

Planning for the Bicentennial began years before the event. As early as 1957, Philadelphia Mayor Richardson Dilworth asked that city's Junior Chamber of Commerce to undertake plans for the Bicentennial celebrations, and Massachusetts established the first state Bicentennial commission in 1964. Efforts began so early, in fact, because of competition among several northeastern cities that hoped to lay claim to the Bicentennial: Boston, the cradle of the Revolution; Philadelphia, the site of the Continental Congress; and Washington DC, the nation's capital.[4]

Official federal plans were underway by 1966 with an ambitious goal: the initial federal agency, the American Revolution Bicentennial Commission (ARBC), considered a proposal for an international exposition—at the projected cost of $1.5 billion and along the lines of the world's fairs held in Seattle in 1962, New York in 1964, and Montreal in 1967—to be held in Philadelphia in 1976. Commissioners hoped that Los Angeles and Denver would be successful in their bids to host the 1976 Summer and Winter Olympics as well. President Lyndon Johnson's White House looked ahead to the Bicentennial and the Philadelphia International Exposition with optimism. In the cold-war era, world's fairs had offered America the opportunity to demonstrate its economic and technological power on the international stage; Philadelphia in the nation's bicentennial year would be no different, and early planning literature highlighted the chance to celebrate the "free world." In the mid-1960s, at the height of Johnson's Great Society, the proposed Bicentennial exposition also carried the promise of federal funds for urban renewal in Philadelphia. Planners, collaborating with the Coalition for a Meaningful Bicentennial, a local community group, developed an "Agenda for Action," which would combine the Bicentennial with urban redevelopment programs aimed at Philadelphia's inner-city poor.[5]

Economic and political upheavals put an end to the proposed fair. Internal White House memos from the early 1970s suggest that the Nixon administration balked at the fair's price tag, and that President Richard M. Nixon had decided as early as 1971 that the Exposition was little more than a Democratic welfare boondoggle. During the economic downturn of the early 1970s, as government budgets shrank at every level, the ax officially fell. "National and international economic hard times," the planners were told, meant that the Philadelphia International Exposition would be scrapped.[6]

Then the Bicentennial ran into a political controversy. In 1972, journalists investigating the ARBC charged that Nixon had stacked the organization with Republican members to further partisan political goals. State and local historical organizations and community groups, shut out of planning for the event, also criticized ARBC as a top-down enterprise. In 1974, as Nixon faced criticism not only of ARBC but of his entire presidency, he disbanded the organization and replaced it with the American Revolution Bicentennial Administration (ARBA), under the direction of Secretary of the Navy John W. Warner.[7]

This was just as well, given the opposition to ARBC's partisan maneuvering and popular demand for greater participation in event planning. The new organization, ARBA, quickly began turning over planning—and payment responsibility—to local governments and voluntary associations. The Bicentennial would be celebrated at the local, not the national, level. Organizers hoped to make a virtue of this necessity. "The Bicentennial was to become a hometown affair," they noted. "The most important Bicentennial undertakings would bring dissidents as well as neighbors and friends together in common purpose." The language of Great Society urban renewal was gone. ARBA now spoke of hometown pride, folksy small-town parades, and local improvement projects paid for with sweat equity and elbow grease. Such nostalgia was appealing, not least because it promised to paper over difficult political divisions facing the nation. Behind the rhetoric, however, were the realities of the 1970s: fiscal crisis and growing opposition to federal planning.[8]

But the Bicentennial still had to be paid for. Florida's Bicentennial Commission raised its funds, nearly $3.5 million, through levies on horse and dog racing; taxes, though, were the exception, not the rule. Instead, the day's events were heavily subsidized by corporate America. ARBA officials forged close connections between government and private industry. Business leaders played prominent roles in the Bicentennial administration; ARBA chairman David L. Wolper was a Hollywood television producer. The officials sought—and received—substantial help with marketing and advertising

Bicentennial events from Madison Avenue firms. The Smithsonian collaborated with American Airlines and General Foods. The Bicentennial Wagon Train Pilgrimage to Pennsylvania, one of the day's most visible events, brought hundreds of covered wagons on an eastward trek to Valley Forge, Pennsylvania; it depended on the organizational leadership of Thelma Gray, an advertising agency executive, and sponsorship by Gulf Oil. Overall, nearly 250 companies chipped in $38.9 million to support official ARBA programs alone.[9]

Businesses, in turn, used the Bicentennial to promote their own products. "Like a sudden swarm of 200-year locusts," noted *Time* magazine, "commemorative kitsch is appearing everywhere." Pharmacy shelves stocked "Minuteman vitamin tablets." The insecticide company d-CON offered a Bicentennial T-shirt to customers to honor "the people who are helping to free America from bugs." One hundred fifty dollars bought a set of red, white, and blue dentures from a Miami dentist who promised to "set dentistry back 200 years." There was even a Bicentennial toilet seat. Robert Williams, executive secretary of the New York chapter of the Sons of the American Revolution, was one of many who defended this commercialism: "There's nothing wrong with making a buck. Free enterprise is the thing that has made this country go zowee." And ARBA certainly depended on the arrangement, which returned between 4 and 15 percent of the sales of licensed products to the organization's coffers.[10]

The commercialism of the Bicentennial was not without its detractors, however. Although ARBA kept tabs on the use of its trademarked logos, plenty of marketing efforts forged ahead without the official seal of approval. Critics mocked the more ludicrous instances, such as the toilet seat, a Bicentennial massage parlor, or a star-spangled whoopee cushion. Other news accounts pointed out that cheap Bicentennial trinkets were often made in overseas factories. The liberal press and radical organizations pushed their critique beyond satire, however. In January 1976, *The Nation* urged "No Sale" on the Bicentennial, noting, "Before it is irrevocably polluted, the Bicentennial ought to be reclaimed."[11]

Overall, the commercialism of the Bicentennial celebrations merely reflected the consumer culture of the country as a whole. Robert Williams was right when he suggested the centrality of enterprise to the nation's "zowee." But the wholesale handover of the Bicentennial to corporate America was part of a larger shift then underway, as the Great Society liberalism of the postwar era collapsed under the burdens of a troubled economy and a hostile public. The story would find echoes throughout the 1970s in taxpayer revolts, antiwelfare agitation, and bitter fights over subsidies for the nation's troubled cities. The economic realities of the Bicentennial, which revealed America's inability to organize a massive national celebration without dependence on private industry, represented just one scene in a drama that played on the national stage during the decade.[12]

"PEOPLE" AND "REVOLUTION"

Money was not the only reason the Bicentennial would be a complicated affair. In the wake of what even official planners acknowledged as "some of the bitterest times in our history," the Bicentennial prompted debates over the meaning of American history and American identity, and the political turmoil of the previous decade made national celebration a challenge. This was ironic, because the Bicentennial itself commemorated divisive and revolutionary events of an earlier era. "The two words most muted during the two hundredth year of American independence," noted historian Richard B. Morris in his presidential address to the American Historical Association, "have been 'people' and 'revolution.'" Both words posed political difficulties in the 1970s. Some believed that the nation's long and ongoing history of discrimination excluded them from "we the people"; others sought to reclaim the nation's revolutionary heritage and shape it to modern-day radical ends. But after a decade of civil rights revolution, no one doubted that the nation's diverse heritage would be part of the Bicentennial conversation.[13]

Among African Americans, there was widespread division over participation in the Bicentennial. Many joined in enthusiastically, including Betty Shabazz, the widow of slain racial justice activist Malcolm X, who joined ARBA's Advisory Council. Some pushed for the inclusion of African American history into the festivities of the Fourth; the Afro-American Bicentennial Corporation, founded in 1970, made inclusion of black history sites on the National Register of Historic Places part of Bicentennial efforts, providing a long-term impetus to African American heritage tourism. Urban African Americans collaborated with other ethnic groups in organizations such as the Bicentennial Ethnic Racial Coalition to lobby for urban renewal programs as part of the nation's Bicentennial agenda. Other voices, however, were more critical. Representative Charles Rangel of New York said, "[I]f the

Bicentennial is some kind of self-congratulatory celebration, it is frivolous and meaningless to the black community." In Philadelphia, community activist Wycliffe Jangdharrie summed up the feelings of many when he noted, "We don't have any reason to have a Bicentennial. The black man is still not free." Reverend Jesse Jackson called for a boycott of the events.[14]

Conflicts over the nation's historic celebrations were particularly visible in Native American communities. In the early 1970s, American Indian reservations had witnessed an upsurge of political activism ranging from courtroom challenges to the radical movement for "Red Power" led by the American Indian Movement. As the Bicentennial approached, some activists chose to commemorate an alternative holiday: the one-hundredth anniversary of the Battle of the Little Bighorn. Beverly Badhorse announced a victory dance to celebrate the defeat of Gen. George A. Custer. "[W]hile the rest of the United States celebrates its bicentennial . . . Northern Cheyennes will hold the traditional victory dance so long denied them. The centennial of an incredible Indian victory. And some will mourn principles of the bicentennial." Federal ARBA administrators actively sought to reconcile America's Indian heritage with its national celebration, with limited success. An Indian group in Portland, Oregon, likened their invitation to join the Bicentennial Wagon Train to Jews joining a celebration for Adolf Hitler; in other communities, however, Native Americans participated in Bicentennial celebrations.[15]

Just as divisive as the debates about the definition of the American people were battles over the meaning of America itself. The political turmoil of the previous years had tempered many Americans' faith in their government—and perhaps, by extension, in the nation itself. The Watergate crisis and the resignation of President Nixon in August 1974 were recent memories, refreshed in the bicentennial year by the premiere that April of the film version of *All the President's Men.* Just a year earlier, in April 1975, the last American troops left South Vietnam. Americans watched on television as South Vietnamese tried desperately to escape as U.S. helicopters evacuated American diplomatic staff from Saigon. South Vietnam fell to the Communists just days later.

Many tried to rein in the federal government after a decade of secrecy, lies, and unauthorized meddling in the affairs of foreign countries. Human rights first emerged as a national (and global) political issue in the 1970s: at the grassroots level, the membership rolls of organizations like Amnesty International grew from the hundreds to the hundreds of thousands; the increasingly savvy organization opened its first lobbying office in Washington DC in 1976. On Capitol Hill, initial congressional hearings on human rights led directly to legislation that made American foreign aid conditional on the human-rights records of overseas regimes. When Jimmy Carter ran for president in the bicentennial year with a promise to make morality part of American foreign policy, he reflected American thinking on human rights more than he shaped it.[16]

Similar criticisms were aimed at an aggressive executive power that historian Arthur M. Schlesinger Jr. termed the "imperial presidency." There was much to be concerned about. Throughout the early 1970s, news reports revealed the political misdeeds of the Central Intelligence Agency (CIA) and the Federal Bureau of Investigation during the Vietnam era. In December 1974, the CIA revealed that it had spied on antiwar protestors through a program called Operation Chaos; in 1975, a 693–page internal memo on the CIA's secret affairs was leaked to the press. Emboldened by its experience challenging President Nixon during Watergate, Congress demanded investigations. Idaho senator Frank Church, chairman of one such investigation, attacked the CIA as a "rogue elephant" and urged closer regulation of the intelligence system. For a few years in the early 1970s, Americans had unprecedented access to the secret inner workings of their government, but few concrete reforms materialized as the Ford administration quickly maneuvered to limit the scope of the inquiries.[17]

The summer of 1974 also saw the release of confidential documents related to the assassination of President John F. Kennedy; later, in March 1975, television audiences first watched the amateur film recorded in Dallas in 1963 by Abraham Zapruder. Throughout 1976 and 1977, a congressional committee reinvestigated the assassination of Kennedy, fueling popular beliefs that the true circumstances of the president's death had been concealed from the American people. From congressional investigations to Hollywood conspiracy films such as *Three Days of the Condor* (1975) and *Marathon Man* (1976), the popular culture of the 1970s expressed the American people's growing sense of disaffection from government, a deep distrust that predated and outlived the specific events of Watergate but would shape American political culture for decades to come.[18]

Probably the most strident and high-profile critique of the Bicentennial came from the People's Bicentennial Commission (PBC), founded in 1971 by twenty-six-year-old Jeremy Rifkin, already a skilled veteran of the 1960s leftist movements. The PBC wanted to reclaim the revolutionary character of the revolution itself. "We will be celebrating radical heroes like Jefferson,

Paine, and Adams, and radical events like the Boston Tea Party," they noted. The PBC bemoaned the "Buy-centennial" and its control by "corporate Tories." It was their investigative legwork that had uncovered the political shenanigans of the ARBC in the early 1970s, and they were among the most prominent critics of the Bicentennial's commercialization. Their visibility showed the continuing appeal of the 1960s assault on big business, but when the organization sought to foment an uprising against corporate power with a far-fetched plan to mobilize whistle-blowing employees in alliance with the wives of Fortune 500 CEOs, their support quickly dried up. Mississippi senator James Eastland denounced the PBC's approach in language that echoed the McCarthyism of an earlier era: "By muscling in on the Bicentennial observance, it seeks first of all to pervert its meaning and, secondly, to exploit it for the purposes of overthrowing our free society."[19]

The decade's distrust of governmental power was not the sole property of the political Left. In fact, the 1970s witnessed a range of grassroots conservative movements in opposition to federal power. President Ford picked up on the rising popular sentiment and linked it to the Bicentennial itself: "The people are about as fed up with the petty tyranny of the faceless federal bureaucrats today as they were with their faraway rulers in London in 1776." In Boston, as the city celebrated the Bicentennial, bitter resentment of court-ordered busing to redress segregation in the city's school districts prompted some city residents to declare another revolution. "The antagonists of forced busing in Boston," noted one commentator, "wear tricorn hats and demand community self-government, like their predecessors of 200 years ago." Members of the antibusing organization ROAR (Restore Our Alienated Rights) attended a 1975 reenactment of the Boston Massacre; when the Redcoats fired their muskets, four hundred protestors fell to the ground in silent protest. A handful went even further in their opposition to busing, setting fire to a replica ship at the Boston Tea Party site and detonating a small explosive at Plymouth Rock in June 1976. They threatened further attacks against Bicentennial sites unless forced busing was halted.[20]

From South Boston to the Little Bighorn to the halls of Congress, the fractured politics of the 1970s played out in a contest over the meaning of America itself. The Bicentennial offered a means for the politically discontented to articulate a critique of the status quo by showing how far the nation had supposedly fallen from its original, noble principles, an approach accessible to people across the political spectrum. But even as Americans appealed to the legacies of their founding Revolution, it was increasingly clear that there would not be another one in 1976. John Warner dismissed the idea. "One revolution," he said, "has proved enough."[21]

THE LOCALIZATION OF AMERICAN PATRIOTISM

For economic, political, and cultural reasons, then, a single grand national celebration was not going to mark the nation's bicentennial. There was no money for a world's fair. There was uneasiness about outspoken patriotism. And in an era of ethnic pride, it had become increasingly clear that one historical narrative could not tell the whole nation's story. There was still plenty of commemoration, much of it observed on the local level and dedicated to local and family history. The Bicentennial return to the past was part and parcel of the "search for self" that characterized much of 1970s culture, as Americans responded to a world that they believed had been disrupted by geographic and social mobility, mass media, and a sense of impermanence fostered by consumer culture. But Bicentennial nostalgia was more than just a search for roots in a rootless world. Celebrating a community's past, or a family's history, could help Americans negotiate the tensions they felt between their local and their national identities. It could also operate as a retreat into the private realm of the family and the community and a rejection of the divisiveness of political life in the period.

Perhaps the Bicentennial's most enduring legacy for American culture was the explosion of interest in local history, genealogy, and American folk culture that it inspired. Americans indulged a newfound appreciation of folk art, Americana, and material culture. Across the country, local history museums sprang up in response to the nation's celebrations, and attendance at sites of heritage tourism increased as well. Similar motives impelled an upsurge of interest in genealogy; what had previously been a minor hobby of Mormons and the Daughters of the American Revolution became a national phenomenon. The revival of the craft of quilting was so widespread that by 1976 the metaphor of America as a patchwork quilt had become one of the central motifs of Bicentennial celebrations.[22]

The most visible symbol of these developments was the publication in 1976 of Alex Haley's novel *Roots*. The novel used Haley's own family histories—from West Africa to the American South—to narrate the story of race and slavery in American history. It was one of the best-selling books of the year and prompted widespread interest in genealogy among Americans of all ethnic backgrounds. The connections between *Roots* and the Bicentennial were even closer than they might at first appear: Alex Haley was an appointed member of ARBA's Advisory Council, and the 1977 television miniseries of *Roots,* watched by more than 130 million Americans, would be produced by none other than David L. Wolper, the chairman of ARBA.[23]

Roots was part of something larger, not so much the cause as the sign of Americans' search for themselves in the 1970s. Those who felt excluded from grand national narratives could find in local history and genealogy a place for themselves in America's history in its celebratory bicentennial year. For those who felt their patriotism tempered or chastised, the quest for roots could express American patriotism from an ambivalent, sideways angle. Finally, Bicentennial nostalgia could also be an avoidance, an embrace of an imagined peaceful past that helped people avoid the fractious present. Equal parts quest and escape, the localism of the Bicentennial gave Americans a way out of failed national narratives without having to take responsibility for answering big national questions.

CELEBRATING THE FOURTH

What, then, do the Bicentennial festivities of July 4, 1976—more than sixty thousand separate events across the country—tell us about American political culture in the 1970s? The Bicentennial's ambivalent mood could be felt in Washington DC; Boston confronted urban renewal along with the decade's fractious politics; the new alliance between business, government, and media spectacle was on display in New York; and in Philadelphia, more than anywhere else, the conflict over the meaning of America itself shaped the day's events.

In Washington DC, the capital celebrated a National Pageant of Freedom with parades and the world's largest fireworks display. Although the city had witnessed numerous marches and public gatherings during the civil rights and antiwar movements of the previous two decades, there was no March on Washington that day, and Bicentennial observances were politically muted. The PBC had hoped that two hundred thousand protestors would march on Washington to declare "Independence from Big Business," but no more than one-tenth of that number appeared at the Capitol steps.

Only a handful joined the protests of the American Nazi Party in Lafayette Park, across the street from the White House; the Nazis themselves even showed up late.[24]

The largest celebrations took place in New York City, where Operation Sail '76 brought 224 historic ships—known popularly as the Tall Ships—to the city's harbor, surrounded by about 10,000 unofficial floating participants that ranged from elegant yachts to humble tugboats. Crowds were estimated at nearly six million. That evening, a fireworks display illuminated the ships in the harbor. President Ford arrived in New York Harbor by helicopter and observed the day's events from the USS *Nashville.*[25]

It was no accident that Ford did not actually set foot in New York City. A year earlier, New York had faced a fiscal crisis that threatened the city with bankruptcy. President Ford's response suggested that the stream of federal funding to cities had dried up; his comments, in fact, were so stern that they prompted a famous headline in the *New York Daily News:* "Ford to City: Drop Dead." New York turned to private industry to stabilize the city's finances in the midst of the fiscal crisis, just as Bicentennial planners had done on a much smaller level.[26]

Collaboration between business and government was also at the heart of Boston's preparations for the Bicentennial. Government funds unavailable for urban renewal could still be obtained to foster historic preservation and heritage tourism. In a 1972 memo, a Boston planner noted the possibilities this shift offered. "The Bicentennial gives us . . . a chance to make the case for cities being good places," she wrote. "We have fallen into the habit of talking about how bad things are in order to convince certain audience [*sic*], particularly the federal government, that Boston and other cities need help." Faced with the disappearance of government aid at a time when it was strapped for cash, Boston learned new ways of asking for money and new ways of thinking about cities, transforming the urban landscape in the meantime.[27]

In Boston, the heritage tourism associated with the Bicentennial reshaped the city, culminating in the construction of the Freedom Trail, a walking tour linking Revolutionary-era historic sites, and the renovation of Quincy Market, a shopping and pedestrian tourist area. Quincy Market was a resounding success; it would later serve as the model for urban redevelopment nationwide as city governments and private industry collaborated to lure suburbanites back downtown.[28]

Nowhere did the politics of the Bicentennial play out more clearly than in Philadelphia, where the Founders had gathered long before to declare independence. The proposed world's fair never took place, but Philadelphia's historical significance guaranteed that it would remain a national focal point for Bicentennial celebrations. Two hundred years after the signing of the Declaration, the city was a reflection of much of the rest of America, especially the urban Northeast: it had experienced the rapid decline of its industrial base and the move of many of its residents to suburbs and the emerging Sun Belt; rising crime and a declining tax base had left the city in financial straits.[29]

Mayor Frank Rizzo, the man in charge of the city, was himself a new phenomenon in Philadelphia politics—and a sign of a shifting political terrain at the national level as well. As police commissioner in the 1960s, he had carefully cultivated a reputation for unstinting commitment to law and order. Once, called away from a formal dinner to respond to an episode of urban unrest, he displayed a nightstick in his cummerbund, in clear view of the news photographers he sought to impress. His toleration of racially motivated police brutality and lines like "I'm going to make Attila the Hun look like a faggot" made enemies in Philadelphia's inner-city neighborhoods (and also, obviously, among its gay residents). In the summer of 1976, Rizzo faced a recall drive prompted by accusations of corruption. But Rizzo could count on fierce support from working-class ethnic whites who felt embattled by the city's urban crisis; they had formed a core constituency of his successful bid for mayor in 1971. As elsewhere across the country, white ethnics in Philadelphia abandoned the New Deal political coalitions that had attached them to the Democratic Party for decades. Although Rizzo served as a Democrat, he also ran against the party that many held responsible for rising crime rates and declining conditions in the city.[30]

In other neighborhoods, many echoed the complaints of one political commentator, who believed that Philadelphia was unfit to host the Bicentennial's leading events because of Rizzo, "a racist whose very existence should be a national embarrassment." Rizzo, however, hoped to turn the Bicentennial to his own uses. In 1972, he announced that his "connections" in Washington— his tough-on-crime conservatism was popular with Richard Nixon—would gain him access to nearly one hundred million dollars in funds to rebuild the city center in preparation for the Bicentennial celebrations. The claim was not entirely outrageous: the federal government spent thirty million dollars just to clean up Independence Hall and the Liberty Bell. The full amount never materialized, but that was the least of Rizzo's exaggerations.[31]

Rizzo made law and order an issue during the Bicentennial. In an interview with the *Philadelphia Inquirer*, he insisted that a plot was underway to undermine the city's Bicentennial celebrations. "[T]he leftists . . . intend to come in here in thousands from all over the country to disrupt . . . how about the rights of the majority who are going to be here to enjoy themselves with their families?" He warned that Philadelphia had become "a target for attempts at disruption and violence by a substantial coalition of leftist radicals" and called on the federal government to provide fifteen thousand troops to protect the city. Washington summarily rejected Rizzo's requests for troops, but on the evening of July 3, Rizzo issued another ominous warning: "I hope and pray that nothing occurs, but I know this—a lot of people are coming to this town who are bent on violence."[32]

In fact, two organizations, the July 4th Coalition and the Rich Off Our Backs Coalition, had both announced peaceful countermarches for the city on the day of the Bicentennial. But had Rizzo received the troops he requested, they would have almost outnumbered the protestors. The Rich Off Our Backs Coalition marched in protest to Norris Park in the largely black neighborhood of North Philadelphia, about one mile from downtown. Another crowd of thirty thousand gathered in Fairmount Park to protest the Bicentennial celebration's triumphant nationalism; they listened as Karen DeCrow of the National Organization for Women read Susan B. Anthony's 1876 Centennial speech. Black Panther Elaine Brown decried the nation's heritage as one of "murder and plunder." Philadelphians of Puerto Rican heritage called for "a Bicentennial without colonies." The violence Rizzo foresaw never materialized: by day's end, not a single protestor had been arrested.[33]

Downtown, official festivities went ahead as planned. President Ford put in an appearance at the Liberty Bell in the afternoon, along with Mayor Rizzo, conservative actor Charlton Heston, and Queen Elizabeth II of England, who caused something of a stir when she touched the Liberty Bell. Marian Anderson, a renowned African American contralto singer who had become a symbol of civil rights after her performance at the Lincoln Memorial in 1939, read the Declaration of Independence at Independence Hall. The Paris Boys' Choir sang, and the Mummers—a city tradition in which residents of the Italian American neighborhood of South Philadelphia parade in outlandish costumes—performed as well. There was even a five-story forty-nine-thousand-pound cake.[34]

Rizzo had succeeded in scaring thousands of people away from the city. Philadelphia had expected seventy thousand to line the route of a festive parade, but only about half that number showed up. Those frightened off included high school marching bands and even entire state parade contingents. Joseph Sakalosky, the principal of Cedar Crest High School in New Lebanon, Pennsylvania, regretted that the school's marching band would not be attending the city's festivities. "After 200 years of liberty, it is disconcerting that the nation cannot celebrate its Bicentennial without a threat of violence sufficiently strong to cause concern for the safety and welfare of our participating youth." Some fifteen thousand marchers stayed home, including the entire delegations of Colorado, Kentucky, and Tennessee.[35]

In the end, most of the viewers of Philadelphia's celebrations watched from the comfort of their living rooms. As Frank Rizzo preened for the cameras, many Americans ignored his antics. That fall, they turned instead to another story of ethnic Philadelphia: *Rocky*. Sylvester Stallone's portrayal of an underdog South Philly boxer won over few critics, but it walked away with an Academy Award for its evocation of the cultural landscape of urban life in the nation's bicentennial year. Its most memorable scene, featuring Rocky Balboa atop the steps of the Philadelphia Museum of Art, was made possible by the Bicentennial: the museum's renovation had been financed as part of the city's Bicentennial cleanup campaign.[36]

Outside the big cities of the Northeast, the day's events were marked by modest celebrations, parades, and fireworks displays. At her summer home on Cape Cod, seventy-nine-year-old Ruth Robinson made only a small notation in her diary: "A fascinating Eve. Watching Bob Hope + all the Fireworks + the BiCentennial 4th of July T.V. programs." Robinson was not the only one who watched the Bicentennial on television. The medium was central to the experience of the Bicentennial; the day's festivities were staged media events broadcast during sixteen hours of coverage (remarkable in an era before round-the-clock programming). But ARBA planners went further, suggesting that "television provided the nation with a great exposition that some felt would be missing during the historic period—an exposition of the nation itself." Here was another paradox of the nation's Bicentennial experience: although many Americans spent the day with their families or marked the event in local community celebrations, they were linked to the Bicentennial on the national level through television, a medium that now claimed to be "an exposition of the nation itself." The media extravaganza of the Bicentennial—from the streets of Philadelphia and the festivities in New York Harbor to the pages of *Roots* and television screens across the nation—contained in its wild array all the contradictions of American political culture in the 1970s. It also signaled a shift in political life that was already underway.[37]

A handful of commentators at the time noticed the interpenetration of politics and entertainment. Jeremy Rifkin of the PBC ominously warned that "corporate America has conceived a bicentennial plan to manipulate the mass psychology of an entire nation back into conformity with its vision of what American life should be." If only the explanation were that easy. There was no psychological war plan hatched in a back room. There was uniformity, to be sure, but not conformity: the Bicentennial fostered the expression of multiple local attachments and filtered them through a mass-media extravaganza that did not so much repress the discordant elements of the day as it did harmonize them into a nonthreatening national spectacle, one that allowed Americans to feel connected and detached at the same time.[38]

In the wake of the Bicentennial, the American news media frequently addressed the issue of national healing. Perhaps the fireworks and small-town parades and the Tall Ships gathered in New York City's harbor had shown the triumph of a perennial American optimism over the Age of Limits. *Time* was happy to see "after a long night of paralyzing self-doubt, good feelings about the U.S." The *Washington Post* saw "a moment of deep and moving reconciliation." The *Birmingham News* went the furthest: "America turned the corner Sunday on a self-induced illness of the spirit and stretched its psyche in a burst of national joy and celebration."[39]

These were, to put it mildly, overstatements. The sense that there was something fundamentally wrong with the country did not fade in the light of the Bicentennial fireworks; it did not disappear with the election of Jimmy Carter. If anything, it would worsen. As the late 1970s brought more inflation, longer gas lines, and a continued sense of national political impotence during the Iran hostage crisis, the idea of the Age of Limits became ever more convincing to many Americans. By 1979, Carter himself would speak of "a crisis of confidence . . . that strikes at the very heart and soul and spirit of our national will." This was hardly the language of a burst of national joy.[40]

But if Americans had embraced their country's contradictions during the Bicentennial and had sought ways to reconcile their skepticism with national festivities, they found a decade later that the choices they made in the 1970s had led them down another path. Their new president, Ronald Reagan, spoke not of crisis or malaise but of "morning in America." He captured for the Right the distrust of big government that a wide spectrum of Americans shared in the 1970s, insisting in his 1981 inaugural address that "government is not the solution to our problem. It is our problem." And by reinvigorating America's sustaining myths as the cure for its alienation, he turned the nation's tentative Bicentennial nostalgia into a principled refusal to confront the difficult questions of American life. Ronald Reagan, needless to say, had not spent the Bicentennial softly singing "Happy Birthday."[41]

A decade later, Ronald Reagan joined thousands of Americans in New York City over the Fourth of July weekend to celebrate the centennial of the Statue of Liberty. The event's planning committee, chaired by the Chrysler Corporation CEO, Lee Iacocca, put on a dazzling show. But it was all spectacle, national heritage as mass entertainment. Unlike the Bicentennial, there was little grassroots participation, no reflective confrontation with the meanings of liberty, and little public dissent. This time, whatever the Bicentennial had done to prompt an engagement with the national past as a source of our common life had been, like American democracy itself, carefully orchestrated away.

ACKNOWLEDGMENTS

For research suggestions and feedback, my thanks to Holly Allen, Beth Bailey, David Farber, David Greenberg, Meg Jacobs, and Ellen Stroud. My siblings, 1970s veterans all, offered oral histories. Zander Capozzola provided invaluable research assistance.

Notes

1. "A Transcript of the State of the Union Address to Congress by President Ford," *New York Times*, January 16, 1975.

2. Raymond A. Schroth, "A 'Feel' for Being American," *Commonweal*, July 1, 1976, 424; "Notes and Comment," *New Yorker*, March 31, 1975, 21.

3. *Peoria Journal-Star*, quoted in American Revolution Bicentennial Administration [ARBA], *The Bicentennial of the United States of America: A Final Report to the People* (Washington: ARBA, 1977), 1:21.

4. ARBA, *Bicentennial of the United States*, 1:58; John Bodnar, *Remaking America: Public Memory, Commemoration, and Patriotism in the Twentieth Century* (Princeton, NJ: Princeton University Press, 1992), 229; Joseph R. Daughen and Peter Binzen, *The Cop Who Would Be King: Mayor Frank Rizzo* (Boston: Little, Brown, 1977), 313. An early proposal from a city planner is Edmund Bacon, "Tomorrow:

A Fair Can Pace It," *Philadelphia Magazine,* October 1959, 236–244. See also Martin W. Wilson, "From the Sesquicentennial to the Bicentennial: Changing Attitudes toward Tourism in Philadelphia" (PhD diss., Temple University, 2000), 174–222.

5. ARBA, *Bicentennial of the United States,* 1:58; Bodnar, *Remaking America,* 230. Histories of other post–World War II world's fairs include Gary M. Bernkow, "Seattle's Century 21, 1962," *Pacific Northwest Forum* 7 (1994): 68–80; John M. Findlay, *Magic Lands: Western Cityscapes and American Culture after 1940* (Berkeley: University of California Press, 1992); and Michael L. Smith, "Making Time: Representations of Technology at the 1964 World's Fair," in *The Power of Culture: Critical Essays in American History,* ed. Richard Wightman Fox and T. J. Jackson Lears (Chicago: University of Chicago Press, 1993), 223–244.

6. Wilson, "From the Sesquicentennial to the Bicentennial," 212; ARBA, *Bicentennial of the United States,* 1:57.

7. Bodnar, *Remaking America,* 230–231; "Documents Link Politics to the '76 Fete," *New York Times,* August 20, 1972; "Reforms Approved by Panel Planning U.S. Bicentennial," *New York Times,* September 9, 1972.

8. ARBA, *Bicentennial of the United States,* 1:9.

9. Ibid., 1:44, 57, 61; Leonard Sloane, "Advertising: The Symbol of '76," *New York Times,* August 17, 1972; James T. Wooten, "Uncertain Course on Bicentennial," *New York Times,* June 16, 1974.

10. "Reconnaissance: World and National News," *Borrowed Times,* late April, 1976, 16; Schroth, "A 'Feel' for Being American," 423–425; "Bucks from the Bicentennial," *Time,* September 29, 1975, 73.

11. James T. Wooten, "Tourism, Commercialization and Rosy Perspective on Bicentennial Stirring Antagonism," *New York Times,* December 1, 1975; "No Sale," *The Nation,* January 10, 1976, 5.

12. For one perspective on these broad shifts, see Steve Fraser and Gary Gerstle, eds., *The Rise and Fall of the New Deal Order* (Princeton NJ: Princeton University Press, 1989).

13. ARBA, *Bicentennial of the United States,* 1:4; Richard B. Morris, " 'We the People of the United States': The Bicentennial of a People's Revolution," *American Historical Review* 82 (1977): 1.

14. Bodnar, *Remaking America,* 232, 237, 241; "The Big 200th Bash," *Time,* July 5, 1976, 14; Wilson, "From the Sesquicentennial to the Bicentennial," 202. See also Benjamin Quarles, "Founding Peoples and Immigrants: A Black Bicentennial Perspective," *Crisis* 82, no. 7 (1975): 244–248; Jean A. McRae and Joyce E. Latham, "Bicentennial Outlook: The Enriching Black Presence," *Historic Preservation* 27, no. 3 (1975): 10–15. For further perspectives, see the series *Black Perspectives on the Bicentennial,* published by the National Urban League in 1976.

15. ARBA, *Bicentennial of the United States,* 1:65, 130; Bodnar, *Remaking America,* 282 n62; Beverly Badhorse, "Century-Late Victory Dance to Be Celebrated June 25–27," *Borrowed Times,* late April, 1976, 5; Grace Lichtenstein, "Custer's

Defeat Remembered in Entreaties on Peace," *New York Times*, June 25, 1976; Edward Tabor Linenthal, *Sacred Ground: Americans and Their Battlefields*, 2nd ed. (Urbana: University of Illinois Press, 1993).

16. Kenneth Cmiel, "The Emergence of Human Rights Politics in the United States," *Journal of American History* 86 (1999): 1231–1250; Peter N. Carroll, *It Seemed Like Nothing Happened: The Tragedy and Promise of America in the 1970s* (New York: Holt, Rinehart, and Winston, 1982), 214–215.

17. Arthur M. Schlesinger Jr., *The Imperial Presidency* (Boston: Houghton Mifflin, 1973); Seymour Hersh, "Huge C.I.A. Operation Reported in U.S. against Anti-War Forces," *New York Times*, December 22, 1974; Kathryn M. Olmsted, *Challenging the Secret Government: The Post-Watergate Investigations of the CIA and FBI* (Chapel Hill: University of North Carolina Press, 1996); Loch K. Johnson, *A Season of Inquiry: The Senate Intelligence Investigation* (Lexington: University Press of Kentucky, 1985); Frank J. Smist Jr., *Congress Oversees the United States Intelligence Community, 1947-1989* (Knoxville: University of Tennessee Press, 1990).

18. Gerald Posner, *Case Closed: Lee Harvey Oswald and the Assassination of JFK* (New York: Anchor Books, 1993), 451–456.

19. Bodnar, *Remaking America*, 234–236, 282 n68; Marilyn Bender, "Staff Informers Offered Reward," *New York Times*, April 12, 1976. PBC members were also prolific writers. See Jeremy Rifkin and John Rossen, eds., *How to Commit Revolution American Style: An Anthology* (Secaucus, NJ: Lyle Stuart, 1973); People's Bicentennial Commission, *America's Birthday: A Planning and Activity Guide for Citizens' Participation during the Bicentennial Years* (New York: Simon and Schuster, 1974); idem, *Voices of the American Revolution: The Story of How the Declaration of Independence Came to Be, in the Fiery Words of the Founding Fathers* (New York: Bantam, 1974).

20. Gerald Ford, quoted in Carroll, *It Seemed Like Nothing Happened*, 186–187; Pauline Maier, "America's Checkered Past," *New Republic*, September 20, 1975, 12; J. Anthony Lukas, "Who Owns 1776?" *New York Times Magazine*, May 18, 1975; Bodnar, *Remaking America*, 234; "Bomb Is Exploded at Plymouth Rock with Little Damage," *New York Times*, June 2, 1976; "Caller Claims Role in Plymouth Blast," *New York Times*, June 3, 1976; "Massachusetts Tightening Security at Historic Sites," *New York Times*, June 6, 1976. Presidential candidate George Wallace was a local hero when he spoke of "community control" in South Boston in the Bicentennial year. B. Drummond Ayres Jr., "Wallace Cheered in South Boston," *New York Times*, February 22, 1976.

21. John W. Warner, quoted in Bodnar, *Remaking America*, 234; Warner, "Bicentennial: The Proper Celebration," *New York Times*, January 11, 1976.

22. Bodnar, *Remaking America*, esp. 226–244; David Glassberg, *Sense of History: The Place of the Past in American Life* (Amherst: University of Massachusetts Press, 2001); Roy Rosenzweig and David Thelen, *The Presence of the Past: Popular Uses of History in American Life* (New York: Columbia University Press, 1998); James C. Olson, "Local History and the Bicentennial," *Missouri Historical Review* 70, no. 2

(1976): 127–133; Robert G. Hartje, *Bicentennial USA: Pathways to Celebration* (Nashville: Association for State and Local History, 1973). On genealogy, see "D.A.R. Aids Family in Tracing Genealogy," *New York Times*, January 25, 1976; Peter Andrews, "Genealogy: The Search for a Personal Past," *American Heritage* 33, no. 5 (1982): 10–17; Carroll, *It Seemed Like Nothing Happened*, 297–301; and Michael Kammen, *Mystic Chords of Memory: The Transformation of Tradition in American Culture* (New York: Vintage, 1991), 641–645. Michelle Hudson provides a local account in "The Effect of *Roots* and the Bicentennial on Genealogical Interest among Patrons of the Mississippi Department of Archives and History," *Journal of Mississippi History* 53, no. 4 (1991): 321–336. On quilting, see Lorrie Marie Weidlich, "Quilting Transformed: An Anthropological Approach to the Quilt Revival" (PhD diss., University of Texas, 1986). Quilting was frequently part of July 4th celebrations; see Muriel Fischer, "Preparing for Yesterday," *New York Times*, June 6, 1976; Fred Ferretti, "The City Throws an All-Day Party," *New York Times*, July 2, 1976; ARBA, *Bicentennial of the United States*, 1:172.

23. Bodnar, *Remaking America*, 232; Matthew Frye Jacobson, "A Ghetto to Look Back To: *World of Our Fathers*, Ethnic Revival, and the Arc of Multiculturalism," *American Jewish History* 88 (2000): 463–474; Bruce J. Schulman, *The Seventies: The Great Shift in American Culture, Society, and Politics* (New York: Free Press, 2001), 77; Carroll, *It Seemed Like Nothing Happened*, 297. The novel was not without its critics, then and later. For an early critical view, see David Herbert Donald, "Family Chronicle," *Commentary*, December 1976, 70–74.

24. ARBA, *Bicentennial of the United States*, 1:47; "People's Bicentennial," *New York Times*, July 5, 1976; John L. Hess, "A Day of Picnics, Pomp, Pageantry, and Protest," *New York Times*, July 5, 1976. For more on Washington's symbolic politics, see Scott A. Sandage, "A Marble House Divided: The Lincoln Memorial, the Civil Rights Movement, and the Politics of Memory, 1939–1963," *Journal of American History* 80 (1993): 135–167; and Lucy G. Barber, *Marching on Washington: The Forging of an American Political Tradition* (Berkeley: University of California Press, 2002).

25. Richard F. Shepard, "Panoply of Sails," *New York Times*, July 5, 1976. In his *And the Band Played On: People, Politics, and the AIDS Epidemic* (New York: St. Martin's, 1987), Randy Shilts begins his account of the AIDS epidemic on July 4, 1976, contrasting the innocence of the festivities with the fact that the HIV virus was already spreading in the United States at that time.

26. "Ford to City: Drop Dead," *New York Daily News*, October 30, 1975; "Transcript of President's Talk on City Crisis," *New York Times*, October 30, 1975. For general accounts of the New York fiscal crisis, see Eric Lichten, *Class, Power, and Austerity: The New York City Fiscal Crisis* (South Hadley, MA: Bergin and Garvey, 1986); Martin Shefter, *Political Crisis, Fiscal Crisis: The Collapse and Revival of New York City* (New York: Basic Books, 1985); William K. Tabb, *The Long Default: New York City and the Urban Fiscal Crisis* (New York: Monthly Review Press, 1982).

27. Gail Rotegard to Kathleen Kane, September 30, 1972, Box 1, Gail Rotegard Papers, Schlesinger Library, Radcliffe College, Cambridge, MA.

28. John Kifner, "A 'New' 1826 Market Joins Boston's Downtown Revival," *New York Times*, August 27, 1976; Thomas H. O'Connor, *Building a New Boston: Politics and Urban Renewal, 1950-1970* (Boston: Northeastern University Press, 1993).

29. For more on social movements in post-1960s Philadelphia, see Carolyn Adams, et al., eds., *Philadelphia: Neighborhoods, Division, and Conflict in a Postindustrial City* (Philadelphia: Temple University Press, 1991); Marc Stein, *City of Sisterly and Brotherly Loves: Lesbian and Gay Philadelphia, 1945–1972* (Chicago: University of Chicago Press, 2000); and Carmen Teresa Whalen, *From Puerto Rico to Philadelphia: Puerto Rican Workers and Postwar Economies* (Philadelphia: Temple University Press, 2001).

30. Dennis Hevesi, "A 'Hero' and 'Villain,'" *New York Times*, July 17, 1991; Schroth, "A 'Feel' for Being American," 426; Daughen and Binzen, *Cop Who Would Be King*. For an account of similar tensions in another city in the 1970s, see Jonathan Rieder, *Canarsie: The Jews and Italians of Brooklyn against Liberalism* (Cambridge, MA: Harvard University Press, 1985).

31. Daughen and Binzen, *Cop Who Would Be King*, 222–223, 314.

32. Daughen and Binzen, *Cop Who Would Be King*, 312–313, 315; "Rizzo Urged to Consult Shapp on July 4 Protests," *New York Times*, June 3, 1976; "Philadelphia Pushes July 4 Troop Plea," *New York Times*, June 13, 1976.

33. "Two Counterrallies in Philadelphia," *New York Times*, July 5, 1976; Daughen and Binzen, *Cop Who Would Be King*, 314; Bodnar, *Remaking America*, 236–237.

34. Staff of the Philadelphia *Inquirer, Millennium Philadelphia: The Last 100 Years* (Philadelphia: Camino Books, 1999), 186–187; ARBA, *Bicentennial of the United States*, 1:28; Daughen and Binzen, *Cop Who Would Be King*, 314; Bodnar, *Remaking America*, 228; Linda Charlton, "A Reporter's Notebook: The Touch of Royalty," *New York Times*, July 12, 1976.

35. John L. Hess, "A Day of Picnics, Pomp, Pageantry, and Protest," *New York Times*, July 5, 1976; Bodnar, *Remaking America*, 236–237; Daughen and Binzen, *Cop Who Would Be King*, 316. ARBA, *Bicentennial of the United States*, 1:19, claims, incorrectly, that all fifty states were represented.

36. Daughen and Binzen, *Cop Who Would Be King*, 316; Vincent Canby, "'Rocky': Pure '30s Make-Believe," *New York Times*, November 22, 1976.

37. Ruth Robinson, diary entry, July 4, 1976, Box 4, Ruth Slocum Tilghman Smith Robinson Diaries, Schlesinger Library, Cambridge, MA; ARBA, *Bicentennial of the United States*, 1:14.

38. Rifkin, quoted in Bodnar, *Remaking America*, 235.

39. All quoted in ARBA, *Bicentennial of the United States*, 1:51.

40. Terence Smith, "A Six-Point Program," *New York Times*, July 16, 1979; Kaufman, *Presidency of James Earl Carter, Jr.*, 144–148.

41. Michael Paul Rogin, *Ronald Reagan, the Movie: And Other Episodes in Political Demonology* (Berkeley: University of California Press, 1987); Garry Wills, *Reagan's America: Innocents at Home* (Garden City, NY: Doubleday, 1987).

3

Affirming and Disaffirming Actions

Remaking Race in the 1970s

ERIC PORTER

On June 28, 1978, the U.S. Supreme Court announced its judgment in *Regents of the University of California v. Bakke,* upholding a California Supreme Court ruling that the University of California–Davis Medical School's affirmative-action policy for admissions was unfair. The *Bakke* case was first filed in 1974 by Allan Bakke, a twice-rejected white applicant who charged that UC–Davis's program, guaranteeing that sixteen of one hundred spots in each class be reserved for minority applicants, violated the equal protection clause of the Fourteenth Amendment and Title VI of the 1964 Civil Rights Act.

The *Bakke* decision was not an easy one for the Supreme Court; there was no majority opinion. The nine justices wrote six different opinions concurring with and dissenting from different parts of the judgment. On the crucial issue, however, they split into two camps: four justices thought the UC–Davis plan was both a constitutionally and statutorily valid means to address the effects of past discrimination, while four other justices affirmed the lower-court ruling, arguing that any consideration of race in admissions violated the "color blind" standard set forth by Title VI. Justice Lewis Powell Jr. cast the fifth and deciding vote, siding with those opposed to the UC–Davis plan, but his opinion split the middle, in a sense. He argued that historical redress was not a constitutionally compelling basis for an affirmative-action program, nor was the pursuit of social or institutional diversity with race and ethnicity as the "determinative factor." But he did believe that some consideration of race in admissions policies was appropriate. Attaching Harvard College's affirmative-action plan as an example, he argued that the goal of attaining a "diverse student body" was constitutionally compelling as long as the definition of "diversity" situated racial or ethnic identity as only one of an array of distinguishing attributes that might be taken into account in admissions decisions.[1] The Court's decision—and Powell's influential, consensus-building opinion— thus validated the concept of diversity as a worthwhile social goal and, in effect, saved affirmative-action programs for the time being while simultaneously scaling back their scope. The *Bakke* decision, however, shaped not only affirmative-action legislation but also Americans' understanding of the meaning and significance of race in the decades to come, and the concept of diversity that Powell successfully used is critical to understanding the larger, complex story of race in the United States during the 1970s.

The 1970s are a decade palpably close at hand yet often obscured by memory and by the nostalgic or retro recycling of 1970s icons in the popular culture of the early twenty-first century. To get a sense of how the 1970s are remembered, take, for example, the film *Austin Powers in Goldmember*—a satire of James Bond films. Austin Powers, a British secret agent, travels back in time to 1975 and returns to the present with CIA agent Foxxy Cleopatra, who, complete with a blond Afro, shakes, shimmies, says "sugar" a lot, and helps save the world from the clutches of Dr. Evil. As with other recent representations of the 1970s, this film accesses the decade through its popular culture texts— in this case, through the imagery of "blaxploitation" films, which present black social identities from the era as a bit silly in their excess and thus makes them palatable, as well as entertaining, to present-day consumers.

The notion that the 1970s were an era of excess when it came to questions of race and racial identities may also be seen in the assessments of the decade by historians and other scholars. As one colleague remembered, when I mentioned this essay to him, people were "way too serious" about their racial and ethnic identities during the 1970s. Paradoxically, many of the same commentators who critique the decade for its excessive attention to race also condemn it as a time of racial retrenchment and missed opportunities. Indeed, the limited gains and profound shortcomings of the antiracist struggles of the postwar era—the civil rights and ethnic empowerment movements in the United States, the anticolonial movements abroad—were keenly felt during the 1970s, which people continue to view as a crucial moment when activists and others made bad decisions regarding race.

Many explain the continuing racial inequalities in U.S. society today as (at least in part) a result of the limitations of the identity-based, group-empowerment programs of cultural nationalists that largely replaced the broader social-change movements of the 1950s and 1960s. Some see the turn to identity as a wrong turn altogether. Others acknowledge the utility of identity-based politics but critique those that emerged in the 1970s. Too often, such critics explain, these movements rejected the notion—even the possibility—of a common good. They did not pay adequate attention to the structural inequalities that had a disproportionate impact on people of color in the United States. The movements missed the bigger picture of global racial inequality. And all too frequently, ethnic chauvinism, sexism, and homophobia pervaded cultural nationalist and identity-based movements. Of course, one might also argue that the key problem with the 1970s was the white backlash that developed over the course of the decade, culminating in the neoconservative revolution that helped bring Ronald Reagan into the White House in 1981.

Although it is important to recognize the limitations of the social movements and political projects of the decade, we should also keep in mind that the 1970s produced some important changes (not always for the worse) in the ways people thought about and acted in relationship to the category of race. The 1970s were nothing less than a critical moment in the world historical development of race as a social, political, and cultural category, and it is important to understand why this was so. In the United States, Americans transformed the ways their society was structured along racial lines during the 1970s; they embraced, rejected, or otherwise negotiated racial identities and mobilized themselves around them in important new ways.

During the 1970s, race was always present. Sometimes it was blatant and in-your-face, at other times it was nearly invisible. Above all, it was increasingly complicated. Although people behaved in ways that are sometimes hard to fathom from today's perspective, we can see in these struggles important shifts in thinking about race that we still struggle with today. Ideas about diversity (articulated in the *Bakke* decision) and of racial or ethnic identity and identity politics remain critical to American culture and social policy. But to understand these important legacies of the 1970s, we must also understand another fundamental concept that underlies them both. We must understand how race, through much of American history, has functioned as a resource that, like material resources of money or property, has not been equally shared by all.

Historically, race is an extremely difficult concept to understand. Today, many biologists and social scientists argue that there is really no such thing as race: it is a fictive social and scientific category. Clearly, the widespread idea that certain small variations in human physiologies signal immutable physical, mental, cultural, or historical differences is a morally and scientifically suspect position. But if we acknowledge that race is a complex and protean concept, defined and used by individuals, groups, and the state in different ways and to different ends, we begin to grasp its continuing importance. Although race may not actually exist as a physiological fact, it is nonetheless a powerful social construct. As put into practice through various political, economic, military, cultural, and intellectual systems, race has played a fundamental role in U.S. history, and it shows little sign of retreating to the background any time soon.

Throughout much of U.S. history, the inhabitants of this land have treated race as a resource—as something of value. Race has conferred or denied privilege. It has been possessed and inherited; it has been used to secure or maintain other resources, whether economic, emotional, institutional, cultural, spiritual, or physical. In the United States, those designated white (and until the mid-twentieth century, Christian whites of northern and western European ancestry) have had the distinct advantage in using race as a resource. Historian George Lipsitz identifies the ways the state, labor unions, corporations, and other entities wittingly and unwittingly gave to European Americans a "possessive investment in whiteness."[2] For much of new-world colonial and U.S. history, European Americans constructed a racial hierarchy that supported the superiority of "whiteness" by ascribing negative qualities to those they defined as nonwhite. Using law in addition to extralegal violence and coercion, European Americans created a race-based system of slavery. The nation's projects of economic expansion and empire building depended on the use of red, black, and brown racial bodies as sources of labor. And when such bodies were defined as impediments in the path of white progress—as in the case of native inhabitants of the land or citizens of northern Mexico—the power of the state was brought to bear, often in the form of war.

During the Fordist industrial order of the twentieth century—characterized by mass production, mass consumption, higher wages, and greater available credit for workers—the economic basis of the continuing "investment in whiteness" shifted as the state played an increasingly large role in creating a "consuming public." After World War II, white privilege was maintained through supposedly race-neutral liberal state policies that allocated resources to citizen consumers and protected their claims on those resources. Federal Housing Administration loan programs, federally funded highway construction projects, urban renewal programs, the move of federal jobs to the suburbs, an expanding criminal justice system, regressive taxation policies, and other factors (even after the gains of the civil rights movement) combined to increase "the gap between the resources available to whites and those available to aggrieved racial communities."[3]

Despite the ways racial investments have generally upheld white supremacy, U.S. history is also rich with examples of other kinds of racial subjects rallying around—although not always successfully—the idea of common biology, geographic origin, or culture as a resource for making better lives for themselves. The pan-tribal, millenarian "Ghost Dance" phenomenon of 1890 (an affirmation of Native American tribal religious and cultural practices in the face of extermination, expropriation of land, and assimilation) and Marcus Garvey's tremendously popular Universal Negro Improvement Association in the 1910s and 1920s (which sought to combat segregation and economic oppression through economic uplift and racial pride) are but two examples.

During the 1970s, more than any time before in U.S. history, people of color claimed race as a resource. It is striking that assertions of the importance of racial and ethnic identities came on the heels of a civil rights movement that had finally succeeded in securing basic constitutional protections for racial minorities, in part by people putting their bodies on the line and in part through a successful rhetorical struggle that emphasized color blindness and a common humanity. But as the civil rights movement became more radical throughout the 1960s and 1970s, activists argued with increasing frequency that a liberal, integrationist approach to combating racial injustice was not enough. Although they usually recognized that the civil rights movement was a noble and important cause, particularly in the segregated South, activists identified other modes of oppression that stemmed not from blatant Jim Crow racism but from the everyday, putatively color-blind practices of the state and of corporate America.

In other words, even as race was generally dismissed as a meaningful biological category, it was embraced as an analytical, political, and cultural concept that was used to understand and explain the fundamental inequalities of American society, deployed as a means of mobilizing people and securing resources, and cherished as a marker of self and group worth. As the black freedom struggle shifted from a focus on civil rights and integration to opposition to the Vietnam War and attacks on institutionalized racism, joblessness, and housing discrimination, the rallying cry of "Black Power" signified a profound inward turn among African American organizations and individuals and quite often a rejection of supposedly color-blind liberalism because of its limitations. In practice, Black Power was an unwieldy concept with multiple, often contradictory meanings—including the Black Panther Party's revolutionary challenges to the status quo; black business ownership; the invention of the African American holiday Kwanzaa; the struggles by black students on university and college campuses to transform curricula and admit more minority students to undergraduate, graduate, and professional schools; and everything in between. Taken together, however, the implementation of Black Power programs in a variety of venues symbolized a growing belief that affirming and organizing along the lines of racial identities was a *sine qua non* for political, social, cultural, or economic advancement.[4]

Black Power was accompanied by assertions of political, cultural, and personal identity by other groups that displayed a similar sense of anger, optimism, and a growing emphasis on their distinctiveness within and sometimes in distinction to the imagined social, political, or cultural framework of the United States. Mexican Americans' embrace of the term "Chicano/a," once a derogatory term for the poor and working class, expressed an oppositional rather than assimilationist sense of identity. And when Chicano/a activists and artists began to invoke Aztlán, a concept first publicly defined in 1969, they further rejected the idea that their identities were rooted in the political and cultural systems of the United States. As described in the manifesto "El plan espiritual de Aztlán," Aztlán was a symbolic homeland encompassing the parts of the southwestern United States that had been seized from Mexico in 1848, which would in the future be a site of political, social, and cultural development.[5]

Not all the projects drawing from cultural nationalism, however, sought to distance racial or ethnic groups from the national political or cultural body. Avery Gordon and Christopher Newfield discuss the ways in which emergent multicultural educational programs of the 1970s had the creation of racial democracy as their goal. Consisting of everything from the diversification of school curricula to bilingual education programs to struggles for adequate minority representation on school boards, multicultural programs of this period often expressed a cultural pluralism that walked the line between assimilation, with its concomitant naturalization of white-majority rule, and cultural nationalism.[6] As one organization said in 1977, "Cultural pluralism is neither the traditionalist's separatism nor the assimilationist's melting pot. It is a composite that recognizes the uniqueness and value of every culture. Cultural pluralism acknowledges that no group lives in isolation, but that, instead, each group influences and is influenced by others." Many believed that investing in cultural difference (mother tongues, dress, history, music, material culture, etc.) would provide a mechanism for achieving racial equity and a more equitable society, especially if members of minority groups created the rules for intercultural exchange themselves. Yet, one also notes in these early multiculturalist agendas the care people took to synthesize a commitment to group demands with those of a national democratic culture. People imagined a democratic society forged not in allegiance to a homogeneous national culture but, in the words of educator Arturo Pacheco, as "a balance of power between competing and overlapping religious, ethnic, economic, and geographical groupings." Proponents of multiculturalism often framed it as an American way of life and rejected the argument that group rights by definition conflicted with individual rights. In their 1974 book *Cultural Democracy, Bicognitive Development, and Education,* Manuel Ramírez III and Alfredo Castañeda argue, "[A]n individual can be bicultural and still be loyal to American ideals."[7]

That such multicultural education programs were often undertaken with governmental funding proves that the 1970s marked a shift in the implementation of race as a resource because of the particular ways political, cultural, and personal affirmations of identity were facilitated by or supported by the state. When the federal and state governments finally implemented more vigorous civil rights protections, minority political participation in traditional party politics increased, and the parties themselves became more responsive to demands that an increasingly heterogeneous electorate be represented by a more diverse set of representatives. In New York, Puerto Rican Bronx Borough president Hernan Badillo was elected to the U.S. House of Representatives in 1968 and named deputy mayor in 1978. Badillo was replaced in Congress by fellow Puertorriqueño Roberto Garcia, and that same year Olga Méndez was elected to serve in the New York State Senate, becoming the first female legislator of Puerto Rican descent in the United States.[8]

Other political movements organized around racial identities defined themselves against the reformist members of their communities, but even some of these would at times conduct programs in dialogue with state institutions or with state support. The relationships of these radical groups to the state were complicated. The federal, state, and local governments were, in effect, waging war against radical organizations through disinformation campaigns, political assassinations, and other measures, most infamously via the FBI's counterintelligence programs (COINTELPROs) of the late 1960s and early 1970s. Still, members of radical organizations found allies in the government for implementing community-specific programs.

The American Indian Movement (AIM), for example, was founded in Minneapolis-St. Paul in 1968 as an alternative to reformist organizations such as Association on American Indian Affairs, the National Congress of American Indians, and the Indian Rights Association. Like the Black Panther Party, AIM's first project was to address police brutality. And like their counterparts in the Black Panther Party, AIM members suffered greatly from government persecution, as its members were murdered, disappeared, or were framed for crimes by the FBI, local police, and tribal authorities over the course of the 1970s. But during the decade they also created a number of public welfare and political programs with government assistance. AIM successfully lobbied the city of Minneapolis to create a center for Indian culture, and with a $4.3 million grant from the Housing and Urban Development Department, the group undertook a project to build almost 250 homes for Indians in Minneapolis.[9]

Affirmative-action programs were, of course, a significant set of vehicles through which the state validated race as something of value and intervened in the struggles over resources between various groups. *Bakke* began to work its way through the courts after a decade of experimentation with and agonizing debates about state- and corporate-sponsored affirmative-action programs. Although governmental and business interests never followed the most radical calls to reconfigure the ways resources were distributed along racial or ethnic lines, a reformist acknowledgment of these critiques shaped a variety of pro–affirmative-action statements, court decisions, and programs during the late 1960s and early 1970s. As the U.S. Commission on Civil Rights defined them, affirmative-action programs were "any measure, beyond simple termination of a discriminatory practice [against a group], adopted to correct or compensate for past or present [group] discrimination or to prevent [such group] discrimination from recurring in the future."[10]

Although some argue that the beginning of a federal commitment to affirmative action may be found in John F. Kennedy's 1961 Executive Order 10925, calling for "affirmative steps" to be taken to create a more diverse government work force, it was during Lyndon B. Johnson's administration that a concrete set of policies emerged. President Johnson's Executive Order 11246 asked federal agencies to "establish and maintain a positive program of equal employment opportunity for all civilian employees and applicants for employment" and established "numerical goals and timetables" as appropriate procedures.[11] Government programs established during the Johnson years were augmented by the Nixon administration, which, among other things, revived the Johnson administration's "Philadelphia Plan," requiring firms with federal construction contracts to demonstrate that they were hiring members of certain racial groups at a rate consistent with that group's representation in the local population. The Supreme Court supplemented such actions with a series of decisions, including 1971's *Griggs v. Duke Power*, in which the Court ruled that "practices, procedures, or tests neutral on their face and even neutral in terms of intent, cannot be maintained if they operate to 'freeze' the status quo of prior discriminatory employment practices."[12]

At the most basic level, race- and gender-specific college admissions and employment programs provided a vehicle and incentive for members of minority groups to invest in their racial or cultural identities as a means of bettering their position in society. For some, the rewards were relatively swift in coming. Between 1969 and 1974, the top 5 percent of nonwhite families saw their earnings grow from just over seventeen thousand dollars to over twenty-four thousand dollars.[13] However, these programs were by definition limited in the range of the social ills they addressed and in the scope of the people that they served. Ironically, although affirmative action is typically understood as a racial issue, various studies have shown that white women have benefited the most from affirmative-action programs as the programs have developed over the past three decades.[14] Moreover, some affirmative-action programs provided a point of entry for those who already had a decent stake in society and did little for the most dispossessed. Affirmative-action programs gave academically oriented students a few more options for college, provided educated or skilled workers with better jobs than they would have received if job discrimination went unchecked, and allowed established businesses to break into the old-boys networks that had a monopoly on government contracts. The programs often did not address the needs of the masses of chronically unemployed workers or schoolchildren unable to obtain a basic education in deteriorating inner-city schools. This inability of affirmative-action programs to address fully the needs of many members of minority communities speaks to another important phenomenon of the 1970s: a growing visibility and awareness of the differences within racial groups, which led to somewhat different kinds of affirmations and disaffirmations of race.

Although class divisions in minority communities were nothing new, the gulf between the haves and have-nots widened during the 1970s. Civil rights reforms had little impact on the private-sector job market and residential segregation, and the economic downturn of the mid-1970s disproportionately hit working-class members of minority communities. Changes to the economy in the late 1960s and early 1970s involved, among other things, a geographical dispersion of capital and sites of production. As American companies experienced more competition from European and Japanese companies, they closed plants and eliminated manufacturing jobs to streamline production and make themselves more competitive. They also tried to save on labor costs by moving production jobs away from union strongholds in the Northeast to the rapidly growing southern and western Sun Belt or overseas. The impact of national deindustrialization and a concomitant disappearance of high-wage, often unionized manufacturing jobs was worsened by a rapid rise of fuel costs resulting from the OPEC oil embargo; rampant inflation and eventually stagflation (inflation combined with a growth in unemployment); and a series of state fiscal crises. With relatively permanent manufacturing jobs disappearing, the 1970s witnessed the rise of a service sector, employing an elite class of technocrats on the one hand and on the other a class of low-wage, often temporary service workers (security guards, janitors, fast-food workers, etc.) to serve them.

New immigration patterns not only changed the composition of the U.S. population but helped enhance the social divisions within various racial and ethnic groups as well. The 1965 Immigration and Naturalization Act eliminated the existing national origins quota system regulating immigration and gave preference for subsequent visas to family members of persons already in the United States. Although the effects of this legislation were felt more keenly during the late 1970s, four million new legal residents entered the country over the course of the decade, the majority from Latin America and Asia. During the 1970s, the overall U.S. population grew 11 percent, while the Asian American population grew 141 percent. The ethnic and class composition of Asian America was transformed by growing numbers of skilled workers or merchants from India, Korea, Taiwan, China, and the Philippines; refugees from Southeast Asia; and unskilled workers from China. In 1960, Japanese, Chinese, and Filipino Americans comprised 90 percent of the Asian American population. By 1980, their share had dropped to 65 percent. The percentage of Japanese Americans in the Asian American population de-creased from 47 percent to 20 percent.[15] Although Mexico continued to be the point of origin for the majority of immigrants heading north, many of the new arrivals were much poorer and less skilled than were the established residents.

Growing internal differences within communities of color, and an increas-ing awareness of those differences, expanded the array of ways people deployed race (or chose not to) in their quests for better treatment but also provoked a fair amount of anxiety. When scholars and activists addressed the growing rifts in their communities, at times they affirmed and at other times they disaffirmed the importance of race in ways that stemmed, in part, from the fundamental question of whether recognition or erasure of differ-ence within racial groups would prove most beneficial to individual or group advancement. Some tried to deny the social divisions in racial com-munities; some sought to create unity across class, ethnic, gender, and re-gional lines while recognizing the importance of these differences; and some began to emphasize other social categories over race in their activist and analytic projects.

As Yen Le Espiritu demonstrates, "Asian American" was a "pan-ethnic" identity developed during the late 1960s and 1970s by politicized members of various Asian ethnic groups in the United States. Before this period, Asian political activism in the United States was generally undertaken through eth-nically specific organizations. However, in a changing context, where broad-based identity movements were organized across the racial spectrum, and the government itself was allocating political and economic resources as well as group rights along broadly conceived racial lines, pan-ethnic organizing became more appealing to radical students and professional service organi-zations alike. Yet many Asian American political or social projects sought to balance an investment in the strategic umbrella category of Asian American with an acknowledgement of the differences within this racial group. In the late 1970s, Asian American activists of different ethnicities joined forces to ensure that members of their group were adequately counted in the 1980 U.S. census as a means of securing government funding and political represen-tation for their communities. But they resisted the government's push to lump all Asian Americans into a single category, for they recognized the need to identify the particular circumstances and needs of different ethnic groups.[16]

Class also informed people's investments and disinvestments in race in a variety of ways. Some turned to working-class culture and politics, or at least what they imagined them to be, as a means of rectifying social divisions and rethinking the basis of political struggle. Chicano/a visual artists working in the 1970s, for example, embraced what Tomás Ybarra-Frausto later called *rasquachismo,* an aesthetic with roots in working-class Mexican and Mexican American culture, which among other things emphasized "ornamentation and elaboration."[17] Others sought to elevate class over race in their analyses of the oppressive conditions facing members of minority communities. Sociologist William Julius Wilson's 1978 book *The Declining Significance of Race* was a controversial disaffirmation of race that sought to show how, in a post–civil rights moment, class was an increasingly important indicator of life chances in the African American population and was bifurcating the black community in significant new ways.

The recognition of internal group differences led some established organizations to change their agendas. Undocumented immigration from Mexico increased during the 1970s and became a national political issue amidst fears that alien workers were taking U.S. citizens' jobs. Only a handful of the Chicano/a activists of the 1960s who had embraced Mexican history and culture as a means of defining themselves against the American mainstream made connections between immigration policy and other pressing social issues. But as the national debate about "illegals" heated up during the early 1970s, support and solidarity for documented and undocumented immigrants played a more central role in the activities of Mexican American organizations across the political spectrum. The United Farm Workers union, established by César Chávez and Dolores Huerta in 1962, had from its inception supported efforts to stem the flow of undocumented and noncitizen workers because they could be used as strikebreakers. But in the early 1970s, the organization found itself at odds with Chicano/a activists hoping to reconstitute their political and cultural community to include recent arrivals. By the end of 1974, Chávez reversed his position, stating that his organization would work for "amnesty for illegal aliens and support their efforts to obtain legal documents and equal rights, including the right of collective bargaining." He declared, "[T]he illegals [are] our brothers and sisters."[18]

Gender was another mode through which race was affirmed and disaffirmed. Many of the racial movements of the late 1960s and 1970s were masculine oriented and sometimes quite sexist and homophobic as well. This is not surprising, given the gender hierarchies in American society in general and the ways that the struggle for full citizenship in the United States had long been equated with a struggle for manhood. Cultural nationalist projects often looked forward to the redemption of men who would not only be liberated politically but would rightfully take their places as the heads of patriarchal families. At the same time, members of racial minority groups participating in second-wave feminist movements and gay rights movements were frustrated by the ways that these struggles seemed to assume the female or feminist and gay or lesbian subject to be white. For example, black women who thought the National Organization for Women did not represent their interests formed the National Black Feminist Organization in 1973.

People had theorized the crosscutting features of race, class, and gender before the 1970s—in part because of the intertwined histories of feminism, working-class movements, and antiracist struggles—but the decade witnessed an increasing number of cultural and political expressions along these lines. In 1977, the Boston-based feminist organization Combahee River Collective produced "A Black Feminist Statement." This document presents an eloquent commitment to feminist and queer politics that go hand-in-hand with broader struggles for human liberation. Although this statement has been characterized as an example of narrowly conceived identity politics, it is better read as an example of the growing sense among activists that racial politics and identities can be viewed only as working in concert with other politics and identities.

Although the Combahee River Collective viewed its work as stemming from its members' identities as black women and the particulars of their own oppression, it was "actively committed to struggling against racial, sexual, heterosexual, and class oppression and [saw] as [its] particular task the development of integrated analysis and practice based upon the fact that the major systems of oppression are interlocking." The group wrote, "The liberation of all oppressed peoples necessitates the destruction of the political-economic systems of capitalism and imperialism as well as patriarchy." The authors of the statement considered themselves socialists, yet they demanded that any successful socialist movement must be antiracist and feminist as well. Ultimately, they voiced what Robin D. G. Kelley has called a "radical humanism," rooted in the particularities of experience but ultimately devoted to the liberation of all human beings and suspicious of any sort of "biological determinism." "The inclusiveness of our politics," the collective concluded, "makes us concerned with any situation that impinges upon the lives of women, Third World and working people."[19]

Affirmations of racial identities and the recognition of differences within groups during the 1970s were facilitated by the electronics revolution and proliferation of media that accompanied the emergence of a postindustrial society. The growing social role of these technologies provided the tools by which, for better or for worse, identities and social rebellion could be commodified and made available to large audiences. During the early years of the decade, there was an increasing commerce in racial or ethnic images, which marked the growing visibility and power of ethnic and racial groups and a wider interest in cultural difference as a social value. This was perhaps clearest in the cinema of the early 1970s, which included Francis Ford Coppola's critically acclaimed and commercially successful *Godfather* and *Godfather, Part II*, which tell the story of an immigrant Italian mobster family, and a spate of domestic and imported martial arts films, the most celebrated featuring Chinese American Bruce Lee.

At least some of these cultural products were popular because people could see themselves in ways that spoke not of assimilation but of identities that stood out against narratives of nation and of larger racial communities. In 1971, Melvin Van Peebles made the low-budget, avant-garde, and sexually explicit *Sweet Sweetback's Baadasssss Song*, a film that tells the story of a small-time hustler and sex worker's violent escape from the Los Angeles police and, ultimately, his politicization. The film was controversial with black critics and activists, who decried its misogyny and its stereotypical representation of its black male hero, while debating whether it presented an adequately revolutionary vision. But it was extremely popular with black urban residents who, while recognizing the problems of the film, saw affirming representations of urban and working-class black communities.[20]

Ultimately, the film's popularity got the attention of Hollywood, which was searching for ways to revive the American film industry after the slump of the late 1960s. The result was a glut of studio-produced blaxploitation films over the next several years. Featuring gangsters, prostitutes, pimps, drug dealers, rogue cops, as well as a good deal of violence, sex, and profanity, these films did not do a lot to challenge stereotypes about black men and women. Sweetback was an oversexed, hypermasculine figure, and many of the heroes of subsequent films were made in his mold. A series of films featuring Pam Grier paid lip service to feminism, although they probably spoke more of anxieties about powerful, independent women. The denouement of the film *Coffy*, for example, shows Grier's character castrating her corrupt, drug-dealing politician boyfriend with a shotgun. But even as these films relied on caricature, the mode of representation was celebration, not ridicule, and they were a significant shift from films of the 1960s that featured noble black characters trying to find their way in a white world.

In these ways and many others, nonwhite persons affirmed their racial identities and had them affirmed by others. But it is important to keep in mind that blaxploitation films and the increasing numbers of people of color appearing on television and film screens were related to the pursuit of profits, as businesspeople devised strategies in the hopes of capitalizing on the rising tide of racial identification. These images may also be explained by the general population's desire to explore the lives of increasingly visible and vocal groups. Witness, for example, the spate of television programs portraying urban, working-class people of color: *Good Times; Sanford and Son; Chico and the Man; Welcome Back, Kotter;* and *What's Happening!!* were all popular with white Americans during the 1970s.

Although the newest and most visible attempts to use race as a resource during the 1970s were those of racial and ethnic minorities, whites were just as invested in race. On the one hand, some whites adopted models of identity similar to those developed by people of color. "Ethnic" Americans especially (who had only recently been considered "white") claimed or reclaimed ethnic identities, pointing out their own histories of exclusion from "mainstream" American society. Such celebrations of ethnic identity contributed to a general cultural validation of ethnic and cultural difference. For example, in 1976, a group of Italian American faculty at City University of New York demanded that Italian Americans be considered for affirmative action in hiring and promotion purposes.[21]

On the other hand, white Americans also defined race (whiteness) as a resource in ways that challenged or undercut the political and cultural struggles of people of color. Although few went so far as to argue for "white rights" in the face of political gains made by people of color, others responded with an apparent sense of victimization and exhaustion. Not only did many think that attempts to ameliorate the sins of the past had gone so far as to discriminate against whites, but many more were simply tired of talking about race and were tired of the critiques that implicated them in the social inequalities that still pervaded American society.

The roots of this backlash run deep in American history. They are evident in a long series of zero-sum interpretations of social equality that reach back to Reconstruction, in which gains made by people of color in the labor force or the political sphere were seen as direct threats to white interests. In the

1970s, many white Americans measured their own interests against the successes and failures people of color had in deploying racial identities to their own benefit. If race was a resource that could be possessed, it was a resource that could be lost. And as people of color succeeded in using their racial identities to gain political power, economic advancement, and cultural pride, many whites saw the privileges historically associated with whiteness in decline. Some of those who saw themselves on the losing end argued that race-based affirmative-action programs discriminated against whites, and government programs that allocated resources on the basis of race were inherently unfair.

During the early 1970s, Richard Nixon and his administration played a curiously complicated role in racial politics, ultimately fomenting a new version of white backlash. The Nixon administration did, in fact, create the first important federal affirmative-action programs for federally funded projects. *Griggs v. Duke Power*, which recognized that "race-neutral" programs could reinforce racial hierarchies, was decided by a Supreme Court stacked with recent Nixon appointees, as was *Swann v. Charlotte-Mecklenburg Board of Education*, a 1971 decision supporting forced busing to achieve racial balance in schools. But at the same time, Nixon played a large role in galvanizing resistance to such programs. His emphasis on "law and order" and his appeal to the "silent majority" during the 1968 presidential campaign—both of which implicitly defined law-abiding whites as the moral center of the nation, put in harm's way by political radicals and by the changes wrought as people of color made legal and political gains during the 1950s and 1960s—helped create animosity toward programs intended to undermine white supremacy.

The Nixon administration also attempted to diminish or dismantle Great Society programs and agencies meant to foster racial equality. Nixon tried unsuccessfully to have Congress pass legislation prohibiting school desegregation; prevented the Department of Education from terminating funding for school districts that had failed to follow court orders to integrate; and, in 1973, abolished the Office of Economic Opportunity. Some have argued that Nixon's support for affirmative action was based on his understanding that it would be a "wedge issue" that could be used to split the Democratic Party's traditional constituency of labor, Jews, and blacks.[22]

The broader context for this backlash against nonwhite people included the transformations in the domestic economy discussed earlier (including job losses, inflation, and stagflation), the domestic political crisis of Watergate, and a series of setbacks in international relations. Nixon's resignation in disgrace, the "defeat" in Vietnam, and the Iran hostage crisis of 1979 to 1981 all contributed to a lack of faith in government. The Nixon, Ford, and Carter administrations were unable to solve these problems, which helped fuel attacks on the liberal state in ways that were explicitly or implicitly racially coded.

The particular forms that affirmations of whiteness and disaffirmations of the identities, gains, and humanity of people of color took depended on a variety of factors. Some were clearly class based, some reflected regional concerns, some were also expressions of masculinity, and some were rooted in specific political ideologies. The backlash was expressed in explicitly white supremacist and neofascist terms in the nearly threefold increase in Ku Klux Klan (KKK) membership during the 1970s and in a series of violent incidents perpetrated by the Far Right at the end of the decade. For example, a November 1979 attack by Nazis and KKK members on an antiracist rally in Greensboro, North Carolina, left five demonstrators dead and eleven injured.[23] When South Boston whites opposing a court-mandated busing plan rained rocks and bottles down on black children—and, in one case, attacked a black parent with an American flagpole—they expressed an antiblack racism inflected with Irish ethnic pride as well as a more general working-class resentment toward the liberal state and elite policymakers who tried to impose an integrated social vision on their community.

Implicit understandings of race and its meanings also shaped American reactions as the nation struggled with foreign-policy failures and its declining position in the world's economy. Racially inflected anger was not confined to whites; members of minority groups at times participated in racism directed at other groups. Powerful anti-Japanese sentiment, including a series of physical attacks on Asian Americans in the late 1970s and early 1980s, stemmed from the perception that Japanese automakers were engaged in unfair competition with U.S. manufacturers, thereby destroying American jobs and livelihoods. But anti-Japanese sentiment also had roots in lingering anti-Asian racism from World War II, renewed in the 1960s and 1970s to motivate a multiracial U.S. military to fight the Vietnam War. This potent brew of class and race resentment culminated in the 1982 murder of Chinese American Vincent Chin, beaten to death with a baseball bat outside a Detroit bar by two white autoworkers who assumed he was Japanese. Anti-Arab and anti–Middle Easterner sentiments, fueled by the OPEC oil embargo, a series of terrorist attacks, and the Iran hostage situation at the end of the decade led to violent attacks on Arab Americans. Although most Americans condemned outright violence against individuals, the song "Bomb Iran," by Vince Vance and the Valiants (sung to the tune of the Beach Boys' "Barbara Ann"), with its suggestion that the United States turn Iran into a "parking lot" via a nuclear strike, was a runaway hit in 1980.

Although some of these reactions to the gains made by people of color and to the limited government sponsorship of such gains are clearly racist, or clearly aimed at preserving the privileges of whiteness, the most pervasive reaction is also the most complex. In the changing racial landscape of the 1970s, many Americans remained attached to notions of "color blindness." Voiced most eloquently by the Reverend Martin Luther King Jr. in his appeal that his children "not be judged by the color of their skin but by the content of their character," color blindness was perhaps the civil rights movement's most powerful rhetorical device. As such, it made its way into civil rights legislation. Title VI of the Civil Rights Act of 1964, for example, made it explicit that people should not be discriminated against because of their race or color. As the Supreme Court considered the *Bakke* case, a key issue was whether the UC–Davis plan and other affirmative action programs, which were often justified by the ideal of color blindness articulated by the act, were actually in violation of Title VI.[24]

Many Americans who embraced the ideal of color blindness during the 1970s believed they were working against racism, adopting the inspirational goals of the civil rights movement itself. But as sociologists Michael Omi and Howard Winant have argued, social ideals (such as color blindness) voiced by minority activists were "rearticulated" during the 1970s in ways that served the group interests of whites. Notions of color blindness were effective in attacking a Jim Crow legal system. But with the triumph over legally mandated segregation and discrimination, color blindness became an increasingly problematic strategy. If the state had ensured that race was no longer a legal impediment to the political aspirations, economic advancement, or social gains by members of minority groups, notions of color blindness worked against further action. King's claim of universal human rights was rearticulated as a bulwark against "preferential treatment" for people of color. It was a short step to the notion that affirmative action and other race-conscious programs victimized whites. This way of thinking, of course, culminated with the "Reagan revolution" of the 1980s.[25]

Films from the 1970s both reflected and encouraged this sense of white victimization. Several tremendously popular films featured white male heroes who were redeemed by standing up to dangerous blacks and Latinos and other social deviants who, the films suggested, had been created by the liberal and permissive society of the 1960s. *Dirty Harry* (1971) and *Death Wish* (1974) both feature characters who take the law into their own hands. Clint Eastwood's Harry Callahan is a rogue cop and Charles Bronson's Paul Kersey is a "bleeding-heart liberal" turned vigilante. Both attempt to rid the world of dangerous criminals created and abetted by an ineffectual liberal state. Although Kersey and Callahan are both equal-opportunity assassins, blacks and Latinos are prominent among their targets. In the *Rocky* series of films from the late 1970s and early 1980s, Sylvester Stallone plays working-class, Italian American heavyweight boxer Rocky Balboa, who battles a series of black and foreign fighters. Most notable is preening, trash-talking champion Apollo Creed, who was patterned on controversial black nationalist heavyweight champion Muhammad Ali. Rocky first loses to Apollo, then defeats him, then gains his support, reconciling Creed to, as film scholar Ed Guerrero notes, "white yearnings for a 'great white hope' and a nostalgic return to a bygone racial order."[26]

Other popular expressions demonstrated that some whites were tired of liberal intervention into racial matters. Southern rock band Lynyrd Skynyrd articulated such sentiments in their 1973 hit "Sweet Home Alabama." In addition to praising its natural beauty, the band defended the homeland against folk-rocker Neil Young, who in his song "Southern Man" criticized a legacy of racial violence and political apartheid in the region. Lynyrd Skynyrd said that a "southern man don't need [Young] around anyhow" and went on to express their love for segregationist governor George Wallace and disdain for the liberal state that had tried to dictate southern racial policy: "Watergate does not bother me / Does your conscience bother you?"

At the end of the decade, the "Disco Sucks" sentiment expressed by radio deejays, in articles in the popular-music press, and, perhaps most frequently, on bumper stickers, voiced legitimate complaints about what had turned into a pretty banal and stultifying genre once it went mainstream (in large part because of the immense popularity of the 1977 film *Saturday Night Fever* and the Australian supergroup the Bee Gees, who figured prominently on the film's soundtrack), but the sentiment also expressed contempt for blacks' and gays' growing visibility in and impact on American culture. This contempt was perhaps expressed most vividly when a 1979 Chicago White Sox baseball game had to be cancelled after a pregame disco-recording burning ceremony turned into an on-field riot by white teenagers.[27]

Television played its own contradictory role both in the backlash against the gains made by people of color and in the growing sense of white victimization. Although situation comedies, after-school specials, made-for-TV movies, and, most famously, the 1975 miniseries *Roots* addressed legacies of oppression and tried to reimagine the United States as a plural, if slightly dysfunctional, society, the messages were quite often complicated. Norman Lear's situation comedy *All in the Family,* which began airing in 1971, continually poked fun at the bumbling patriarch Archie Bunker's racism, sexism, and general ignorance, particularly through his ongoing ideological war with his feminist daughter, Gloria, radical Polish American son-in-law, Michael, and African American neighbor, George Jefferson. Yet Bunker also was a somewhat likeable character, certainly capable of redemption and perhaps responding in an understandable way to the social transformations that threatened him.

A sense of white victimization was also consolidated through the evening news. As the violent-crime rate rose during the 1970s, in part because of rising unemployment and deteriorating conditions in inner cities, more and more Americans were relying on television news instead of newspapers and radio for their information. By 1975, according to one report, over one-third of Americans said they received all their news from television.[28] As television news coverage expanded, it brought lurid criminal images into people's living rooms and helped transform the image of black protest from the noble civil rights demonstrator of the early 1960s to the urban rioter of the late 1960s and to the urban criminal of the 1970s. Also contributing to a sense that black protest had gone bad were a series of highly publicized acts of mayhem with vague political overtones directed toward whites, including the "zebra murders" of 1973 and 1974 in which four African Americans murdered fourteen randomly selected whites and injured seven others in San Francisco.

Ideas about criminality helped feed a widely held notion that at least some people of color simply did not have the character to participate fully in American society. Although this was not a new argument, the basis had changed from assumed biological or moral failings to a culturalist understanding of racial difference forged in a new social moment. And this was the flipside of the cultural nationalist's embrace of difference, as black commentator Albert Murray cautioned in his 1970 book *The Omni-Americans,* a work that rejected cultural nationalism and tried to position African Americans at the center of American life.[29] Social theorist Etienne Balibar has theorized a global transition from a biologically based to a culturally based racism during the late twentieth century. This "new racism," or "differentialist racism," is based not so much on biology, and not necessarily on assumptions about the superiority of certain groups in relations to others, but on immutable differences between groups of human beings and the "incompatability of life-styles and traditions."[30] Indeed, since the 1970s in the United States, "cultural explanations" have increasingly supplanted structural analysis when people seek to understand emergent social problems and, in particular, the continued marginal position of people of color in the post–civil rights United States.[31]

Ultimately, the *Bakke* decision and Powell's validation of diversity refracted these complicated and overlapping affirmations and disaffirmations of race during the 1970s. Powell's opinion helped define racial diversity as a national resource and spoke of profound changes in racial discourse and race relations. Certainly one of the important changes this 1970s version of diversity offered was a level of inclusion missing from many previous definitions of U.S. pluralism. But Powell's pragmatic attempt to scale back yet preserve affirmative-action programs also spoke of the struggles around race as a resource during the 1970s. His validation of diversity accommodated increasingly visible and powerful minority groups, but it was also framed in a way that spoke of how white Americans were themselves invested in race. Powell's definition of diversity not only broadened the concept so that whites could benefit from it, it also positioned whites as the primary beneficiaries of social diversity. Powell wrote, "[I]t is not too much to say that the 'nation's future depends upon leaders trained through wide exposure' to the ideas and mores of students as diverse as this Nation of many peoples."[32] Affirmative-action admissions programs that created a more diverse student body were in a sense being justified by defining diversity as a resource for the elite (i.e., white, or at least majority white) members of society. Thus, Powell's opinion referenced the way the state played a contradictory role in managing race during the 1970s—on the one hand, responding to the affirmative demands of minority groups, and on the other hand, affirming its historical racial function by placating white interest groups that saw minority struggles and the reallocation of resources as a distinct threat to their own interests—and it also spoke of the competing individual and group investments in race as a resource that continue to define and divide American society today.

But this does not mean our assessment of the decade need pronounce it a failure. I believe we can look back on the 1970s in a cautiously positive light. Powell's definition of diversity as a social goal that includes but is broader than racial difference may also be seen, at a symbolic level at least, as representative of the ways that many people were balancing a variety of identities and affiliations. It also disaffirms the limitations of certain kinds of racial identities, even as such identities seemed to hold increasing value as vehicles for personal affirmation, political mobilization, and commercial exchange.

Writing about 1970s super soul group Earth, Wind & Fire, Paul Gilroy suggests that their music was "dominated by the desire to find a new political and ethical code in which the contradictory demands for blackness on one side and postracial utopia on the other could be articulated together under the bright signs of progress, modernity, and style." They "strove to be both nationalist and internationalist. The tension between those two commitments was resolved into a universalistic appeal to spirituality on the one hand and to shared human characteristics on the other. . . . The music framed these possibilities by creating spaces of pleasure and discovery."[33] With their sonic invocations of Africa ("Africano," "Zanzibar") and their messages of affirmation ("Devotion," "Keep Your Head to the Sky," "Shining Star"), the group's music certainly carried forward Black Power's emphasis on individual and group empowerment. It is also noteworthy that one of their earliest recordings was the soundtrack to the ur-blaxploitation film *Sweet Sweetback's Baadasssss Song.*[34]

Still, the band's affirming love songs, commitment to spiritual healing, and sometimes otherworldly and futuristic album cover imagery made them deeply inclusive. The Earth, Wind & Fire concerts I attended in the 1970s were decidedly multiracial affairs and clearly sites of intercultural sharing and communion. They remind me that striking a balance between a group focus and other affiliations could still be a powerful weapon in the hands of oppressed groups and a means of both rectifying the particularist errors of identity-based social movements and state racial projects alike.

Despite the continuing existence of narrowly conceived identity formations, the 1970s were a time when many people questioned the utility of race as a resource in itself and as a tool for obtaining resources. As the examples of the Combahee River Collective and other activists illustrate, in new, important ways people were coming to terms with the manner in which social hierarchies were determined by multiple categories of experiences and were trying to balance ethnically particular politics with both national civic and broader political human modes of affiliation.

Viewing the variety of affirming and disaffirming actions mentioned above helps us understand how race was remade and rethought during the 1970s.

These events, ideas, and processes also help us understand how and why people continue to struggle for racial resources today through political movements, social policy debates, ballot initiatives, the competition for public space, and so on. But beyond merely helping us understand the present, we might contemplate the words and deeds of those who affirmed the need to hold on to race, yet disaffirmed race when it was limiting. Such visions suggest ways of negotiating the pitfalls of a postmodern relativism, an essentialist cultural nationalism, and a white supremacy that is often cloaked in color blindness. For they call upon people to move toward a progressive, humanist vision that is always concerned with the particulars of the experiences of racial subjects and the multifaceted history of racial inclusion and exclusion in the modern world.

Notes

1. Robert Post, "Introduction: After *Bakke*," in *Race and Representation: Affirmative Action*, ed. Robert Post and Michael Rogin (New York: Zone Books, 1998), 14–16; Howard Ball, *The Bakke Case: Race, Education, and Affirmative Action* (Lawrence: University Press of Kansas, 2000), 112–140.

2. George Lipsitz, *The Possessive Investment in Whiteness: How White People Profit from Identity Politics* (Philadelphia: Temple University Press, 1998), 1–23.

3. Thomas C. Holt, *The Problem of Race in the 21st Century* (Cambridge, MA: Harvard University Press, 2000; paperback edition, 2002), 59–85; Lipsitz, *Possessive Investment in Whiteness*, 5.

4. Manning Marable, *Race, Reform, and Rebellion: The Second Reconstruction in Black America*, rev. 2nd ed. (Jackson: University Press of Mississippi, 1991); William L. Van Deburg, *New Day in Babylon: The Black Power Movement and American Culture, 1965–1975* (Chicago: University of Chicago Press, 1992).

5. David G. Gutiérrez, *Walls and Mirrors: Mexican Americans, Mexican Immigrants, and the Politics of Ethnicity* (Berkeley: University of California Press, 1995), 184–185.

6. Avery Gordon and Christopher Newfield, "Multiculturalism's Unfinished Business," in *Mapping Multiculturalism*, ed. Avery Gordon and Christopher Newfield (Minneapolis: University of Minnesota Press, 1996), 76–96.

7. Gordon and Newfield, "Multiculturalism's Unfinished Business," 95–97; The ASCD Multicultural Education Commission, "Encouraging Multicultural Education," in *Multicultural Education: Commitments, Issues, and Applications*, ed. Carl A. Grant (Washington DC: Association for Supervision and Curriculum Development, 1977), 3; Arturo Pacheco, "Cultural Pluralism: A Philosophical Analysis," *Journal of Teacher Education* 28, no. 3 (1977): 16–20; Manuel Ramírez

III and Alfredo Castañeda, *Cultural Democracy, Bicognitive Development, and Education* (New York: Academic Press, 1974), 23.

8. Virginia E. Sánchez Korrol, *From Colonia to Community: The History of Puerto Ricans in New York City*, rev. ed. (Berkeley: University of California Press, 1994), 234.

9. Marable, *Race, Reform, and Rebellion*, 138–141.

10. Quoted in Ball, *The Bakke Case*, 8. Language in brackets is Ball's.

11. Ibid., 8.

12. Quoted in David Frum, *How We Got Here: The 70's; The Decade that Brought You Modern Life (For Better or Worse)* (New York: Basic Books, 2000), 242–243.

13. Marable, *Race, Reform, and Rebellion*, 151.

14. Barbara T. Christian, "Camouflaging Race *and* Gender," in *Race and Representation*, 227–228.

15. Yen Le Espiritu, *Asian American Panethnicity: Bridging Institutions and Identities* (Philadelphia: Temple University Press, 1992), 54, 95.

16. Ibid., 10–13, 25, 35, 82–83, 112–133.

17. Alicia Gaspar de Alba, *Chicano Art Inside/Outside the Master's House: Cultural Politics and the CARA Exhibition* (Austin: University of Texas Press, 1998), 10–14.

18. Gutiérrez, *Walls and Mirrors*, 183–199.

19. The Combahee River Collective, "A Black Feminist Statement," in *This Bridge Called My Back: Writings by Radical Women of Color*, ed. Cherríe Moraga and Gloria Anzaldúa (New York: Kitchen Table, 1981), 210–218. Robin D. G. Kelley, *Yo' Mama's Dysfunktional* (New York: Beacon Press, 1997), 103–124. In addition to analyzing "A Black Feminist Critique," Kelley offers his own important critique of revisionist interpretations of late-twentieth-century social movements that suggest everything fell apart in the 1970s when black, Chicano/a, and other activists ignored the commonality of class struggle and looked only to racial issues.

20. Ed Guerrero, *Framing Blackness: The African American Image in Film* (Philadelphia: Temple University Press, 1993), 69–111.

21. Kathleen Conzen et al., "The Invention of Ethnicity: A Perspective from the U.S.A.," *Journal of American Ethnic History* 12, no. 1 (1992), 29–30; Frum, *How We Got Here*, 273.

22. See Troy Duster, "Individual Fairness, Group Preferences, and the California Strategy," in *Race and Representation*, 111–133. Duster bases his analysis, in part, on Kenneth O'Reilly, *Nixon's Piano: Presidents and Racial Politics from Washington to Clinton* (New York: Free Press, 1995).

23. Marable, *Race, Reform, and Rebellion*, 174–175.

24. Ball, *The Bakke Case*, 5–6.

25. Omi and Winant, *Racial Formation in the United States*, 117–118. As they put it, "This new injustice conferred group rights on racial minority groups, thus granting a new form of privilege—that of 'preferential treatment.' . . . In this

scenario, the victims of racial discrimination had dramatically shifted from racial minorities to whites, particularly white males."

26. Guerrero, *Framing Blackness*, 104–105, 116.

27. Schulman, *The Seventies: The Great Shift in American Culture, Society, and Politics* (New York: Free Press, 2001), 72–75.

28. Frum, *How We Got Here*, 35.

29. Albert Murray, *The Omni-Americans: Some Alternatives to the Folklore of White Supremacy* (New York: Outbridge and Dienstfrey, 1970; repr., New York: Da Capo, 1990).

30. Etienne Balibar, "Is There a 'Neo-Racism'?" in *Race, Nation, Class: Ambiguous Identities*, ed. Etienne Balibar and Immanuel Wallerstein (London: Verso, 1991), 21–22, 25.

31. George Lipsitz writes: "The increased possessive investment in whiteness generated by disinvestment in U.S. cities, factories, and schools since the 1970s disguises as *racial* problems the general social problems posed by deindustrialization, economic restructuring, and neoconservative attacks on the welfare state. It fuels a discourse that demonizes people of color for being victimized by these changes, while hiding the privileges of whiteness by attributing the economic advantages enjoyed by whites to their family values, faith in fatherhood, and foresight—rather than to the favoritism they enjoy through their possessive investment in whiteness." *Possessive Investment in Whiteness*, 18.

32. *Regents of University of California v. Bakke*, 438 U.S. 265 (1978), 311–313, quoted in Post, "Introduction," 15.

33. Paul Gilroy, *Against Race: Imagining Political Culture beyond the Color Line* (Cambridge, MA: Harvard University Press, 2000), 342, 350.

34. As Craig Werner writes, "Earth, Wind & Fire preached a soul sermon on the theme that united the new black cities, the most serious sixties revolutionaries, and the members of Ella Baker's beloved community: the moral imperative of creating a better world for the blessed children." *A Change is Gonna Come: Music, Race & the Soul of America* (New York: Penguin, 1998), 187.

4

"Vigorously Left, Right, and Center"

The Crosscurrents of
Working-Class America in the 1970s

JEFFERSON COWIE

❖ ❖ ❖ ❖ ❖ ❖ ❖ ❖ ❖ ❖ ❖ ❖ ❖ ❖ ❖

"If we read our stars right, the seventies ought to see, not the dawning of the age of Aquarius, but a new era for the workingman," prophesized two labor intellectuals at the dawn of the decade. "If history moves on its present course, the worker and his union will again have a place in the sun." Other contemporary commentators struck similar chords as they bore witness to a "huge, crude astonishment" at the rediscovery of the "working/forgotten/average man" or spoke, as did *Newsweek,* of "a far-ranging, fast-spreading revolt of the little man against the Establishment." The difference between the 1960s and the 1970s might well be summed up by one writer in *Commonweal,* who colloquially declared that "workers is in, blacks and poor is out." All the attention on the working class was for a good reason. Beneath the preoccupation with the urban crisis, the bombing of Cambodia, and the collapsing Days of Rage was a nation riding the biggest wave of strike activity since the end of World War II (and 1946 was the biggest strike year in U.S. history). The chronology of labor unrest in 1970 alone is remarkable: a national strike against General Electric at the beginning of the year was followed by an unprecedented work stoppage by the New York City postal workers in March (for which President Nixon had to call in the National Guard); the Teamsters then halted interstate trucking in May, after which the United Auto Workers (UAW) took on the massive General Motors (GM) in the fall; and hundreds of thousands of railroad workers walked off the job and paralyzed the nation's rail system at the year's end. These strikes were only the major landmarks in a year that saw over 2.4 million workers engaged in large-scale work stoppages in addition to all sorts of wildcats, slowdowns, union democratization movements, and aggressive stands in contract negotiations.[1]

The new worker emerging in the 1970s was not, however, a simple reincarnation of the 1930s proletarian of popular historical imagination. Rather, an amalgam of politically complex, and at times quite contradictory, forces defined the blue-collar revival of the 1970s. The Gordian knot of 1970s working-class history bound together two sociological strands: the economic and workplace struggles that gave shape to the dramatic strike wave, and, equally important, the politics of culture and race that shaped post-1968 America. Scholars have typically tried to make sense of only one or the other of these trends, but pulling on one strand inevitably tightens it around the other. To understand the full complexity of 1970s blue-collar America, the young militants of the auto shops must be placed in an analytical tension with those who declared their allegiance to segregationist presidential candidate George Wallace. The truck drivers struggling to democratize their union must be squared with their official leaders enlisting in the legions of Richard Nixon's silent majority. The picketers outside the plant gates that rocked the nation must be contrasted with the construction workers pouring into Manhattan's financial district, bloodying anti-war protestors, and declaring their allegiance to Nixon and the establishment. The institutional achievements of the previous generation—from labor law to the building of big unions—must be framed as both a source of power as well as a system of constraint on the advancement of workers. Whether rechristened as the "hardhats," the "blue collars," the "disenchanted workers," the "unmeltable ethnics," the "lower middle class," or the "new militants," blue-collar Americans clearly had returned to the national stage; where their movement was headed was much less clear.

Workers were back, but in ways that were simultaneously profound and strange, militant and absurd, traditional and new, insurgent and reactionary. Commenting on the political confusion swirling about him in 1976, Michael Harrington declared that "America is moving vigorously left, right, and center, all at once." Urban jazz poet Gil Scott-Heron may have best captured the ambivalence in his acid-dipped lyrics: "America doesn't know whether it wants to be Matt Dillon or Bob Dylan." Indeed, whether the country wanted to be led, tall in the saddle, to a restoration of the ancien régime, cowboy style, by Marshall Matt Dillon of television's *Gunsmoke* or wanted to meld the workerism of Woody Guthrie with the new politics of the 1960s á la Bob Dylan marked a fundamental tension among American workers in the 1970s. These dual political strains, one of insurgency and one of backlash, often overlapped in their criticisms of the failures of the liberal consensus. Both pointed to unfulfilling work and declining economic opportunity; both also built on concerns about traditional morality and the highly charged issue of race. Even when that overlap was strong, however, finding ways to tap into it proved politically elusive.[2]

Despite well-reasoned hope, history did not continue to move "on its present course" toward a new working-class future. By the end of the decade, although the backlash workers found some political outlet in new strategic plans of the Republican Party, the insurgent workers fell prey to the newly and cohesively reorganized powers of business, the crush of inflation, and the destruction of key parts of the industrial heartland. The Democrats experimented with new formulas to draw white workers back into the orb of the New Deal coalition, but those attempts to stake out a common foundation for an interracial working-class coalition ended in failure by 1978. Economic crisis, racial tensions, and political failure added up to what one writer called a "sociological 'perfect storm'" that overwhelmed and finally submerged the place of workers in civic life by the dawn of the 1980s. Despite predictions of a "new era for the working man"—or woman—the 1970s ended not as a revival, but as a swan song. Just as the 1960s were a period of crystallization for race and gender issues, the 1970s and early 1980s were important years for the dissolution of what once held place as one of the fundamental problems of political economy, the "labor question."[3]

❖ ❖ ❖

THE INSURGENCY

In 1966, *Fortune* foreshadowed the dissident democratic strains in the labor movement that would reach their crescendo in the early 1970s. "The news about organized labor is a dramatic shift in the balance of power, from the familiar faces to the faceless men of the rank and file," explained the magazine. "The change signifies an entirely new era in labor relations; in the particular year ahead, it implies a round of very large wage increases—possibly accompanied by strikes—like nothing the U.S. has seen in the last decade." *Business Week* concurred, proclaiming that the new worker was "militant, confident, and loaded for bear. He intends to press for substantial wage increases—as a matter of justice, to match booming profits, and as a matter of need, to compensate for rising living costs. He is remarkably well informed about both these phenomena." The restless workers of the early 1970s focused on three issues: rising inflation eating away at their postwar wage gains, mind-numbing working conditions, and the decrepit state of rank-and-file control over their unions and their workplaces. They also took action. In the nine-year period from 1967 through 1976 the average number of workers on strike rose 30 percent, and the number of days lost to work stoppages rose 40 percent over the eighteen-year period from 1948 to 1966. "At the heart of the new mood," reported the *New York Times*, "there is a challenge to management's authority to run its plants," as workers sought to recast the constraints of the postwar labor relations regime.[4]

The 1970s began with postal workers raising all three of these issues in the first substantial strike against the federal government in U.S. history. A New York City postal worker with twenty-three years on the job still made 25 percent less than the income level necessary for a moderate standard of living as defined by the federal government. The job site was hazardous, the positions were oversupervised, and working conditions were antiquated. As the postmaster general admitted before a Senate committee, supervision practices "smack more of a Dickens novel than of intelligent use of fine (and costly) human talents." Longstanding complaints about poor wages remained unheard, and many feared that Nixon's plan to turn the U.S. Postal Service into an independent government corporation held out little promise to change the situation. Despite these issues, postal workers were an unlikely group of militants. They were typically regarded as good and loyal civil servants, and their union, like those of other federal employees, was little more than a toothless lobbying organization that, neither able to bargain nor legally strike, could partake only in, as the workers called it, "collective begging." Joining an illegal strike against the federal government was not without substantial risk: postal workers risked fines of up to one thousand dollars, jail time as long as one year, and automatic dismissal.[5]

In March 1970, however, postal workers shocked the nation as they walked off the job in New York, New Jersey, and Connecticut in demand of wage increases and collective bargaining procedures; stoppages in major cities across the country soon followed. The Nixon administration declared, "What is at issue then is the survival of a government based upon law." Although the administration carefully called the action a "work stoppage" rather than a strike so as not to exacerbate the situation, Nixon sent in twenty-five thousand unarmed members of the National Guard to move the mail (though without much success). The federal government's intervention sparked a back-to-work movement in most sites except for New York City, which remained out in defiance of the federal government. George Schultz, Nixon's secretary of labor, captured fears of rank-and-file power in the early 1970s in his opening salvo in the conflict. "There's only one thing worse than a wildcat strike," he declared, "a wildcat strike that succeeds." And this *was* a wildcat that largely succeeded, potentially tipping the balance toward a runaway rank and file rather than the sober and statesman-like leadership on which the postwar paradigm of labor relations depended. In the end, although they did not gain all they were promised when they returned to work three weeks later, the workers had won a hefty raise that hedged their inflation problems, a concession in the number of years necessary to reach top rates of pay, and, most important, collective bargaining rights (although without the right to strike or create a union shop).[6]

By the fall of 1970, *Business Week* explained, "Already this year, union truculence has halted the mail and snarled air travel, establishing dangerous precedents of militant government workers in the process. Twice the country has come to the brink of a nationwide railway strike. . . . A trucking strike is still a possibility." The magazine continued, "This is only the beginning." It was, indeed, only the beginning as the autumn brought a titanic struggle between the UAW, the largest industrial union, and GM, the largest corporation in the world—the type of struggle that had not been seen since 1946. It was one of the largest and costliest strikes in U.S. history, an immense affair—more than "just a strike . . . a crusade," explained journalist William Serrin—that lasted fifty-eight days. Yet the showdown was one that took place largely within the predictable boundaries of postwar collective bargaining—a "civilized affair" following the strict rules of engagement. The union won substantial gains in wages and benefits, pensions, cost-of-living protections, and—especially popular with the rank and file, "thirty and out": those who had served thirty years on the job could take their pensions and escape the life-draining labor of the assembly line.[7]

The 1970 GM-UAW struggle, as central as it may have been to the U.S. economy in its loss of one billion dollars in profits for the company and the near bankruptcy of the UAW, was not the most historically significant conflict between the company and the union. The agreement did not address the demands of groups such as the League of Revolutionary Black Workers, which drew together African American militants from Detroit-area auto shops to criticize the union's complicity in the auto "plantation"; it did not alter the balance of power between the workers and their employers; and it did nothing to challenge the mind-numbing working conditions of the assembly line. Quite the opposite, the GM strike confirmed the stale rules of postwar collective bargaining. As Serrin explained in his in-depth look at the strike, the union and the corporation "are not enemies, nor, in a large sense adversaries;" they have a "great[er] community of interest than of conflict." The prolonged strike actually masked many of the conflicts brewing below the otherwise progressive patina of the UAW. The work stoppage, as big as it was, confirmed David Brody's fundamental insight into postwar bargaining: "The contractual logic itself actually evolved into a pervasive method for containing shop-floor activism."[8] The system delivered more money but no more voice.

The rules of the game were more directly challenged two years later in a set of state-of-the-art auto plants built in the cornfields of the Ohio River Valley. In events that would later be called "the Woodstock of the workingman," automobile workers at GM's Lordstown, Ohio, plants launched a rank-and-file movement that became a national symbol for worker alienation and brought to national prominence a new, young and enlightened working class, whose face had been hidden from the public behind the likes of television's Archie Bunker. As Lordstown local president Gary Bryner explained about his membership, "[T]he young black and white workers dig each other. There's an understanding. The guy with the Afro, the guy with the beads, the guy with the goatee, he doesn't care if he's black, white, green, or yellow." They smoked dope, socialized interracially, and dreamed of a world in which work had some meaning. These Lordstown screw turners regarded the Volvo plant in Sweden, where workers performed a variety of tasks and learned multiple skills, as some sort of distant industrial nirvana. "They just want to be treated with dignity," said Bryner. "That's not asking a hell of a lot."[9]

Production, not dignity, however, was on the company's agenda. GM had reorganized assembly into an aggressive, authoritarian management system (appropriately named General Motors Assembly Division [GMAD]) in order to build a subcompact car, the Vega, to compete with foreign imports in the 1970s. Under the new system cars flew down the assembly line at a rate of 101.6 cars per hour, producing one vehicle every thirty-six seconds, the fastest assembly line in the world. The workers balked at the speed and discipline by working strictly to rules, letting production slip by unfinished, and engaging in occasional sabotage. The grievance machinery clogged up, and workers reached the breaking point as management pushed cars through the plant with its get-tough policy. The local strike vote of March 1972 polled a rare 97 percent in favor of walking off the job, not for more money, but for a more humane production and industrial relations system. All the other plants that fell under the purview of GMAD organization had the same issues, but it was Lordstown that came to symbolize for the nation a new kind of industrial unrest.[10]

Consumer advocate Ralph Nader proclaimed that Lordstown would do for workers "what the Berkeley situation of 1964 did for student awareness." Although the strike lasted only three weeks, it quickly became emblematic of alienation, the need for work reorganization, and what the press liked to call the "blue-collar blues." Across the nation, insurgent labor forces applauded the Lordstown strike; periodicals—from *Harper's* to *Life* to *Newsweek* to *Playboy*—angled for its meanings; and business leaders fretted about its implications. The Nixon administration even launched a national commission to study the problems raised by the strikers. The report, *Work in America,* confirmed that "many workers at all occupational levels feel locked in, their mobility blocked, the opportunity to grow lacking in their jobs, challenge missing from their tasks." The strike and the ensuing report initiated the "quality of work life" movement that sought to redesign work, introduce automation, and invest in "human relations" strategies, most of which continued to empower management, not workers—albeit with a gentler hand.[11]

Lordstown was but a small part of a larger pattern of rank-and-file unrest that rocked not just the corporations but also organized labor. Several large unions in the postwar era had been shaped around leaders who, wielding power, charisma, and strategic vision effectively, often won the hearts and minds of the rank and file and outbargained the bosses. Although often undemocratic, authoritarian, and even overtly corrupt, these union leaders—such as John L. Lewis of the United Mine Workers and Jimmy Hoffa of the Teamsters—delivered the goods. When their less-competent lieutenants took over in the 1960s, however, often all that remained was corruption and authoritarianism—minus charisma, strategic vision, and rank-and-file support. As one student of the reform movement put it, "Great tyrants, jealous of their power, often surround themselves with men much less capable than themselves, men who do not pose a threat to their kingdom. The result is often disastrous." Proponents of democratization movements faced down violence, intimidation, and entrenched bureaucracy to bring rank-and-file voice into the leadership. In the case of Miners for Democracy, the obstacles even included the murder of its leader, Jock Yablonski, and his family. The reform movements met with mixed success, but their gains included substantial local victories for the steel workers, the laying of groundwork for eventual democratization of the Teamsters, and the transformation of the mine workers' national leadership for the indefinite future. The spirit of the reform movements, as labor lawyer Thomas Geoghegan explained, "was like nothing else in labor. It was Union Democracy, the New Politics, the whole Sixties Enlightenment. It was the whole sixties experience come at last to organized labor."[12]

A final example of the remarkable insurgency of the 1970s is the organizing drive at J. P. Stevens. The struggle, part of which was fictionalized in the film *Norma Rae*, stands, in the words of one historian, as "a defining confrontation between labor and capital in the United States." The South, where organizing had been hobbled by the problems of race and employer militancy, had been the labor movement's weak link for generations. An unorganized South meant that the unions' power in the North was vulnerable to runaway shops and interregional competition to lower business costs (i.e., wages and working conditions). In a dramatic interracial struggle in 1974, the workers broke through the textile industry's vicious antiunionism and won the election at the Stevens plant in Roanoke Rapids, North Carolina. It looked as though the South would finally be organized. "It was a new day in Dixie— first J. P. Stevens, then the textile industry, then the South," proclaimed a Carolina unionist. Rather than a new day, however, the victory in Roanoke Rapids came to symbolize the futility of working within the tangled web of a legalistic industrial relations system because the employer simply refused to bargain and entered into a war of attrition in the courts. The U.S. Court of Appeals concluded that the company's "campaign has involved numerous unfair labor practices, including coercive interrogation, surveillance, threat of plant closing and economic reprisals for union activity. Moreover, the threats have been made good by extensive discriminatory discharges." Despite winning case after case in the courts and before the National Labor Relations Board, the union ended up wasting its resources on litigation, establishing the high moral ground but gaining few new union members.[13]

However, other breakthroughs suggested that a multicultural and multi-issue "age of the worker" would become a reality. In 1975, César Chávez and the United Farm Workers obtained what was once unimaginable—California's Agricultural Labor Relations Act, which codified ten years of struggle and promised a new day to agricultural workers excluded from the postwar system of labor relations. Similarly, the Coalition of Black Trade Unionists, founded in 1972, provided a forum for African Americans to maintain the struggle for civil and employment rights as well as to support rank-and-file efforts to fight discrimination *within* the labor movement. The Equal Employment Opportunity Commission (EEOC) took on entrenched racism and sexism both in unions and the workplace, even though many of these important efforts to ensure fair employment practices were checked by shrinking economic opportunity during the decade. Occupational safety and health took an apparent great leap forward when the Occupational Safety and Health Administration came to life under the Nixon administration. However, the 1974 killing of union activist Karen Silkwood, who was on her way to the *New York Times* to deliver important documents about horrific safety and health violations at Kerr-McGee's Oklahoma plutonium plant, made clear how difficult it could be to regulate what happened behind the fortress-like walls of the workplace.[14]

Women's issues certainly became more central to the labor movement as a result of more women working in the formal sector, the decline of many male-dominated occupations, and the feminization of politics in the 1970s. Two organizations founded in the decade, the Coalition of Labor Union Women (CLUW) and 9 to 5, sought to meld women's rights and occupational rights into a single movement. CLUW provided a forum for women already in unions, and 9 to 5 became a forum for nonunionized women to discuss occupational issues and problems. Through organizations like 9 to 5, once-subservient female office workers found an outlet for combining workplace rights and feminism in the pink-collar ghettos. These changes, however, often occurred in an uneasy relation with unions. "When we started," explained Karen Nussbaum, founder of 9 to 5, "the union people scorned women. They didn't care to take the time with us women, who didn't know anything about unions." Similarly, flight attendants struggled both within the unions and against the notorious sexism of the airlines. Flight attendants had often been used as sex objects to sell seats on airplanes; National Airlines' ad campaign featured stewardesses with captions such as, "Hi, I'm Linda, and I'm going to FLY you like you've never been flown before," and Continental Airlines claimed, "We really move our tail for you." Consequently, airline workers launched Stewardesses for Women's Rights and, in conjunction with the

EEOC, were able to redefine their work from the realm of the sexualized "sky muffin" to that of flight attendant. As one attendant explained to *Ms.* magazine, "I don't think of myself as a sex symbol or a servant. I think of myself as somebody who knows how to open the door of a 747 in the dark, upside down and under water."[15]

All these groups and others survived to build lasting institutions, but most of the insurgency of the first half of the 1970s ground to a halt with the 1974–1975 recession. The economy shrank, industrial capacity plummeted, unemployment rose to its (then) postwar high, foreign competition eroded market position, rising interest rates prevented plant modernization, and holding down wages and benefits became the central goal of corporate strategies as inflation became political enemy number one. The combination of high unemployment and high inflation, factors that should have been in an inverse relationship with one another, meant that any policy designed to boost employment or wages would be likely to exacerbate inflation. The 1970s ended up as the first decade in which, according to critics, organized workers simply made too much money and their high rates of pay caused a national crisis. Union members remained relatively immune to inflationary pressures because they typically had cost-of-living adjustment mechanisms in their contracts, but the majority of the nation's employees were not so fortunate. In previous decades the unionized sectors pulled the wages and benefits of nonunion workers upward, but with union members reigning as a new aristocracy of labor in inflationary times, the interests of the organized and unorganized diverged more dramatically than at any other time in the postwar era. Resentment and fear between the two groups replaced the hope for solidarity. Joshua Freeman's description of New Yorkers who became "hard hearted" in "the harsh climate of prolonged recession and austerity politics" held true for much of the nation in the mid-1970s. Hope began to fade for renewing the postwar blue-collar dream by breaking out of the structure that had simultaneously fostered and fettered it.[16]

THE BACKLASH

The most salient image in 1970s working-class iconography is not the insurgent striker warming himself by a picket-line barrel fire but the beer-slugging bigot of the blue-collar backlash. The two images coexisted in the first half of the 1970s and, surprisingly enough, shared some common political terrain. While working people challenged the industrial relations system in record-setting strikes that sought to democratize their unions, bring dignity to the job, and maintain wages and benefits in the midst of stagflation, other workers openly challenged the liberal political structure that once seemed the (white) workers' stalwart ally. The Democratic Party, which had won workers' allegiance by delivering the National Labor Relations Act, the Social Security Act, and the Fair Labor Standards Act in the 1930s, began to appear to many in the white working class to have drifted too far from bread-and-butter liberalism by the end of the 1960s. The EEOC and the courts pushed issues such as affirmative action, busing, and welfare rights, which offered the promise of equal opportunity for women and minorities, but helped to foster a politics of class and racial resentment as well. The Vietnam War catalyzed the reaction of an already volatile political chemistry.

In 1968 and 1972, third-party presidential candidate George Wallace drew together segregationist southerners and antiliberal northerners who feared the prospect of blacks moving into their neighborhoods; questioned the protests and the urban riots; and, above all, simply felt forgotten. Just a month before the 1968 election, Wallace rode those sentiments to a 21 percent share in a national poll, only 7 points behind Democratic candidate Hubert Humphrey. "The support he was drawing in 1968," suggests historian Michael Kazin, "looked to many liberals like a fascist movement on the rise." In the end, Wallace won 13.6 percent of the vote, and his segregationist message helped him carry five southern states (four of which Goldwater had carried in the previous presidential election). His earlier gains among white ethnics in the urban North, which suggested something fundamentally new and troubling in U.S. politics, had largely eroded by election day. Some of the reasons for the erosion of his support are suggestive of the character of the blue-collar backlash. Among northern wage earners, Wallace's populist antielitism and anticrime messages (including the implicit racial issue embedded in law-and-order language) worked best, but his overt embrace of segregation, his selection of a vice presidential candidate who appeared ready to push the button, and his snarling rhetoric and petty resentments failed him. When the UAW launched a campaign against him—exposing the dismal level of workers rights and compensation in Wallace's Alabama—it helped turn the tide in the industrial North.[17]

Disentangling George Wallace's race baiting from his "stand up for the common man" theme is as impossible as untangling race from class in U.S.

history. Undoubtedly, however, his common-man rhetoric spoke to themes that no one else on the national stage addressed, tapping into sentiments that paralleled the blue-collar insurgency along the way. "Can a former truck driver who married a former dime-store clerk and whose father was a plain dirt farmer be elected president of the United States?" he asked in explicitly class terms.[18] In another stump speech, Wallace asked:

> Now what are the real issues that exist today in these United States? It is the trend of pseudointellectual government where a select elite group have written guidelines in bureaus and court decisions, have spoken from some pulpits, some college campus, some newspaper offices, looking down their noses at the average man on the street, the glass workers, the steel workers, the auto workers, and the textile workers, the farm workers, the policemen, the beautician, and the barber, and the little businessman, saying to him that you do not know how to get up in the morning or go to bed at night unless we write you a guideline. . . .[19]

Similar questions would have occupied the minds of postal workers denied the right to strike by the federal government, textile workers dragged through the courts for the better part of a decade, and autoworkers subjected to the innovations of industrial engineers. As one welder noted in 1970, "Now people say we're only out for ourselves and we're against the Negroes an [*sic*] all that. Well, I don't know. I've never been asked. If they did come around and talk with us at work and ask us their question, I'll bet we'd confuse them. One minute we'd sound like George Wallace, and the next we'd probably be called radicals or something." A promising political space seemed to exist between the race and the class dimensions of the 1970s labor problem. As Oklahoma populist Fred Harris speculated, the "blue-collar worker will be progressive as long as it is not progress for everyone but himself."[20]

The problems of work and class languished in the Democratic Party, but the Republicans proved more effective in tapping into the spirit of the moment. When newly elected President Nixon happened to read "The Revolt of the White Lower Middle Class," a *New York* magazine article by Pete Hamill, the pieces began to fall into place for conservatives to take the lead on the labor issue. "The working-class white man is actually in revolt against taxes, joyless work, the double standards and short memories of professional politicians, hypocrisy and what he considers the debasement of the American dream," wrote Hamill. In final words that proved to be the Rosetta stone for Republican strategists, the author wrote, "Any politician who leaves that white man out of the political equation does so at very large risk." Republican strategist Kevin Phillips calculated that the Republican votes for Nixon in the 1968 contest, combined with the Wallace votes (which he figured were disillusioned Democrats en route to the Republican Party), equaled a "new Republican majority" that would finally triumph over the New Deal coalition. Having been inspired by Hamill's thinking about workers as "the forgotten man," Nixon commissioned a report on the "blue-collar issue" to add a more distinct class hue to his "silent majority" strategy. The result helped lay the groundwork for moving the Republican Party out of the country club and into the neighborhood tavern. The strategy included courting labor leaders to the president's side (especially on the war), rhetorically promoting the dignity of work and the struggle of the wage earner, and swearing off any form of antiunion action that might alienate workers (and fighting off Republican traditionalists who wanted to come out swinging). The administration's goal was to make the party open, at least rhetorically, to the working class. As Charles Colson explained in an administration memo, "[O]ur immediate objective is to keep Labor split away from the Democrats. Our long-range target is to make them part of our 'New Majority.' "[21]

When the notorious "hard hat" revolts shook Manhattan in May of 1970, workers seemed to be the shock troops for the emerging New Right. New York City construction workers violently descended on antiwar protestors gathered to condemn the killings at Kent State University. After storming the steps of City Hall and chasing students through the financial district, the workers gained national notoriety as the avant-garde of an authoritarian working class. Nixon recalled the degree to which the protests bolstered his spirits for his policies in Southeast Asia and his faith in the new blue-collar strategy. "The workers," Nixon exclaimed, "were with us when some of the elitist crowd were running away from us. Thank God for the hard hats!" The protests continued all month, culminating in a final demonstration of over one hundred thousand proclaiming their support for the administration and the establishment. H. R. Haldeman noted in his journal that the president "thinks now the college demonstrators have overplayed their hands, evidence is the blue collar group rising up against them and P[resident] can mobilize them."[22]

Like the Wallace movement, the hard-hat protests and the stereotype of the hawkish working class deserve a more complex treatment. Certainly, numerous blue-collar Americans agreed with John Nash, a Newark printer who, when interviewed during the protests, chalked up participation in the war as simple duty to country. "I'm backing the president all the way. My boy goes into service Dec. 7. . . . I'm proud of him. It's a chance we all had to take. It's his turn." But polling data gave lie to the myth of a uniquely pro-war working class and consistently showed, in fact, that manual workers were more opposed to the war and more in favor of withdrawal than were the college educated. An amalgam of polls, interviews, and reports suggest that sentiments such as Nash's did not reflect support for the war so much as reveal class resentments of workers toward the protestors' methods, privilege, and apparently nonexistent sense of duty. In an era in which many families were barely more than one generation out of poverty, the college draft deferment created a fairly distinct class divide between those who were forced to serve and those who were not. Thus, much of the psychology of the backlash trended more toward class antagonisms, guilt, and victimization than toward an actual stand on foreign policy. According to historian Christian Appy, "To many veterans, the protest of college students felt like moral and social putdowns, expressions not of principle and commitment but simply of class privilege and arrogance."[23]

Andrew Levison reported watching his neighbor, a member of Vietnam Veterans against the War (VVAW) who had seen the worst the war had to offer, boldly approach another veteran who was screaming and venting his venom at antiwar protestors:

"Look, we were over there—we know what was going on," the protestor explained.

"Damn right," the heckler replied.

"Well, hell, you know we should have never gotten in there in the first place—you know we didn't belong there."

"Yeah," the guy replied uncertainly.

"Well, that's all we're saying," explained the VVAW member.

"Yeah, but I just can't take them damn kids who don't know what we went through, saying we're all a bunch of killers, and that the Viet Cong are all saints."

"I got six ounce of lead in my ass that shows that's not true. But I just don't want anyone else killed in that mess."

"I agree with you on that, but I just can't stand these hippies."[24]

While the Republicans effectively tapped into such tensions, the Democrats groped for solutions to the labor question but could never quite assemble the pieces into a strategic vision. When *U.S. News and World Report* interviewed Democratic standard bearer Hubert Humphrey on "How will the common man's revolt change politics?" he condemned a "kind of snobbishness" creeping into liberalism and sought out ways to return the Democrats to their blue-collar base through a renewed focus on jobs and the workplace. Humphrey believed that only workplace issues could serve as the "common denominators" that would enable people to duck the divisiveness of the 1960s by discussing "mutual needs, mutual wants, common hopes, and the same fears" across a fragmented political landscape.[25] Here Humphrey hit the right note, but he was already the political symbol of all the failings of the liberal establishment. Despite Humphrey being the Democratic heir apparent for 1972, the nomination fell to Senator George McGovern, who, instead of mobilizing supporters around the class cleavage in U.S. politics, deepened the divide.

The success of postwar Democratic politics traditionally depended on an alliance between labor and liberals, but on that ground the McGovern campaign proved a dismal failure. Given the intransigent pro-war stance held by leaders of the American Federation of Labor and Congress of Industrial Organizations (AFL-CIO), maintaining the labor-liberal alliance would have been difficult, but the McGovern strategy guaranteed defeat. In the 1972 primaries, McGovern supporters actually framed their strategy around defeating organized labor and pushing social issues rather than finding ways to patch the old coalition. Nixon's "Assault Book" for the fall presidential contest sought to take advantage of the Democrats' weakness:

> As the campaign progresses, we should increasingly portray McGovern as the pet radical of Eastern Liberalism, the darling of the New York Times, the hero of the Berkeley Hill Jet Set; Mr. Radical Chic. The liberal elitists are his—we have to get back the working people; and the better we portray McGovern as an elitist radical, the smaller his political base. By November, he should be postured as the Establishment's fair-haired boy, and RN postured as the Candidate of the Common Man, the working man.[26]

Although many refugees from the New Left ended up working as important organizers and staffers to colonize the labor movement in the 1970s, others seemed mostly to have helped Nixon's strategists by savagely criticizing the embourgeoisment of the American working class and by issuing blanket condemnations of postwar liberalism. Historian Jack Metzgar's description of arguments with his father, a union steel maker, are telling, as he remembers the condescension with which he formulated his New Left denunciations of his father's generation and its accomplishments and takes stock of their consequences: "I helped George Wallace get a hearing with that man, and then I helped Ronald Reagan get his vote. I helped make him part of the problem when he should have been part of the solution."[27]

Stuck between the courtship of Richard Nixon and the social issue liberalism of George McGovern, for the first time the AFL-CIO simply refused to endorse a candidate. George Meany, president of the labor organization, announced, "I will not endorse, I will not support, and I will not vote for Richard Nixon. I will not endorse, I will not support, and I will not vote for George McGovern." Hinting at the profundity of the labor problem in the 1970s, he added, "If Norman Thomas was only alive—." Of course, Meany never did and never would have endorsed Socialist Party candidate Norman Thomas, but his joke speaks to the volatile nature of working-class politics in the 1970s. The split between laborers and liberals helped usher in the biggest landslide in American history, with over 60 percent of the popular vote, 57 percent of the manual-worker vote, and 54 percent of the union vote going to Nixon. He was even the first Republican to receive a majority of Catholic votes. The president himself certainly believed he had achieved a strategic breakthrough. "Here's to you Chuck," exclaimed the victorious president as he toasted Charles Colson, his blue-collar strategist. "Those are your votes that are pouring in, the Catholics, the union members, the blue collars, your votes, boy. It was your strategy and it's a landslide!"[28]

STAYIN' ALIVE IN POPULAR CULTURE

The multifaceted resurrection of blue-collar America resonated in commercial popular culture from Nashville to Hollywood. In 1970, the most popular television shows included the traditional escapism of *Marcus Welby, Flip Wilson, Here's Lucy, Ironside,* and, of course, *Gunsmoke.* By the middle of the decade, in contrast, the list of top shows was a multicultural working-class ghetto in all its complexities: *All in the Family* (backlash worker versus the new politics); *The Waltons* (return of the Great Depression); *Good Times, Welcome Back Kotter,* and *Sanford and Son* (life and poverty in the inner city); *The Jeffersons* (black upward mobility); *Laverne and Shirley* (working girls in the classless Fifties); and *One Day at a Time* and *Alice* (working women face life after divorce). For eight consecutive nights in January 1977, the nation even glued itself to the set to confront the most oppressive labor system in U.S. history, slavery, by watching the epic miniseries *Roots.*[29] Reporters descended on factories to record special programs explaining the "blue-collar blues," and filmmakers turned their lenses toward working-class themes at a rate five to six times that of the previous decade. Bruce Springsteen brought the greaser back into rock and roll with his portrayal of working-class characters "sweating it out on the streets of a runaway American dream," and in country music Johnny Paycheck led his audiences in mass choruses of "Take This Job and Shove It!"

The revival of working-class characters in American popular culture was actually fairly complex and interesting, often showing workers moving "left, right, and center, and all at once," but it was the backlash characters that have since received the lion's share of attention. The early 1970s began with what might be called a "revenge sequence," in which scriptwriters seemed set on a misplaced retaliation against working people for their alleged conservatism. Media creations such as the title character in the 1970 film *Joe,* a machinist played by Peter Boyle, fostered the worst of the backlash stereotype. "All you gotta do is act black and the money rolls in," Joe rants. "Set fire to the cities, burn a few buildings, throw a few bombs and you get money and jobs," he exclaims before teaming up with an advertising executive in an armed hunt for hippies. In a gentler mood, *All in the Family* featured the comic malapropisms of Archie Bunker, who defends his president and his nation against the criticisms of his own "little goil" and her "Meathead" New Left husband. In yet another example, the ending of *Easy Rider* was explicitly designed to incriminate reactionary working-class politics: a redneck pulls a shotgun off the rack and blows the hippie protagonists off their motorcycles. As Terry Southern, a screenwriter for *Easy Rider,* explained in incredibly tortured logic, "In my mind, the ending was to be an indictment of blue-collar America, the people I thought were responsible for the Vietnam War."[30]

Although Archie Bunker faced layoffs and went on strike, the insurgent worker never got equal time in 1970s popular culture. The main exception is the Academy Award–winning film *Norma Rae,* a fictionalized portrayal of the real life of Crystal Lee Sutton, who played an extraordinary (but hardly solitary) role in organizing J. P. Stevens in Roanoke Rapids. Arguably, the movie's popularity stemmed more from the representation of a woman's rising social consciousness than from the theme of triumphant labor organizing, thus par-

tially explaining why *Norma Rae* was the exception in its unapologetic celebration of working-class heroes. *Norma Rae* aside, most films were much more
ambivalent on their subjects, and many were openly hostile to workers. The
centrifugal forces playing on working-class representation made the labor
problem in the 1970s into a bit of a political Rorschach test. Argued one critic,
"We have let the working man (or woman) become a transparent, hollow
mannequin," into whom we pour our own politics, our own hopes, and our
own prejudices.[31]

Paul Schrader's 1978 dramatic film *Blue Collar* provides a case in point.
Inspired by the events at Lordstown, the film follows three autoworkers—
two black, played by Yaphet Kotto and Richard Pryor, and one white,
played by Harvey Keitel. These workers are alienated from their work
beyond measure, caught in the grip of inflation, and barely able to keep it
all together. As *Cineaste* opined, "The three heroes of the movie are the kind
of workers who abound in cities like Detroit. They have an ingenuous
American moral sincerity, a camaraderie that transcends personal racism,
drive that defies resignation, and refusal to be suckered. They have only the
common illusions about their place in capitalist society: that one person or
a bunch of buddies can beat the system." At first they seem like perfect
1970s workers. They defend their union, they despise their foreman, and
they support each other. Although they seem primed to be characters in a
story of rising class consciousness, Schrader made his film about cynicism,
as the workers turn to robbing their union, not standing up to the company
or the labor leadership. Schrader believed the film was an exploration of
"self-destructiveness" of workers who "attack the organization that was
supposed to defend them. And how that kind of dead-end mentality is fostered and engendered by the ruling class in order to keep the working class
at odds with itself."[32]

Although that plot is far from any form of 1970s reality other than, maybe,
the democratization movements in unions like the Teamsters, the political
feel of the film does capture the decade well. "Its politics are the politics of
resentment and claustrophobia, the feeling of being manipulated and not in
control of your life," Schrader explained. The otherwise claustrophobic sets
are heavy with symbols of past struggles that haunt the present moment—
photos of Martin Luther King Jr., John F. Kennedy, the sit-down strikes, and
deceased UAW leader Walter Reuther. But those are images of a once mighty
past; in the film the 1970s class war is against the union, not the company (or
even, potentially, both the company *and* the union). By the end of the film,

the interracial solidarity is destroyed. The union has the streetwise militant (Yaphet Kotto) murdered; Richard Pryor's character sells his soul to the union bosses, who sold theirs long ago; and Harvey Keitel's character turns to the FBI out of fear for his life. In the final scene, former friends Keitel and Pryor, having called each other every racial slur in their imaginations, pick up tools and go after each other in open conflict. The movie ends in a freeze-frame of worker against worker, the earlier class solidarity dissolved into racial hatred. The prophetic words of Smokey, Yaphet Kotto's character, echo over the image in his deep gravely voice: "They pit the lifer against the new boy, the young against the old, the black against the white. Everything they do is to keep us in our place." In a complete inversion of 1930s social realism, the working class is in the midst of meltdown, not unification. Nonetheless, Schrader strangely called the violent freeze-frame a product of the film's *"Waiting for Lefty* moment"—a "classic social realist poster," he suggested without any hint of irony, that "should be in a post office somewhere."[33]

The theme of solid, blue-collar America shattering in the face of the problems of the 1970s is not limited to straight proletarian films like *Blue Collar,* but carries through to such emblematic movies as *Saturday Night Fever.* As two critics described John Travolta's character, "Tony Manero is a high-powered fusion of sexuality, street jive, and the frustrated hope of boy-man who can't articulate his sense of oppression." The film, they argued, gives "the impression that it knows more about the working-class psyche and ethos than it is willing to risk showing us."[34] At his job at the paint store, Tony works the customers with the same grace and ego that he later reveals on the dance floor of Club 2001. His slick salesmanship and confidence is interrupted only by the realization that he could be stuck selling paint for the rest of his life like his broken-down co-workers. Begging his boss for an advance so he can buy a new shirt for the weekend festivities in the disco, Tony gets instead a lecture on not frittering his money away. "Fuck the future!" Tony angrily retorts. The boss fires back ominously, "The future fucks you."

The workplace is only a minor set in this blue-collar drama, as the plot centers on Tony's attempt to conquer the discotheque, win over Stephanie (Karen Lynn Gorney), an upwardly mobile dancer, and deal with his gang of futureless buddies. Stephanie rejects Tony at first, telling him, "You're a cliché. You're nowhere on your way to no place." Tony's attempt at impromptu self-improvement quickens as he tries to fake his way through a conversation with someone who is trying to fake her way rather pathetically across the river to wealthy Manhattan. Looking "as sharp as [he] can look without turning into a nigger," Tony bursts with creativity and sense of self that he cannot find elsewhere as the crowds part in celebration of his prowess. Among the swirling lights, he gets the attention and adulation missing both at work and at home. Enraged when the first-place trophy in the dance contest is awarded to him rather than the obviously better Puerto Rican couple, he turns over the trophy to the reviled Latinos and storms out of the club.

This is the turning point in the film. Tony then harangues his partner, Stephanie, with a furious, primitive, Marxist sociology that explains gender, race, and class in a few easy pieces: "My Pa goes to work, he gets dumped on. So he come home and dumps on my mother, right? Of course, right. And the spics gotta dump on us, so we gotta dump on the spics, right? Even the humpin' is dumpin' most of the time." Tony proceeds to prove his point about oppression rolling downhill when, in a rage, he attempts to rape Stephanie. By the time an insane night of gang-banging and suicidal behavior has ended, however, the drama concludes with a tightly wrapped, if largely improbable, plot resolution. Unable to contend with either dwindling economic opportunity or the racial, ethnic, and gender challenges around him, Tony chooses to sever all ties to his blue-collar community and create himself anew. "They're all assholes," he declares as he escapes the limits imposed by Brooklyn for the promise offered by Manhattan.

The nation as a whole was asked to make a similar journey by the dawn of the 1980s, but like Tony's new girlfriend, Stephanie, Americans had to fake it. A new day is dawning at the end of the film and a Matisse print hangs on the wall to symbolize their new status, but the characters are sitting in a borrowed apartment. They are literally inhabiting somebody else's world—a world in which their identity as members of a class is either denied or covered up and their blue-collar community is relegated to some forgotten past. The theme is echoed by the Bee Gee's disco anthem "Stayin' Alive," which is featured on the film's soundtrack. "Life goin' nowhere. Somebody help me," sing the Bee Gees. In another contribution to 1970s social realism, they declare in their trademark falsetto, "I've been kicked around since I was born." But then comes the twist—rather than a call to act, the Bee Gees offer permission to forget: "And now it's all right. It's OK. And you may look the other way" as Tony, Stephanie, and the audience turn their back on the unseemly race-class stew of Brooklyn and face a future purged of the working class.

❖ ❖ ❖

THE SEARCH FOR BLUE-COLLAR UNIVERSALISM IN THE ME DECADE

Saturday Night Fever invites its audience to place workers in the past, but some activists and politicians sought to find more realistic routes out of the race-class conundrum of the 1970s As the major social questions of the 1960s moved off the campuses and beyond the sites of the major civil rights struggles, they entered blue-collar communities at a moment of shrinking economic opportunity. Overcoming this recipe for backlash would require the political equivalent of a hat trick: (1) the maintenance of the economic needs of the Democratic Party's blue-collar base; (2) the integration of new expressions of 1960s racial and cultural change; and (3) the achievement of both amid hard times. Simply slapping affirmative action onto a world of shrinking hope and opportunity appeared to many as a zero-sum game. The key was to meld the energy of the insurgency and the resentments of the backlash into a renewed political vision. As Andrew Levison made the connection in the the *New Yorker* in 1974: "Until progressives deal seriously with the idea of full employment and government-guaranteed jobs, black representation in skilled jobs will remain a question of throwing a white carpenter out of work in order to employ a black, or making a Pole with seniority continue to tend the coke ovens while a black moves up to a better job."[35] A few years later, when such plants shut down in the late-1970s wave of deindustrialization, the problem would be more complex than the author could have imagined.[36]

Consider the problem of the consent decree signed in the steel industry. Union seniority had been the bedrock of contractual protection for industrial workers in the postwar era, but it was also a system that protected a host of ills, not the least of which was racism. Although the old CIO unions backed the civil rights movement with financial and political support, they typically dragged their feet in their own workplaces, forcing black workers and civil rights groups to pursue justice through federal intervention. In 1974, nine steel companies and the United Steel Workers signed a consent decree with the federal government in the face of over four hundred discrimination cases pending before the EEOC. The consent decree was designed as a preemptive strike to avoid having the courts impose a Byzantine hiring and promotion system on the companies and the union, but the system remained complex nonetheless. The decree provided simpler paths to advancement (seniority accruing plantwide rather than by department), more transparency in hiring and promotion, goals and timetables for the admission of women and minorities to the skilled positions, and over thirty million dollars in back pay to the women and minorities covered by the agreement. The consent decree, of course, fueled plenty of George Wallace–like sentiments against the government, the company, and the union as white workers believed their job security and skin privilege were under attack. Even those who benefitted were dismayed by the complexity of the settlement. The problem, however, was even more complicated.[37]

Just a few years after the new system of racial hiring and promotion was set up, the steel mills began to shut down across Ohio and Pennsylvania, creating Depression-like conditions in communities that once appeared to be incontrovertible proof of a stable and affluent working class. For African Americans and women, the right to equal-employment opportunity, as fundamentally important and hard won as those struggles were, suddenly became irrelevant in the old steel towns where there were no jobs. The steel industry had already been cutting back on employment throughout the 1970s. Then on "Black Monday," September 19, 1977, the shutdown of the Campbell Works of Youngstown Sheet and Tube was announced. The mills kept folding "like broken promises" into the early 1980s. One journalist described "the dead steel mills . . . as pathetic mausoleums to the decline of American industrial might that was once the envy of the world." Individual rights to nondiscrimination smacked head-on into the need for industrial planning or structural adjustment at a time when capital was either being withdrawn from basic industry or relocated out of the Rust Belt. As historian Judith Stein contends in her study of the industry, "liberalism lacked an economic blueprint to match its social agenda."[38]

The central theme in employment rights had moved from collective economic rights, celebrated by the labor movement and codified by the Wagner Act and other New Deal legislation, to a world of individual rights and identity politics guaranteed by new institutions such as the EEOC and a changed Democratic Party. In essence, the political goal had shifted—the goal was no longer to change how the economic pie was divided, but to give everyone an equal chance to compete for a slice of the pie. Both were laudable goals, but in the midst of the economic crisis of the 1970s, neither approach worked without the other. Historian Nelson Lichtenstein has criticized this "rights consciousness" in the workplace for exactly the type of failure experienced in the steel sector: as a political strategy, it could redistribute jobs to workers who were historically denied access to them, but it could not create more jobs in a world of shrinking opportunity. The approach also depended on the courts, the state, and professional expertise for enforcement rather than on the direct control of workers themselves, fueling the type of hostility toward liberal elites that wound its way through blue-collar politics in the 1970s. The "rights revolution" also did little to encourage unionization and had no impact on the actual structure of the economy. It could change the complexion of the wealth and power pyramid, but not its shape.[39]

It was exactly at the stormy intersection of the politics of race and class in the 1970s that the idea of national economic planning for full employment and the federal guarantee of a job reemerged from its postwar slumber. Senator Hubert Humphrey, who found himself outflanked on the common-man theme by Nixon and Wallace back in 1968, believed he could save his party and the New Deal coalition by pushing the idea. His cosponsor in the project was Congressman Augustus Hawkins, an African American who strongly believed in the linkage between civil and economic rights and who represented the riot-torn district of Watts in Los Angeles, California. Together, they embarked on an ambitious agenda to confront their party's race-class problem. Their plan, typically called the Humphrey-Hawkins bill, despite numerous official iterations, combined two key elements: nationally coordinated economic planning to bring about full employment at "prevailing" (i.e., high) wages and a federally mandated and legally enforceable right to a job for every American. The umbrella of economic planning required that the president annually submit to Congress a nationwide full employment and production program to ensure an adequate demand for labor, as well as an expanded role for the congressional Joint Economic Committee in reviewing and challenging the program. To support national planning efforts that focused largely on the private sector, the bill also expanded the federal role in providing jobs through the creation of local reservoirs of public service and private employment projects.[40]

The Humphrey-Hawkins bill, first proposed in 1974, was a cause célèbre among those interested in placing progressive politics back on an economic footing. The clever bill worked within the rights-consciousness framework prominent after the 1960s but provided an economic right, that of a job, and built a floor under all workers—not just workers who faced a history of discrimination. It thus avoided the alleged "special interest" legislation problem prominent in 1970s politics ("targeting within universalism," Theda Skocpol called it). Yet the legislation harkened back to the unfinished agenda of the New Deal (the last full-employment act was contemplated in 1945 but was gutted and passed as a largely meaningless political gesture in 1946). The bill also sought to unite the alienated civil rights and labor groups at a moment when unemployment rates set postwar records and the rate for black youth hovered at 40 percent. The labor–civil rights linkage was best symbolized by the cochairs of the national mobilization committee: Coretta Scott King, wife of Martin Luther King Jr., and Murray Finley, head of the Amalgamated Clothing and Textile Workers of America. The political struggle to extend the right to a job to all citizens lasted for over four years. Declared the number one legislative priority by the Congressional Black Caucus, civil rights groups, and the AFL-CIO, it was actually signed into law in 1978 despite monumental opposition based on fears it would create inflationary pressures.[41]

The final law was so full of commitments to balanced budgets, competitiveness, business incentives, and anti-inflation measures, however, that it could only be regarded as a failure. The AFL-CIO characterized the law as "more symbol than substance," and the *New York Times* editorialized that it was "a cruel hoax on the hard-core unemployed, holding forth the hope—but not the reality—of a job." The Carter administration chose to drain the bill of real economic content, rather than openly reject it and thus subject the Democratic president to bruising punishment from his core constituents. The destruction of the bill was part of a longer tempestuous relationship between the administration and the old New Deal coalition—particularly around issues important to workers, unions, civil rights groups, and the Congressional Black Caucus.[42]

Carter was hardly the figure to lead American workers out of the wilderness of the 1970s and into a new New Deal. Carter had always understood race much better than class, did not understand unions at all, and felt caged rather than empowered by coalitional politics. Stuart Eizenstat, Carter's domestic policy advisor, explained, "Carter saw unions as just another interest group—they did not have a special call on his heartstrings. They were a group that had to be dealt with, but that was all." As Charles Schultze, chair of Carter's Council of Economic Advisors, recalled, the administration was at best hamstrung by the Democratic base, and at worst in open battle with its major constituencies. "Exactly where one came down between the necessities of the times and the political necessities of holding the coalition together and having had no experience in national politics on this would make it even tougher," said Schultze. It was a problem Reagan would not have to face, because he could essentially afford, politically, to put the economy "through the ringer" rather than try like Carter to achieve a "modest austerity balancing act" designed not to upset the labor and civil rights communities (which it did anyway). Essentially, concluded Schultze, "the Democratic Party has never quite sorted out what its image is in those kinds of [inflationary] times."[43]

The same year, 1978, saw another attempt to reunite old-school blue-collar politics through labor-law reform, which met a similar fate as the Humphrey-Hawkins bill. U.S. labor law had long been ineffectual at best and twisted toward the employers' side at worst. The 1947 Taft-Hartley amendments, the courts' evisceration of the right to organize, the National Labor Relations Board's weakness, and the new business climate that saw unfair labor practices, fines, and the courts as the price to pay for a nonunion environment all added up to an incredibly hostile legal climate for unionization. The struggle at J. P. Stevens, a notorious recidivist labor-law violator since the 1960s, was the touchstone in the debate for the need for reform (they had been in the courts since the union's 1974 victory and would remain there for several more years). The bill that Congress contemplated was pretty tepid; it did not even include the brass ring for many unionists, the repeal of 14b, the infamous right-to-work provision that helped the South remain nonunion. Nonetheless, the bill called for expedited elections and increased punishment for employers unlawfully discharging activists; demanded an enlarged Labor Board; encouraged good-faith bargaining; and denied federal contracts to labor-law violators. The bill only tinkered around the edges of a deeply flawed and legalistic labor-relations regime. As one wag said, "[T]hat's the state of labor today: no working-class heroes, just lawyers on floats waving to the crowd." The legislation sailed easily through the House in 1977 but faced death by filibuster the following year in the Senate, lacking only two votes to build the sixty-vote super majority necessary for cloture.[44]

When reflecting on the 1970s' cynicism about the capacity of the government, fears of inflation, and increasingly conservative economic policy (particularly in the second half of the Carter administration), it is interesting to speculate on what almost happened in the near misses of Humphrey-Hawkins bill and labor-law reform. In their defeat, however, they suggest something of an end to an era. Admittedly, labor-law reform was vanquished by the traditional intransigence of southern Democrats, but it also fell victim to a changed political climate in which business lobbies had taken command. The Business Roundtable, the National Right to Work Committee, the National Federation of Independent Business, and the U.S. Chamber of Commerce had launched a very effective organizing campaign backed by an immense growth of pro-business political action committees.[45]

Doug Fraser, president of the UAW, understood the moment. "I believe leaders of the business community, with few exceptions, have chosen to wage a one-sided class war today in this country—a war against working people, the unemployed, the poor, the minorities, the very young and the very old, and even many in the middle class of our society," he openly declared in 1978. Feeling betrayed and angry, he used these words in an open resignation letter to the Labor-Management group, a national body characteristic of postwar labor-management negotiations that sought to work out problems between labor and business in a respectful and consensual manner. "The leaders of industry, commerce, and finance in the United States have broken and discarded the fragile, unwritten compact previously existing during a past period of growth and progress." He declared businesses' effort to defeat labor-law reform the "most vicious, unfair attack upon the labor movement in more than thirty years"; where "industry once yearned for subservient unions, it now wants no unions at all."[46]

This was tough talk from a postwar labor leader, from the likes of whom the term "class war" was rarely heard (and even then, only when it was waged *on* them). But Fraser also understood what the insurgents of the first half of the decade were trying to say: labor had to reshape the system that caged its freedom to experiment and had to reimagine the limits of the possible. His final point in his resignation sought to resurrect the insurgent worker in a coalition of the struggling and dispossessed. "I would rather sit with the rural poor, the desperate children of urban blight, the victims of racism, and working people seeking a better life than with those whose religion is the status quo, whose goal is profit and whose hearts are cold," he wrote. "We in the UAW intend to reforge the links with those who believe in struggle: the kind of people who sat down in the factories in the 1930's and who marched in Selma in the 1960's." He was a decade too late.[47]

THE SILENCE

Despite a complex revival of labor issues that resonated from Detroit to Hollywood to Washington DC, by the end of the 1970s, workers—qua workers—had eerily disappeared from the national scene. Some went right, some left, some to the center, but workers as a subject worthy of political, social, cultural, or economic attention seemed to have been drowned by the crosscurrents, and thus swept from a once-significant place in national civic life. The aging labor intellectual J. B. S. Hardman, reflecting on his involvement in organized labor since the beginning of the century, predicted such a fate when he declared that labor stood "at the Rubicon" at the start of the 1970s. The crossing, he cautioned, would be fraught with treacherous obstacles, but he believed that, win or lose, the decade would represent a watershed in the fortunes of workers. It did. The 1970s whimpered to a close as the labor movement failed in its major initiatives, deindustrialization weakened the power of the old industrial heartland, market orthodoxy eclipsed all political alternatives, and promising organizing drives ended in failure. Workers occasionally reappeared in public discourse as "Reagan Democrats" or the victims of another plant shutdown or as irrational protectionists and protestors against free trade, but rarely did they appear as workers. So began what one journalist called "the era of the forgotten worker."[48]

Just as the opening of the 1970s working-class revival was marked by a federal strike, so was its last gasp: the Professional Air Traffic Controllers Organization (PATCO) disaster. One of Ronald Reagan's first major acts as president was his mass firing of the members of PATCO, who went on strike against the federal government in the summer of 1981. Facing extraordinary mental strain, inadequate staffing, and incredible levels of burnout, the air-traffic controllers demanded workplace reform and increased staffing from their federal employer. During the 1980 campaign, candidate Reagan declared his sympathy with the "deplorable state of our nation's air-traffic control system." He claimed that if elected, he would act in a "spirit of cooperation" and "take whatever steps are necessary to provide our air-traffic controllers with the most modern equipment available and to adjust staff levels and work days so that they are commensurate with achieving a maximum degree of public safety."[49] Given Carter's failures, PATCO even backed Reagan in 1980. It would have been difficult to predict, however, that Reagan's solutions would have included firing more than eleven thousand striking workers, smashing the entire organization designed to represent both public safety and employees' interests and giving the nod to business to declare open season on organized labor. Overt warfare against unions spread like wildfire across the country; although almost all unions, like PATCO, displayed incredible levels of local and even national solidarity, the organized power of American workers ended in disaster.

The 1970s turned out to be the key turning point in the history of labor and the working class after the Great Depression, but not because it fulfilled the promise of "a new era for the working man"—quite the opposite. The decade marked a type of defeat for working people that differed from the lost battles littering the historical landscape: battles ranging from the Haymarket Tragedy to the Ludlow Massacre. After a complex and multilayered revival of working-class issues in the 1970s, a sense existed that it was not simply that specific groups of workers were defeated at specific places, but that the very *idea* of workers in civic and popular discourse was defeated. Strike rates plummeted to insignificance, wages and working conditions were restructured along management's lines, politics took on an almost exclusively middle-class turn, and J. R. Ewing from *Dallas* replaced Archie Bunker as the media's new totem for the next decade. Even the dramatic efforts to defend unions in the Reagan era, such as those of the copper workers in Clifton-Morenci, Arizona, and the meatpackers in Austin, Minnesota, seemed to happen in distant outposts of the industrial wilderness—missing from the central place in national discourse that they deserved.

Bruce Springsteen, one of the few working-class heroes to survive into the 1980s, hinted at how the new blue-collar silence worked. In his enormous 1984 hit "Born in the USA," the narrator attempts to straddle the breach of an incongruously dual narrative. The main story line is that of a 1970s worker "born down in a dead man's town" who burns in the despair of deindustrialized, post-Vietnam America. That tale, however, is all but completely drowned out by a chant that is part burden, part pride, and all destiny: "I was born in the USA." These two strands form an indivisible unity as this working-class hero is left with a birthright unfulfilled, an American promise broken, and a voice that speaks only in echoes of a betrayed social patriotism. On the landscape looms the refinery that offers no job for him and the penitentiary that may hold his fate. You may end up "like a dog that's been beat too much," he explains, but the response is neither action nor solidarity with other workers. Lacking any civic outlets for his pain ("nowhere to run, ain't got nowhere to go," he explains in a Motown reference), the character is lost in the chorus of Ronald Reagan's America. Pain is internalized " 'til you spend half your life just covering it up"—a public silence that speaks of the collective unconscious about working-class America after the 1970s.

Notes

1. Brendon Sexton and Patricia Cayo Sexton, "Labor's Decade—Maybe," in *The Seventies: Problems and Proposals [Dissent* compilation], ed. Irving Howe and Michael Harrington (New York: Harper and Row, 1972), 269; Barbara Ehrenreich, *Fear of Falling: The Inner Life of the Middle Class* (New York: Pantheon, 1989), 97; "The Troubled American," *Newsweek,* October 6, 1969, special edition; *Commonweal,* February 2, 1973; description of various strikes from *Fortune,* July 1970 and September 1970. Strike data may be measured in many ways; my statistics are from Bureau of Labor Statistics, *Handbook of Labor Statistics* (Washington DC: GPO, 1983), 380, and Bureau of Labor Statistics, "Work stoppages involving 1,000 workers or more, 1947–2002," table, March 26, 2003, http://www.bls.gov/news.release/wkstp.to1.htm.

2. Michael Harrington, "Two Cheers for Socialism," *Harper's Magazine,* October 1976, 78; Gil Scott-Heron lyrics from "B Movie," on the album "Reflections" (Arista Records, 1981).

3. Steve Fraser, "The Labor Question," in *The Rise and Fall of the New Deal Order,* ed. Steve Fraser and Gary Gerstle (Princeton, NJ: Princeton University Press, 1989), 55–84.

4. Murray J. Gart, "Labor's Rebellious Rank and File," *Fortune,* November 1966; "Boom Gives Labor Its '67 Leverage," *Business Week,* May 1967, 40–41; Aaron Brenner, "Rank-and-File Teamster Movements in Comparative Perspective," in *Trade Union Politics: American Unions and Economic Change, 1960s–1990s,* ed. Glenn Perusek and Kent Worcester (Atlantic Highlands, NJ: Humanities Press, 1995), 112; *New York Times,* June 1, 1970 and April 21, 1970.

5. On the postal workers' strike, see Aaron Brenner, "Rank-and-File Rebellion, 1966–1975" (PhD diss., Columbia University, 1996), 112–146; National Association of Letter Carriers, *Carriers in a Common Cause* (1989), 72–77.

6. Ibid.; *New York Times,* March 24, 1970; *Newsweek,* March 30, 1970.

7. *Business Week,* September 26, 1970. William Serrin, *The Company and the Union: The "Civilized Relationship" of the General Motors Corporation and the United Automobile Workers* (New York: Knopf, 1973), 19.

8. Serrin, *The Company,* 306; Brody, *Workers,* 185.

9. Gryner quoted in Studs Terkel, *Working* (New York: Pantheon, 1972), 193; Barbara Garson, "Luddites in Lordstown," *Harper's Magazine,* June 1972, 68–73.

10. For the broadest overview of Lordstown, see David F. Moberg, "Rattling the Golden Chains: Conflict and Consciousness of Auto Workers" (PhD diss., University of Chicago, 1978), 321.

11. Moberg, "Rattling," 321 (Nader quote), and passim; Paul F. Clark, *Miners for Democracy: Arnold Miller and the Reform of the United Mine Workers* (Ithaca, NY: ILR Press, 1981), 19, 15, 89.

12. Thomas Geoghegan, *Which Side Are You On?* (New York: Farrar, Straus and Giroux, 1991), 15.

13. James A. Hodges, "J. P. Stevens and the Union: Struggle for the South," in

Race, Class and Community in Southern Labor History, ed. Gary M. Fink and Merl E. Reed (Tuscaloosa: University of Alabama Press, 1994), 59; Clete Daniel, *Culture of Misfortune: An Interpretive History of Textile Unionism in the United States* (Ithaca, NY: Cornell University Press, 2001), 264.

14. See Cletus E. Daniel, "César Chávez and the Unionization of California Farm Workers," in *Labor Leaders in America,* ed. Melvyn Dubofsky and Warren Van Tine (Urbana: University of Illinois Press, 1987), 350–351; Richard Rashke, *The Killing of Karen Silkwood* (New York: Houghton Mifflin, 1981).

15. Ruth Milkman, "Women Workers, Feminism and the Labor Movement Since the 1960s," in *Women, Work & Protest,* ed. Ruth Milkman (Boston: Routledge and Kegan Paul, 1985), 307–318; Dorothy Sue Cobble, " 'A Spontaneous Loss of Enthusiasm': Workplace Feminism and the Transformation of Women's Service Jobs in the 1970s," *International Labor and Working-Class History* 56 (Fall 1999): 23–44; Louise Kapp Howe, "No More Stewardesses—We're Flight Attendants," *Redbook,* January 1979, 65, 70–74; Lindsy Gelder, "Coffee, Tea, or Fly Me," *Ms.,* January 1973, 86–91.

16. Joshua Freeman, *Working-Class New York* (New York: New Press, 2000), 281.

17. Michael Kazin, *The Populist Persuasion* (New York: Basic Books, 1995), 238, 240–241; on Wallace, see Dan T. Carter, *The Politics of Rage: George Wallace, the Origins of the New Conservatism, and the Transformation of American Politics* (Baton Rouge: Louisiana State University Press, 1995).

18. Quoted in Barbara Ehrenreich, *Fear of Falling,* 125.

19. Quoted in Richard M. Scammon and Ben J. Wattenberg, *The Real Majority* (New York: Coward-McCann, 1970), 62.

20. Welder quoted in Kazin, *Populist Persuasion,* 221; Harris quoted in Jonathan Rieder, "Politics and Authenticity," *Dissent* (Summer 1975): 292. Doug Fraser, UAW president, remarked that the backlash was real but not hard to overcome. The workers "accepted the inevitability" of integration. "Now that it's integrated and they meet the blacks and socialize with the blacks and they say, 'What the hell was the fuss about? They're human beings just like me, or much like me.' " Doug Fraser, oral history interview by John Barnard, Archives of Labor and Urban Affairs, Walter P. Reuther Library, Wayne State University, Detroit, Michigan, 86.

21. Pete Hamill, "The Revolt of the White Lower Middle Class," *New York Magazine,* April 14, 1969, 28–29; reprinted in Louise Kappe Howe, ed., *The White Majority, Between Poverty and Affluence* (New York: Random House, 1970), 10–22; Jefferson Cowie, "Nixon's Class Struggle: Romancing the New-Right Worker, 1969–1973," *Labor History* 43 (Summer 2002): 257–283; quote 268.

22. Cowie, "Nixon's Class Struggle," 264–265.

23. *New York Times,* May 21, 1970; Christian G. Appy, *Working-Class War: American Combat Soldiers and Vietnam* (Chapel Hill: University of North Carolina Press, 1993), 299.

24. Andrew Levison, *The Working-Class Majority* (New York: Coward, McCann and Geoghegan, 1974), 157.

25. *U.S. News and World Report,* November 24, 1969; remarks by Hubert Humphrey at Civil Rights Symposium, LBJ Library, December 11, 1972, box 3, Subject Files 1971–77, Hubert Humphrey Papers, Minnesota Historical Society, St. Paul, Minnesota.

26. Buchanan/Kachigian, "Assault Strategy," June 8, 1978, in *From the President: Richard Nixon's Secret Files,* ed. Bruce Oudes (New York: Harper and Row, 1989), 466.

27. Jack Metzgar, *Striking Steel: Solidarity Remembered* (Philadelphia: Temple University Press, 2000), 197–198.

28. Archie Robinson, *George Meany and His Times* (New York: Simon and Schuster, 1981), 322–323; Charles Colson, *Born Again* (Old Tappan, NJ: Chosen Books, 1986), 15. Voting calculations made from Gallup poll, "Vote by Groups, 1968–1972" archived at http://www.gallup.com/poll/trends/ptgrp6872.asp. The southern vote provided the most dramatic increase of any category for Nixon—35 points—but the gain can be attributed largely to the absence of George Wallace, who garnered 33 percent in 1968. High-school-educated voters, a reasonable proxy for "manual workers," increased their support for Nixon by 23 percent at the polls. The only other substantial jump was the disproportionate 26-point increase provided by voters between the ages of thirty to forty-nine.

29. Others, such as Bruce Schulman, regard viewers' experience of *Roots* as less of a history of African Americans than as part of the fragmented and self-absorbed search for ethnic roots that defined the decade. "They looked back—but almost exclusively at themselves," he argues. See Schulman, *The Seventies: The Great Shift in American Culture, Society, and Politics* (New York: Free Press, 2001), 77.

30. Southern quoted in Peter Biskind, *Easy Riders, Raging Bulls: How the Sex-Drugs-and-Rock-'n'-Roll Generation Saved Hollywood* (New York: Simon and Schuster, 1998), 68. For classic interpretations of workers in popular culture, see Ehrenreich, *Fear of Falling,* 114–121; Stanley Aronowitz, *False Promises: The Shaping of Working-Class Consciousness* (New York: McGraw-Hill, 1973), 103–118.

31. *Book World,* September 3, 1972.

32. "Blue Collar: An Interview with Paul Schrader," *Cineaste* 8 (Winter 1977–1978): 34–37; Kevin Jackson, ed., *Schrader on Schrader* (London: Faber and Faber, 1990), 142.

33. *Schrader on Schrader,* 148; Paul Schrader, director's comments on "Blue Collar," DVD release, Anchor Bay Entertainment/Universal City Studios, 1978.

34. "Blue Collar," *Cineaste* 8 (Summer 1978): 36–37.

35. Andrew Levison, "The Working-Class Majority," *New Yorker,* September 2, 1974, 48.

36. On deindustrialization, see Barry Bluestone and Bennett Harrison, *The Deindustrialization of America* (New York: Basic Books, 1982); Jefferson Cowie and Joseph Heathcott, eds., *Beyond the Ruins: The Meanings of Deindustrialization* (Ithaca, NY: Cornell University Press, 2003); on the current debate over identity politics versus class politics, good primers are Todd Gitlin, "Beyond Identity Politics," and Michael Eric Dyson, "The Labor of Whiteness, the Whiteness of

Labor, and the Perils of Whitewashing," in *Audacious Democracy,* ed. Steven Fraser and Joshua B. Freeman (Boston: Mariner Books, 1997), 152–172.

37. The complexities of steel, race, and public policy are best understood through Judith Stein, *Running Steel, Running America* (Chapel Hill: University of North Carolina Press, 1998), 169–195; see also Bruce Nelson, *Divided We Stand* (Princeton, NJ: Princeton University Press, 2001), 280–286.

38. Dale Maharidge and Michael Williamson, *Journey to Nowhere: The Saga of the New Underclass* (New York: Hyperion, 1996), 17, 20; Stein, *Running Steel,* 195.

39. For further development of problems with "rights consciousness," see Nelson Lichtenstein, *State of the Union* (Princeton, NJ: Princeton University Press, 2002), 207–211.

40. See Tim Thurber, *The Politics of Equality* (New York: Columbia University Press, 1999), 223–247.

41. Theda Skocpol, "Targeting Within Universalism: Politically Viable Policies to Combat Poverty in the United States," in *The Urban Underclass,* ed. Christopher Jencks and Paul E. Peterson (Washington DC: Brookings Institute, 1991), 411–436; Thurber, *Politics,* 244–247.

42. *AFL-CIO News,* October 21, 1978; *New York Times,* February 21, 1978; W. Carl Biven, *Jimmy Carter's Economy* (Chapel Hill: University of North Carolina Press, 2002), 32–34.

43. Eizenstat quoted in Taylor Dark, "Organized Labor and the Carter Administration: The Origins of Conflict," in *The Presidency and Domestic Policies of Jimmy Carter,* ed. Herbert D. Rosenbaum and Alexej Ugrinsky (Westport, CT: Greenwood Press, 1994), 775; Charles Schultze, interview, January 8–9, 1982, Miller Center Interviews, Carter Presidency Project, 11:2, 38–39, 80, Jimmy Carter Library, Atlanta, GA. Schultze's reasoning contrasts with Secretary of Labor Ray Marshall's. Marshall believed that the administration should have built a consensus, especially with labor, early on in order to have the political goodwill to do what was necessary. See Ray Marshall, interview, May 4, 1988, Miller Center Interviews, Carter Presidency Project, 25: 20–21, Carter Library.

44. Thomas Geoghegan, *Which Side Are You On?* 163. The story of labor-law reform is told in Gary Fink, "Fragile Alliance: Jimmy Carter and the American Labor Movement," in *The Presidency,* ed. Rosenbaum and Ugrinsky, 788–790.

45. For an argument that explores the historical continuities between 1978 and the postwar era, see Taylor Dark, *The Unions and the Democrats* (Ithaca, NY: Cornell University Press, 1999), 112–113.

46. For a copy of the letter and a full discussion of the Fraser resignation, see Jefferson Cowie, "'A One Sided Class War': Rethinking Doug Fraser's 1978 Resignation from the Labor-Management Group," *Labor History* 44, no. 3 (2003): 307–314.

47. Ibid.

48. Maharidge, *Journey to Nowhere,* 7.

49. Ronald Reagan to Robert E. Poli, President, PATCO, October 20, 1980, reprinted by UAW-CAP, author's possession.

5

She "Can Bring Home the Bacon"

Negotiating Gender in Seventies America

BETH BAILEY

In 1975, Arizona senator and 1964 Republican nominee for president Barry Goldwater was asked in a public forum whether he supported the equal rights amendment (ERA) to the Constitution. The ERA, which had been passed by both houses of Congress in 1972, was at the center of an enormous and controversial battle for ratification by the required two-thirds of America's fifty states. According to the newspaper account, Goldwater answered: "I don't think it is needed." It was a politically savvy answer for a conservative politician speaking in the South. Such an amendment could only stir up trouble, many argued, by mandating that men and women be treated identically—and the notion that women, like men, might be subject to the draft had been a powerful argument during the Vietnam War. Women, according to the position Goldwater was claiming, were already guaranteed equal rights and protections, along with all Americans, under the Constitution. Goldwater, however, did not stop there. "I was for it at one time," he told the audience, "but then I saw the women in Washington who were pushing it, and I said, 'Hell, I don't want to be equal to them.'" The audience laughed and applauded.[1]

The campaign for the ERA failed, expiring in 1982 (after an extension) and falling three states short of ratification. But even as the ERA stalled in the face of organized opposition and grassroots resistance, opportunities for women in American society were growing almost exponentially. The calls for revolution had begun in the 1960s, and much of the legal and political groundwork for change had been laid during that era. But it was during the 1970s that Americans confronted what was arguably a revolution in gender roles. For as women's lives changed—whether by choice or simply as a result of the larger social forces that were transforming the nation—men's lives changed, too. And it was not easy. Looking back to the 1970s, it is striking how very hard the struggles over change were, how angry and ugly and confused the public culture was, as Americans debated the transformation of American life and of American lives "from bedroom to boardroom," as the saying went, and just about every place else. These struggles over gender roles and expectations, set in motion during the 1960s, played out in a society divided by the struggles over race relations and the Vietnam War, fragmented by Watergate and the crisis of political authority, riven by cultural conflict, and angered and dispirited over the collapse of what had seemed an endless cycle of economic growth. The 1970s were an era of new freedoms and opportunities for many Americans—women, people of color—but at the same time, they were the years in which Americans confronted a future that no longer seemed limitless.

In many ways, the transformations of the 1970s appear to be the triumph of the liberal wing of the women's movement, which had worked hard since the early 1960s to secure political and legislative equality for women. In 1973, *Roe v. Wade* guaranteed women's right to choose abortion, and as of 1972, the unmarried could no longer be denied access to birth control. In 1975, new legislation ended practices that made it impossible for a married woman to obtain a credit card or a loan without her husband's written permission.[2] Title IX of the 1972 Education Act amendments prohibited discrimination by sex in any program receiving federal aid, thus guaranteeing funding for women's athletics in high schools and colleges. Girls' participation in high school athletics increased almost fivefold by the end of the decade. And during the 1970s, women flooded the workplace. Some were drawn by new opportunities: the *U.S. News and World Report* article "The American Woman: On the Move—But Where?" noted that the percentage of female law students had risen from 4 percent in 1960 to 19 percent in 1974, gains similar to those made in medicine.[3]

However, larger structural forces also were critically important in changing the landscape of gender in America. Seventies-era deindustrialization meant the loss of well-paid blue-collar jobs, most of them held by men. The vast majority of the new jobs created in the service sector paid less than the jobs they replaced, and by 1976, according to one estimate, only 40 percent of the nation's jobs paid enough to support a family. The energy crisis that began in 1973 sent oil prices skyrocketing 350 percent, and as inflation topped 11 percent in 1974, many families were struggling to make ends meet. Women's earnings became critical. The influx of women into the job market was not a new trend, for the percentage of wives and mothers working outside the home had been growing throughout the past two decades. However, the economic crisis of the 1970s—along with better job opportunities for women—was a powerful catalyst for change. In 1970, 30 percent of women with children under six years of age held paid jobs. That total jumped to 43 percent by 1976 and then to 50 percent by 1985. Many women also found themselves in the paid labor force because of changes in family circumstances, as the divorce rate doubled between 1966 and 1976.[4]

The importance of the economy, as opposed to ideology, in changing gender roles complicated matters. If women's liberation demanded equality in the workplace, did that mean that women who held jobs were "women's libbers"? If a great many women who held relatively conservative views about gender roles nonetheless worked outside the home, where did they fit in the angry debates about women's proper roles? In a special report on women in 1975, *U.S. News and World Report* heralded the "millions of unreconstructed housewives" who rejected "women's lib" and instead signed up for "full-time duty as chauffeurs, cooks, cleaning ladies, repair specialists, nurses, laundresses, baby-sitters and counselors—all for their own families" while at the same time noting that several million of these "career homemakers" were employed full or part time outside the home and that many found their jobs a "welcome change" from household duties.[5] In such a complicated landscape, Americans sought ways to make sense of the changes taking place in men's and women's lives.

The women's movement provided one arena for discussion. But during the 1970s, feminists had no easy or clear answers. The movement was confronting its own divisions, and its most radical statements and occasionally rancorous exchanges were eagerly reported in the media, sometimes to discredit the movement, and sometimes simply because they were sensational.[6] Thus, the women's movement influenced the ways Americans understood gender in this period, but its positions were not coherent enough to offer a firm foundation to sympathizers and were various enough to provide a multiplicity of targets for opponents.

Throughout most of the decade, a variety of competing frameworks for understanding gender circulated in the public sphere, sometimes claimed by one group or another, sometimes highly politicized and strategic, sometimes vaguely coloring the oceans of ink spilled on the topic. Although discussions ranged widely, struggles over gender during this era were most commonly framed around the notion of liberation or around the critical question of difference: are men and women essentially different or essentially the same? And, significantly and somewhat surprisingly, changes in gender roles were negotiated and reconciled in the American consumer marketplace as much as in the realm of politics or of ideas.

"Women's lib" is a phrase that has disappeared from common usage, but it was omnipresent shorthand, usually derogatory or condescending, throughout most of the 1970s. Liberation, appended to the name of a movement in the 1960s, signaled that its members sought more than equal rights in the existing society. Liberation meant freedom from oppression, but it also meant fundamental change. Adherents of liberation rejected the existing structures of power and declared common cause with a host of other movements, united in a vision of a more just world. Of course, even those within the specific movements for racial justice, gay liberation, and class revolution did not share the exact same vision of justice and liberation, but the term served its purpose of positioning groups beyond the limits of liberal reform. The Liberation News Service, for example, provided a leftist alternative to mainstream news outlets.

In the grand tradition of Sixties protest, the women's liberation movement had its symbolic beginning in a media-savvy and slightly wacky protest organized by very serious activists. On September 7, 1968, members of New York Radical Women gathered on the boardwalk in Atlantic City to protest the Miss America Pageant, which, they argued, perpetuated "an image that has oppressed women." Carrying banners proclaiming women's liberation, they crowned a sheep Miss America (remember, Yippies had nominated a pig for president in protests at the Democratic National Convention in Chicago the previous month). They distributed a pamphlet protesting the fact that "women in our society find themselves forced daily to compete for male approval, enslaved by ludicrous 'beauty' standards we ourselves are conditioned to take seriously." And they threw "instruments of torture"—hair curlers, high heels, girdles, bras, copies of magazines such as *Playboy* and *Cosmopolitan*—into a "Freedom Trashcan." The protesters had hoped to burn the contents but decided not to run the risk of setting fire to the wooden boardwalk. Robin Morgan, one of the organizers, told a reporter that the mayor of Atlantic City had expressed concern about fire safety: "We told him we wouldn't do anything dangerous—just a symbolic bra burning." (For context, think draft-card burning.) No bras were burned that day—or girdles, or magazines, or false eyelashes. But Morgan's statement would plague the women's movement for more than a decade.[7]

On August 26, 1970, *ABC Evening News* concluded its coverage of Women's Strike for Equality, which was at that point the largest demonstration in American history for women's rights, with a comment from West Virginia senator Jennings Randolph. Senator Randolph dismissed the women's movement as "a small band of bra-less bubbleheads," and ABC News closed the segment with that phrase projected on the screen beside anchorman Howard K. Smith.[8] In 1972, Amitai Etzioni, professor of sociology and director of the Center for Policy Research at Columbia University, published a "Test for Female Liberationists" in the *New York Times Magazine*. "Are you inclined to believe that bra-burners are the most effective flag-carriers of a major social political revolutionary movement but that those who keep theirs on, while marching, despoil the image of American womanhood?" read question 5. Question 6 read, "Is believing that there are more important issues—Vietnam, pollution, crime, and the oppression of blacks—than who leaves what hankies where, a true sign of male pigheadedness?"[9] As feminists Kate Swift and Casey Miller noted in a *New York Times Magazine* article later that year, "The word 'liberation' itself, when applied to women, means something less than when used of other groups of people."[10]

How was women's liberation defined in American public culture during the 1970s? The original meanings of the term survived, as is evident in Etzioni's question 6 above. Women's liberation sought to free women from oppression. Many of the young women who helped initiate the women's liberation movement had begun their journey in the civil rights movement or the New Left, seeking social justice for African Americans or for the poor and dispossessed, and had gradually come to recognize that women, too, were an oppressed class within American society. But "oppression" was complicated territory; it invited comparisons. How could the sorts of oppressions claimed by women (symbolized in Etzioni's question by the issue of house-work, reduced to the slightly ridiculous "who leaves what hankies where") compare with the oppression of black people in America?

Opponents of women's liberation tended to see oppression as all-or-noth-ing: if women, as a group, were not so oppressed as black Americans, as a group, then claims of oppression were misplaced at best and ludicrous at worst. This position did not rule out the oppression of women altogether. Women of color might be oppressed because of their race; poor women might be oppressed because of their class. But women per se were not oppressed. This tendency to marginalize race and class (shared by parts of the women's movement) was further complicated by a tendency to treat "women" interchangeably with "married middle-class women with chil-dren." How could American women, supported comfortably by their hus-bands and able to stay home and care for their children and to gather with friends to drink coffee in the morning, claim to be oppressed? Compared with whom? Even allowing for the millions of women who did not fit this description, it was a significant sleight of hand. If oppression was measured primarily in terms of material comfort, then issues of choice, autonomy, and human dignity became largely irrelevant. With such self-defined parameters, skeptics found it easy to reduce many of the less tangible claims of the women's liberation movement to what they saw as parody.

Life magazine, for example, offered readers "a women's lib exposé of male villainy," a parodic portrait of Hyperia, a woman once "just like any other downtrodden female living a perfectly contented enslaved life." Awakening to her exploitation (while putting her husband's clothes in the washing machine), however, she became "so conscious of the sexism rampant in our society that she finds it in the most outlandish places." Although the piece's female narrator cherishes her own "fond memory" of the time a New York construction worker called her a "knockout," Hyperia rages about the "sex-ual oppressor" who referred to her as a "real tomato."[11]

Another would-be parodist, writing in *Harper's* magazine in 1976, com-plained that the women's movement was putting satirists and parodists out of business by introducing ludicrous claims, such as the feminists' new issue of sexual harassment "or, as some of us would call it, flirting." Most women, she claimed, given a petition on "sex in the office," would "put a check next to 'not enough.'" But the author's larger target was the twinned notion of liberation and oppression. Unable to resist the satirical tone, she scoffed, "The feminists are to be congratulated for having rooted out still another area of injustice." Sexual harassment was a false issue, she concluded, not likely ever to make the evening news, but it was still a "graphic illustration of what's wrong with much of feminism":

> "Women's liberation," ironically, exists on its ability to persuade its adherents that, despite appearances, they are miserable and weak. With jesuitical ingenuity, they go about convincing white, middle-class, college-educated women that society has done them wrong, like the snake-oil salesmen whose suggestible listeners began to feel all the symptoms of sciatica, dropsy, and the botts. This way of thinking, of course, is not without appeal. Persons whose affluence and civility ensure they will never be beaten as punishment may find flagellation an interesting vice.[12]

The author obviously was not prescient—sexual harassment has claimed a great deal of time on the evening news, in the nation's courts, and in congressional hearings over the past few decades. However, she was laying one more brick in the wall of arguments about comparative oppression and the meaning of liberation. The truly oppressed risked beatings. Women risked . . . flirting?

The network news programs, with tens of millions of viewers, also found ample opportunity to compare women's claims of oppression with "real" oppression. On ABC, anchor Howard K. Smith contrasted American women with "Indians and Negroes," who had been "genuinely mistreated." NBC's coverage of the 1970 Women's Strike for Equality cut from a black woman singing, "And before I'll be a slave, I'll be buried in my grave . . . Yes, goodbye slavery, hello freedom," to footage of well-dressed white women, lounging in the park, eating ice cream as they listened. And CBS concluded its three-part series on women's liberation that year: "So far, the women's rights movement has had one fundamental problem; not so much to persuade men, but to convince the majority of American women that there is something basically wrong with their position in life."[13]

In the early 1970s, surprisingly, women's liberation tended to receive its most generous hearing (in the mainstream media) in traditional women's magazines such as *Redbook, Good Housekeeping,* and *Ladies' Home Journal.* (In July 1976, the month of America's bicentennial, thirty-five women's magazines produced special issues on the ERA.) Earlier in the decade, the editors of *Redbook* launched a series of articles on women's liberation, describing it as an issue that "matters very much to all of us." In the heading to each of the substantial articles, the editors stated straightforwardly that *Redbook* believed "every human being should have the right and the opportunity to make her own or his own choices in every area of life." They continued, "This seems to be a very simple and obvious point of view. But, of course, it is not, and it may not ever be a popular one. Yet we do not see how, in a free nation, freedom can be defined otherwise."[14]

In several of the articles, *Redbook* confronted the tricky question of oppression and liberation for an audience made up largely of homemakers. The first article was an eight-page interview with feminist Gloria Steinem, who made an eloquent case for the women's movement. When asked whether she really believed women were exploited, she responded with statistics about how many hours per week the American housewife worked (ninety-nine and six-tenths, she said). When asked "what does the Movement have to say to those women who insist—as so many do—that they like being wives and mothers and are perfectly happy in these roles?" Steinem replied that the point of the movement was choice: all individuals, men and women, should be able to choose how to live their lives. With inset photographs and quotes from women such as Susan B. Anthony and Eleanor Roosevelt, the article gave the women's movement a full, respectful, and supportive hearing.[15]

For the second installment, published in February 1972, *Redbook* sent writer Vivian Cadden to travel the nation and ask women what they thought about women's liberation and their own lives. The reporter's conclusions were grim, given *Redbook*'s own position: "Except in the larger cities and on the campuses, liberation does not yet seem to be an aspiration of young women."[16]

Nonetheless, the complex picture of women's fears and desires offered in this article sheds light on the difficulty of framing a movement for women's rights around a framework of oppression and "liberation." A thirty-something-year-old farm wife in Indiana was bemused:

Women's Liberation? I just laugh when I hear them talk about it. Today's women have all the freedom they please to come and go. Husbands have been brainwashed into letting women do anything. I suppose it's the economic thing—women having to go to work to help make ends meet. But it's not good for the family. I think the trouble with these women who complain about their lives is that they're disorganized. With a washer and a dryer, I don't see how any woman can get behind.

"I *like* what I'm doing," said one young housewife. "If I really wanted to go back to work, my husband would let me," said another. And another: "I don't want to go out and do what my husband is doing."

For many of the women Cadden interviewed, "women's lib" really meant going out to work. That "liberation," she noted, was not so appealing "to the wives of truck drivers and farmers and salesmen and auto workers and struggling small businessmen and beginning lawyers." Such women told her that "[n]o woman in her right mind who didn't have to" would trade her life of homemaking, mothering, gardening, the PTA, community politics, and bridge for a routine office job or worse. "For these women," Cadden explained, "cooking and marketing and child rearing are pleasant jobs"— much more pleasant than what they saw as their alternatives in paid employment. Cadden acknowledged that low-level, routine jobs might not seem like "liberation," but she suggested that women were perhaps steered from an early age toward a narrow range of possibilities, that the weight of sexism and discrimination in American society narrowed their own sense of possibility as well as their practical options. At the same time, she conceded, most of these women did not see the problem as sex discrimination or oppression. "By comparison to their husbands' work," she wrote, these women saw their work as "not a bit menial and not very hard."

If housewives in the heartland thought the term "liberation" was shorthand for working outside the home, it might seem that women already in the paid workforce would be more enthusiastic about its possibilities. Here, though, the slippery set of meanings attached to liberation complicated matters. Most of the employed women Cadden interviewed believed in equal pay for women, and many believed in equal job opportunities. But for them, women's liberation carried other connotations and threatened other sorts of loss. "I don't think men and women ought to be the same," explained a nineteen-year-old woman who worked in an insurance company office. A twenty-four-year-old factory worker at a General Electric plant in Warren, Ohio, scoffed: "This whole Women's Liberation thing is a crock of you-know-what. . . . I suppose you're going to start opening car doors for them. Next thing you know it'll be my turn to . . . pick him up on Saturday night. Before you know it, it'll be my turn to pay." Liberation, it seemed, meant different things to different people.

Liberation's most complicated association, and one scarcely touched in the *Redbook* series, was with sex, and it was in the realm of sex that notions of liberation were most confused and contradictory. During the 1970s, some women sought liberation from the oppressions of sex. "A large part of our oppressions stem from the sexual exploitation of our bodies," asserted a women's liberation article in a midwestern underground paper in 1970. "Women are viewed as objects. It is difficult for a woman to walk down the street without being weighed, measured, and judged."[17] *Life*'s parody of the "real tomato" and *Harper's* satirical rendering of sexual harassment show how mainstream—and controversial—such claims became as they spread from radical collectives to suburban consciousness-raising sessions and the mainstream media.

But some women also found another form of oppression in the American sexual landscape. If, as most believed, a woman's future status and material well-being depended on marriage to a successful man, she was in a difficult position. She must be sexually alluring enough to attract a man (hence the Miss America protest rejected "ludicrous beauty standards") while maintaining her marriageability through a "good reputation." Consider the terms "ruined" and "spoiled." Some women—most of them young—sought liberation from a system that equated a woman's value with her sexual virtue. And, finally, some sought liberation in sex itself, whether with men or with other women: sex on their own terms, sex for pleasure, sex as a way to explore previously forbidden experiences. Liberation was not always just an escape from oppression; sometimes it was an affirmative embrace of new freedoms.

Some of the most difficult struggles within the women's movement came over issues of sex and sexuality, and it was in the vexed relation of sex to liberation that many skeptics found their best targets. Throughout the 1970s, in American public life, women's liberation was frequently conflated with the sexual revolution. "Are you liberated?" did not mean "Do you believe that an individual should have the freedom to choose his or her own path?" It did not mean "Do you work outside the home?" It meant "Do you have sex?"

Sex sells, of course, and titillating images of bra-less women and sexual freedom made for livelier stories than statistics about women's wages and the lack of affordable childcare. The mainstream media—and often for reasons no more Machiavellian than a desire to attract viewers or readers—often treated women's liberation and sexual freedom interchangeably. But opponents of women's liberation also purposely conflated women's liberation with the sexual revolution to brand the women's movement as radical, immoral, and antifamily. A woman attending an anti-ERA rally at a Palm Beach, Florida, movie theater in 1977 asked Phyllis Schlafly, the wife and mother (and attorney and prominent conservative activist) who spearheaded the campaign against the amendment, "Wouldn't you say that the majority of these so-called females who are for ERA are AC-DC or lesbians who are naturally very loud, very vociferous, very wealthy? I mean, they are backed by the media." Her voice trailed off, "And unisex." As the *New York Times Magazine* correspondent who covered the rally noted, Schlafly found the question embarrassing, but only because it was too bald and incoherent a statement of themes her movement had been using in its quest to stop ratification of the ERA.[18]

The conflation of the women's liberation movement with the sexual revolution, however, reached beyond the ranks of avowed antifeminists. Many who were somewhat sympathetic to the claims of the women's movement found the sexual revolution troubling, and the conflation of movements made it easier for them to draw a line between "reasonable" demands for decent wages and (as they saw it) the sex-obliterating role reversals and illegitimate intrusions into the "private" spheres of home, marriage, and the family demanded by "radical" women's libbers.

In the fall of 1977, Americans flocked to see the film *Looking for Mr. Goodbar,* which stars Diane Keaton as Theresa Dunn, a young woman confronting the new freedoms of the age. Leaving her conservative Catholic family to live on her own, Theresa begins a new life: by day, she is "Saint Theresa," the generous and nurturing teacher of deaf children; by night, she is "swinging Terry," prowling the singles' bars for sex on her own terms. But Theresa's initial sense of independence, control, and erotic adventure collapses as her night life overwhelms her day life. The small apartment of which she'd been so proud becomes filthy and cockroach infested, sex on her own terms degenerates into a series of drunken or drug-befuddled fumblings, and her sexual freedom is misinterpreted as prostitution by a paunchy middle-aged conventioneer who tries to pay her after they have sex. Even her students lose trust in her. On New Year's Eve 1976, just as she resolves to escape this cycle, she is brutally murdered by the last man she picked up at a bar.

The film (which director Richard Brooks described as a story "about freedom, commitment, and women in the seventies"[19]) offers a confusing abundance of explanations for Theresa's descent into self-destruction: childhood scoliosis and her resulting physical "imperfection," the repressive weight of the Roman Catholic Church, the patriarchal rage of her father, even disappointment in love (her first lover, a married professor, tells her, "I can't stand a woman's company right after I've fucked her"). But none of these individual or psychological explanations are compelling, for all other adults in the film—men and women—are equally confused and damaged. Instead, as Arthur Schlesinger Jr. noted at the time, the director "hauls in television shots of the women's liberation movement as if to prove Theresa the victim of the sexual revolution and the permissive society."[20]

Like Schlesinger, the film conflates women's liberation and the sexual revolution. On New Year's Eve 1975, Theresa is still living with her parents, home babysitting her small nephew while the rest of the family celebrates at the Knights of Columbus party. "Nineteen seventy-five has just become history," the television announcer says. Theresa, in a fuzzy bathrobe, is doing breast enhancement exercises. "It was only five years ago that ten thousand women marched for liberation. They carried books, signs, and babies. They called for free abortions, equal education, equal job and equal pay opportunities and [significant pause] sexual freedom. This was to be THE DECADE OF THE DAMES."

It is an odd scene, and its importance is not immediately obvious. But *Looking for Mr. Goodbar* is structured around two New Year's Eves: the first is when women's liberation is something Theresa watches on TV; the second, when the liberated Theresa is murdered. On that first New Year's Eve, she begins her movement toward "liberation," leaving home after a confrontation in which her father sarcastically asks, "By the way, I'm not breaking any of the rules of the women's holy crusade to burn the brassiere?" In the logic of the film, it is women's liberation—here thoroughly conflated with sexual liberation—that kills Theresa.

Theresa's killer is not simply any psychopath; he is a sexually confused gay psychopath. Victim of a homophobic attack upon gay revelers (a public display newly possible in the wake of the gay liberation movement), this unnamed character (played by Tom Beresford) strikes out against his older lover: "We're a couple of freaks," he tells him, violence close to the surface. He then flees, ending up in the bar where Terry has just told the bartender, "This is it—my last night cruising bars." Theresa, ambivalent about her resolution, flirts with Beresford's character, seeking his help in warding off the boyfriend who has been stalking her. He walks her home and tries to prove his heterosexual manhood by having sex with her. But he fails. "Goddamn women, all you gotta do is lay there," he rages. "A guy's gotta do all the work." And Theresa laughs, pushing him over the edge. As the strobe light above the bed flashes, he rapes her, then stabs her repeatedly. Terry's screams are orgasmic; her last words are "Do it."

Most reviewers at the time saw *Looking for Mr. Goodbar* as a morality play, a cautionary tale for the liberated woman. One reviewer, writing in *Ms.* magazine, speculated that the director may have wanted to explore "the contradictory feelings he, as a good liberal, has about women. (They have the right to be independent and yet they need protection.)"[21] At the same time, the circumstances of Theresa's death are more complicated. She's not simply done in by a modern-day Jack the Ripper, is not the victim of a sexual predator. Instead, her killer is portrayed as a man damaged by sexual liberation, pushed to violence by his impotence and the laughter of a liberated woman.

Here, as much as anywhere in the film, *Looking for Mr. Goodbar* depends on 1970s debates about liberation and gender roles. "What Is the New Impotence, and Who's Got It?" asked *Esquire* in 1972. Citing a range of experts who testified to a "flood" of impotence (even among "previously immune non-Caucasian machos"), as young men suddenly "shrank" before "liberated" women, the author explored the possibility that women's liberation had "upset the sexual applecart." Even more directly, *Vogue* raised the question "Is Women's Lib Ruining Orgasms?" (The article is about men's orgasms, not women's.)[22]

Once again, the meaning of liberation was complicated. *Esquire,* like *Looking for Mr. Goodbar,* focused on the realm of sex itself, where women's new "aggressiveness" or "overassertiveness" in sexual realms left men unmanned. *Vogue*'s "Is Women's Lib Ruining Orgasms" looked beyond sex to the larger question of competition between men and women. The author soundly rejected what he called "the orgasmic fallacy" (the notion that women's liberation had brought about an epidemic of male impotence) but nonetheless found in it a powerful explanation for male resistance to change in other spheres of life. Men, he explained, have somehow convinced themselves that sex is "rooted in some fixed relationship between men and women, that orgasm is dependent on a certain established balance," not only in the rituals of seduction and the sexual act but in all spheres of life. As women successfully "compete" with men, he argued, in terms that seem to overstate his argument that gender equality will not destroy the possibility of good sex, "it is time for men to learn that love and sex have nothing to do with work, talent, and success."[23]

For many Americans, the crux of the problem was that liberation freed women to compete with men and, in so doing, upset what they believed was the proper relationship between the sexes. Discussions about liberation, pro and con, were usually focused on women and their changing roles. But as the decade wore on, people were increasingly concerned not only about women but about women, men, and the relationship between the sexes. In these debates, competition was a key issue and not only in the bedroom. In 1973, Americans witnessed a tennis match between the aging star Bobby Riggs (then fifty-five years old and with a Wimbledon victory in 1939) and women's champion Billie Jean King (twenty-nine years old). The event drew more than fifty million television viewers to what was billed as the "Battle of the Sexes." King won. Feeding the flames, *Science Digest* explored the "facts" in "Biological Superiority: Female or Male." (The proponent of male superiority mused, "If a woman claims superiority on a genetic basis, must she exclude genetic females with characteristics of male behavior?")[24]

When *Ladies' Home Journal* asked a male and a female author to respond to the question "Do Strong Women Frighten Men?" both answered with a qualified "yes." "As more and more women enter the workforce," the female author noted, "men are finding a frightening new challenge to their jobs and futures: a whole new crop of ambitious and serious people—women. Added to this new competition, men now have to wrestle with their conditioned feelings that the people they're forced to compete with are, well, inferior." (The author eventually circled back to *Vogue*'s "orgasmic fallacy," noting that "when a man perceives competition in his marriage or love life, the fear engendered may have repercussions in the most intimate areas of his life.")[25] Thus, *Readers Digest* offered advice for the working woman on "How to Support Your Husband's Ego" (she should avoid making him feel "inadequate by flaunting her own contribution to the family income"),[26] and a host of articles explored the phenomenon of the woman boss, giving advice on how to handle the situation when a woman "wears-the-pants-in-your-office" or "when the 'man at the top' is a woman."[27] *Time*'s contribution to the genre was a portrait of "business bitches." Top female executives, *Time* explained, had "shelved their femininity" in "blind striving" for success; the most successful of them managed to reclaim femininity in midcareer and become more "open and effective," while those who continued "to act as much like men as possible" became "closed, bitter, defensive, and unhappy."[28]

Emotionally charged debates over the changing relationships between men and women usually hinged on the vexed question of difference. Were men and women fundamentally and essentially different from one another? Or were they fundamentally the same? Difference was not just the fallback of traditionalist opponents of women's lib; many feminists embraced an essentialist vision during the 1970s, rejecting what they called patriarchal values for a more body-centered, noncompetitive, nurturing "women's culture." But in much of mainstream American thought, "difference" was the final answer to the challenge of feminists, the line drawn against the rapidly changing gender roles symbolized by the ERA. House Judiciary Committee chairman Emmanuel Celler, who had buried the ERA in committee for twenty-three years until Representative Martha Griffiths engineered a discharge petition supported by some of the most influential members of the House, fumed when confronted with the Congressionally passed ERA: "There is no equality except in a cemetery. There are differences in physical structure and biological function. . . . There is more difference between a male and a female than between a horse chestnut and a chestnut horse."[29]

It was not a new concept. One major strand of the women's movement historically had strongly supported various forms of protective legislation for women—all based on women's biological and physical differences from men and the responsibilities of motherhood that were closely associated with those differences. Many opponents of the ERA feared that the amendment would overturn protective legislation that limited the physically strenuous tasks women could be required to do in the workplace and that defined support of the family as the man's responsibility and guaranteed (at least legally) alimony and child support in the case of divorce. Senator Sam Ervin, a wily opponent of the ERA, crafted a different version of the amendment that centered on the notion of the difference of the sexes. "Equality of rights under the law shall not be denied or abridged by the United States or by any state on account of sex," the amendment began, as did the original, but continued, "This article shall not impair, however, the validity of any law of the United States or any state which exempts women from compulsory military service or which is reasonably designed to promote the health, safety, privacy, education or economic welfare of women, or to enable them to perform their duties as homemakers or mothers." The second half of the amendment, in effect, nullified the first.[30]

Difference was a complicated concept, especially for a society that had, until recently, allowed racial segregation predicated on the notion of difference embodied in "separate but equal." Opponents of the women's movement, therefore, had to square the assertion of difference with some understanding of equality. Reverend Billy Graham, the nation's most influential clergyman, offered one of the most eloquent arguments to that end in a *Ladies' Home Journal* article, "Jesus and the Liberated Woman." He portrayed mid-twentieth-century American gender roles as God-given and timeless, but his logic held outside the theological framework. Resuscitating an old argument, Graham and others like him attempted to reorient the debate. Men and women have different roles in society and in the family, but those roles are complementary. Abstract notions of equality are not the issue, for each role is dependent on the other, the survival of the family and of society itself dependent on both. To the skeptic, it seemed that men were allotted all the real power in society and beyond (Graham did not pull his punches, advising women to subordinate themselves to their husbands).[31] But for many, the notion of complementary roles was an excellent answer.

It was an answer, however, that left an opening. In 1970s America, men and women did not occupy separate spheres. In the scheme of complementary roles, where did a woman fit if she were not a wife or mother? Where did the woman fit who worked outside the home? What about the woman who was her own sole support or the sole support of her family? Once again, the economic transformations of the 1970s made such issues more pressing. The framework of oppression had allowed a loophole for economic issues: most who scoffed at calls for liberation were willing to accept calls for equal pay for equal work. But the notion of complementary roles had no such loophole. What about those who, by choice or necessity, did not fit easily into such a predefined notion of women's sphere?

In the women's movement and its opposition alike, during the 1970s, notions of women as a class (whether an oppressed class or as males' complementary sex) confronted the old notions of American individualism. As *Redbook* asserted from the beginning of its pro-ERA campaign, "every human being should have the right and the opportunity to make her own or his own choices in every area of life." *Redbook*'s big push for the ERA, in the bicentennial month of July 1976, focused squarely on the issue of individual choice. "It is the individual," argued *Redbook*, "under Federal law, who will determine whether to play football, work a graveyard shift or join the Marines."[32]

Although the debate over gender roles was largely waged in the language of liberation and oppression or of difference and competition, another framework would become dominant by the end of the decade. Magazines that had previously trotted out scores of experts to demonstrate the fundamental differences between men and women began offering expert condemnations of "sex roles." It was a short step from individual choice to individual difference and from there to a suspicion of gender roles entirely. "Androgyny vs. the Tight Little Lives of FLUFFY WOMEN AND CHESTY MEN," offered the widely read magazine *Psychology Today.* "Learning to Be a Boy, a Girl, or a Person," contributed *PTA Magazine.* Over and over, throughout America's public culture, the deadening effects of sex roles were condemned. "We need a new standard of psychological health for the sexes," wrote a Stanford professor in *Psychology Today,* "one that removes the burden of stereotype and allows people to feel free to express the best traits of men and women."[33] What of the stereotypes that have created "agony for the countless 'sissy' boys and 'tomboy' girls[?]" asked a *Mademoiselle* columnist, advocating a society that "tolerated, even prized, individual variety over the dubious intellectual and social convenience of categories." And even Dr. Spock ventured the opinion that all people have a mixture of male and female identities.[34]

In 1974, *New York Times Magazine* published, without editorial comment, the new guidelines distributed to all eight thousand authors and to editorial staff at the McGraw-Hill Book Company. Going well beyond suggestions for gender-neutral language, the lengthy guidelines began, "Men and women should be treated primarily as people, and not primarily as members of opposite sexes. Their shared humanity and common attributes should be stressed, not their gender difference." The memo reiterated, a few hundred words later, that both men and women should be "represented as whole human beings with *human* strengths and weaknesses, not masculine or feminine ones."[35]

The new focus on common humanity finessed some of the tensions associated with gender oppression and liberation, for in this framework it was not women who needed liberation from men but men and women who needed liberation from the stifling stereotypes and confining sex roles that thwarted their true human potentials. Difference here was individual, falling along a continuum of masculine and feminine traits. And choice remained central. As the McGraw-Hill memo emphasized,

> Though many women will continue to choose traditional occupations such as homemaker or secretary, women should not be typecast in these roles. . . . Teaching materials should not assume or imply that most women are wives who are also full-time mothers, but should instead emphasize the fact that women have choices about their marital status, just as men do: that some women choose to stay permanently single and some are in no hurry to marry; that some women marry but do not have children, while others marry, have children, and continue to work outside the home.

(The memo also pointed out that statements such as "Jim Weiss allows his wife to work part-time" should be avoided, replaced with "Judy Weiss works part-time.")

The issue of language—"firefighter" versus "fireman," for example—was one of the issues most parodied by those who found women's claims of oppression ridiculous and their proposed solutions more so. However, in the context of common humanity, these claims had weight. McGraw-Hill was a major educational publisher, and this memo signaled a transformation. The language of common humanity, the emphasis on avoiding gender-role stereotypes, was becoming a central part of America's public culture. And this new framework, encompassing and surpassing the frameworks of liberation and of difference, offered a fairly revolutionary path to the future.

The turmoil over gender was not put to rest in the 1970s, though women's role and power in American society continued to expand throughout the decade and beyond. What that meant, however, remained uncertain, and people relied on complicated and often incoherent combinations of these various frameworks—liberation and oppression, competition and difference, and common humanity—to make sense of changes that came rapidly and often without being sought.

While tensions remained high in the political realm and in the private lives of American men and women, those who managed the American consumer marketplace tried to avoid or, at the very least, negotiate the troubled ground. Struggles over changing gender roles threatened to divide and disrupt the mass market for consumer goods. In a 1970 article on advertising and women, *Time* described "liberationists" as embracing "oddball causes—from ban-the-bras to communal child rearing" but noted nonetheless that many (implicitly non-oddball) women were also unhappy with advertising. "Though nearly one-half of American women hold jobs," noted *Time*, "they are still depicted in many ads as scatterbrained homebodies, barely able to cope with piles of soiled laundry, dirty sinks and other mundane minutiae."[36] Surveys by *Redbook* and *Good Housekeeping* also found high levels of dissatisfaction. But in such a contested atmosphere, how could companies appeal to the working woman? How could they avoid alienating the traditionalists who still saw themselves as homemakers despite having full-time jobs, while appealing to the liberationists who were perhaps more likely to hold well-paid, higher-status positions, and still manage the anxieties about gender roles that seemed to pervade American society?

Advertisers purposely set out to negotiate the complexities of the new gender relations and the new sex roles. Marketing research focused on women, making discoveries such as "Working Women No Monolith" (*Advertising Age*, 1975), and "New Era Women Need Fragrance to Define Their Roles" (*Product Marketing*, 1977).[37] Advertisers and their clients were no more progressive than any other sector of American society, but they had a major stake in figuring out how to manage changing gender roles. Their task, as they were increasingly aware, was to avoid sexism and the portrayal of women as idiots while assuaging or at least not increasing the fears about changing gender roles that remained widespread even among many women in the workplace. Advertisers had to figure out how, for the sake of profit, to negotiate the fact that stagflation and desire for liberation had led women by different paths to a similar consumer position: the working woman. As Franchellie Cadwell, president of the Cadwell David advertising agency, explained in 1970, as she was building her agency's reputation on the notion that "the lady of the house is dead," replaced by a "new woman" (who had neither "the mentality of a six-year-old" nor "acute brain damage") to whom advertisers must learn to appeal: "This campaign we've got going is strictly a business thing. We've got the best interests of business at heart."[38]

In their attempts to have it all, to belay anxieties about competition between men and women, and to portray women as both competent and liberated working women and competent and traditionalist homemakers, the advertising industry invented the superwoman. Her apotheosis came in the long-running Enjoli commercial, created for Charles of the Ritz in the late 1970s by the agency Advertising to Women. "I can bring home the bacon, fry it up in a pan, and never, ever, let him forget he's a man," sang the Enjoli woman (remember, "New Era Women Need Fragrance to Define Their Roles").[39]

The Enjoli woman has survived, in American public culture, as a symbol of the 1980s superwoman. But the Enjoli woman was not a product of the 1980s; she was, instead, the best attempt of American advertising to manage the gender anxieties of the 1970s. As Americans struggled to make sense of the rapidly changing roles brought about by the complex combination of feminist activism and economic necessity, American advertising agencies and their clients in the business world had begun to portray a new image of the American woman—the superwoman. She was created from no particular ideological commitment; her all-encompassing role was simply a ploy to manage and neutralize the divisive debates over gender—in order to sell freeze-dried coffee, dishwasher detergent, and perfume.[40] American advertisers, of course, did not create the phenomenon. However, as an industry with little ideological investment in women's equality or social change, American advertising nevertheless played a huge role in *normalizing* for the American public a world in which women can—and do—do it all.

❖ ❖ ❖

ACKNOWLEDGMENT

I am grateful to Kate Lehman for meticulous and good-humored assistance in research for this piece.

Notes

1. Quote from the *Charlotte Observer*, published in "No Comment," *Ms.*, February 1974, 76.

2. For an interesting article on women and credit, see "Women Move Toward Credit Equality," *Time*, October 27, 1975, 63–64.

3. "The American Woman: On the Move—But Where?" *U.S. News and World Report*, December 8, 1975, 57.

4. Statistics from Peter N. Carroll, *It Seemed Like Nothing Happened: The Tragedy and Promise of America in the 1970s* (New York: Holt, Rinehart, and Winston, 1982), 284–285; Bruce J. Schulman, *The Seventies: The Great Shift in American Culture, Society, and Politics* (New York: Da Capo Press, 2001), 134,161–162.

5. "Special Section/Women: To Many, Happiness Still Means Staying At Home," *U.S. News and World Report*, December 8, 1975, 63.

6. Periodicals that chronicle the divisions include *U.S. News and World Report*. In a "special section," titled "The American Woman: On the Move—But Where?" (December 8, 1975, 54–64), the author explains: "Clearly women have come a long way in a few years. But they have a longer way to go, not just in achieving external goals, but more basically—in mastering the historic problems of women's movements: uncompromising factionalism and escalating rhetoric, leading to schism and a long period of dormancy" (54–55).

7. The Miss American protest is chronicled in various places. The "No More Miss America" manifesto appears in Robin Morgan, *Sisterhood is Powerful* (New York: Vintage, 1970). For the best account of the protest, see Ruth Rosen, *The World Split Open* (New York: Viking Press, 2000), 160.

8. Susan J. Douglass, *Where the Girls Are: Growing Up Female with the Mass Media* (New York: Random House, 1994), 163.

9. Amitai Etzioni, "Test for the Female Liberationist," *New York Times Magazine*, February 27, 1972, 23. Etzioni's credentials are listed prominently just below the title.

10. Casey Miller and Kate Swift, "One Small Step for Genkind," *New York Times Magazine*, April 16, 1972, 100.

11. Ann Bayer, "A Women's Lib Exposé of Male Villainy," *Life*, August 7, 1972, 62.

12. Rhoda Koenig, "The Persons in the Office: An Ardent Plea for Sexual Harassment," *Harper's*, February 1976, 87–90.

13. Susan Douglass has a wonderful analysis of network news portrayals of the women's movement in *Where the Girls Are*. Quotes appear on 179, 182, and 175.

14. Editors, headnote to Liz Smith, "Gloria Steinem, Writer and Social Critic, Talks about Sex, Politics, and Marriage," *Redbook*, January 1972, 69. The wording of the statement varied slightly from issue to issue, but the editors maintained a firm commitment to women's liberation. The bicentennial-month features in women's magazines are discussed in "Marketing Blitz to Sell Equal Rights," *Business Week*, April 19, 1976, 146.

15. Liz Smith, "Gloria Steinem, Writer and Social Critic, Talks about Sex, Politics, and Marriage," *Redbook*, January 1972, 72.

16. Vivian Cadden, " 'Women's Lib? I've Seen It on TV'," *Redbook*, February 1972, 93.

17. "Down the Drain . . . ," *Vortex* (Lawrence, Kansas), July 1970, n.p.

18. Joseph Lelyveld, "Should Women Be Nicer Than Men?" *New York Times Magazine*, April 17, 1977, 126.

19. T. Johnson, "Who Else Is Looking for Mr. Goodbar?" *Ms.*, February 1978, 26.

20. Arthur Schlesinger Jr., "The Movies: Mr. Goodbar and The Goodbye Girl," *Saturday Review*, December 10, 1977, 62.

21. T. Johnson, "Who Else Is Looking for Mr. Goodbar?" 26.

22. Philip Nobile, "What is the New Impotence, and Who's Got It?" *Esquire*, October 1972, 95. The author, to his credit, chose to emphasize that it was not women's liberation, per se, that caused the "new impotence," but men's reactions to it. "Through no fault of his own," he wrote of young men, "he was born into the empire and now must live through the Balkanization of the masculine mystique. It's a rough passage for potency" (98); Michael Korda, "Is Women's Lib Ruining Orgasms?" *Vogue*, May 1972, 146–147.

23. Korda, "Is Women's Lib Ruining Orgasms?" 146–147. Korda was the author of *Male Chauvinism: How It Works* (New York: Random House, 1973).

24. "Biological Superiority: Female or Male," consisted of two articles by "well-known medical writers," Ruth Winter and Ken Anderson, in *Science Digest*, August 1971, 44. Quote is from Anderson, p. 51.

25. Linda Bird Francke, "Do Strong Women Frighten Men?" *Ladies' Home Journal*, July 1978, 48.

26. James Lincoln Collier, "How to Support Your Husband's Ego," *Readers Digest*, January 1970, 109 (condensed from *Woman's Day*).

27. Quotes from Letty Cottin Pogrebin, "When Men Have Women Bosses," *Ladies' Home Journal*, May 1977, 24.

28. "Madam Executive," *Time*, February 18, 1974, 77. This article was paired with one on the "role reversals" of "male homemakers," titled "Men of the House."

29. Robert Sherrill, "That Equal-Rights Amendment—What, Exactly, Does It Mean?" *New York Times Magazine*, September 20, 1970, 26 (ellipses in original).

30. Ibid., 110.

31. Billy Graham, "Jesus and the Liberated Woman," *Ladies' Home Journal*, December 1970, 40.

32. Cathleen Douglas, "You Can Be Anything You Want to Be!" *Redbook*, July 1976, 127. This section also contained a well-argued piece by Maureen Reagan, who "happens to be the daughter of Ronald Reagan," and sidebar quotes from actresses such as Brenda Vaccaro, who wrote, "You must have the freedom to make choices for yourself. It's only fair; it's only human."

33. Sandra Lipsitz Bem, "Androgyny vs. the Tight Little Lives of FLUFFY WOMEN AND CHESTY MEN," *Psychology Today*, September 1975, 58; Margaret Conant, "Learning to Be a Boy, a Girl, or a Person," *PTA Magazine*, March 1972, 18–21. The Stanford psychology professor is Sandra Lipsitz Bem.

34. Karen Durbin, "Who Knows Anymore What Is Masculine and What Is Feminine?" *Mademoiselle*, June 1975, 156. See Dr. Benjamin Spock, "How My Ideas about Women Have Changed," *Redbook*, November 1973, 29; "Male Chauvinist Spock Recants," *New York Times Magazine*, September 12, 1971, 98.

35. "'Man!' Memo from a Publisher," *New York Times Magazine*, October 20, 1974, 38. See also Joseph J. Seldin, "'A Long Way to Go, Baby,'" *The Nation*, April 16, 1977, 464. The *New York Times Magazine* article, which ran six pages (with advertisements), was excerpted from "Guidelines for Equal Treatment of the Sexes in McGraw-Hill Book Company Publications."

36. "Advertising: Liberating Women," *Time*, June 15, 1970, 93.

37. "New Era Women Need Fragrance to Define Their Roles," *Product Marketing*, January 1977, 13; "Working Women No Monolith," *Advertising Age*, November 3, 1975, 22–23.

38. "Women's Libs Fume at 'Insulting' Ads; Ad Gals Are Unruffled," *Advertising Age*, July 27, 1970, 32. *Time* magazine reported on Batten, Barton, Durstine & Osborn's efforts to rethink portrayals of women, quoting a psychologist on the BBDO staff: "In advertising . . . we will have to show women less as women and more as people." "Advertising," *Time*, June 15, 1970, 93.

39. PR Newswire, September 27, 1982, Dateline Chaska, Minnesota (press release on Minnetonka, Inc., and Advertising to Women agency); Lynn Langway, "The Superwoman Squeeze," *Newsweek*, May 19, 1980, 72.

40. For interesting commentary, see Laurie Ashcraft, "Ads Start to Roll with the Social Punches," *Advertising Age*, July 26, 1982, M-24.

6

"Adults Only"

The Construction of an Erotic City in New York during the 1970s

PETER BRAUNSTEIN

New York has many toys for its slaves to play with. And yet, there had to be more.
—Marco Vassi, *The Stoned Apocalypse*

During an early scene in the controversial film *Cruising,* a crime thriller set entirely in the 1979 gay sadism and masochism (S&M) underground, a police car cruises down Hudson Street in Manhattan's West Village. Two patrolmen scan the streets and sidewalks that are brimming over with leathermen, hustlers, and assorted thrill seekers in front of such hardcore gay clubs as the Ramrod. "This whole city is about to explode," exclaims one cop. "You used to be able to play stickball on these streets. Now look at these guys. Christ, what's happening?" The two cops then proceed to pull over a pair of leather queens and shake them down for blowjobs in the squad car. It was a uniquely 1979 New York City dilemma: succumbing to a gay impulse, whether or not you were avowedly gay. Gay life had gone surface level and was quite brazenly occupying various sectors of Manhattan: the Meatpacking District, the Hudson Piers, the Rambles in Central Park, parts of Times Square.

The branding of certain sections of the city as territorially gay was only one component of a sweeping cultural shift that occurred in New York City during the Seventies, transforming the metropolis into an Erotic City that became both the epicenter and world marketplace of the sexual revolution. In the Sixties, Mayor John Lindsay had christened New York "Fun City" to lure tourists to the Big Apple, but for the most avid consumers of "adult entertainment" it was not until the Seventies that the city began to earn Lindsay's moniker. In the mid-1960s, Times Square "adults only" movie theaters still eschewed hardcore pornography, gay life remained both cloistered and illicit, and the cult of thrill seeking by way of exhibitionism, voyeurism, and drug use was limited to certain cultural vanguards like Andy Warhol's "Factory" coterie. By the early Seventies, entire sectors of the city became effectively closed off to families, as red-light districts led by Times Square teamed with massage parlors, live "sex shows," peep shows, porno theaters, as well as record levels of brazen street prostitution. During this same period, gay life acquired a new visibility and, indeed, notoriety through the proliferation of discos and gay bathhouses. With its ever-expanding red-light districts, graffiti-sprayed subway trains, and record homicide rates, New York City in the Seventies was regarded by the country at large as a latter-day Sodom teetering on the verge of ruin, a perception inscribed in such films as *Death Wish* (1972) as well as network television comedies like *The Odd Couple.* Although New York City's descent into unfettered raunch was abetted in part by a landmark fiscal crisis that sapped the city's resources and left it on the verge of bankruptcy, its vertiginous transformation into an adults-only mecca actually predated its fiscal woes (which crested in mid-decade) and was the product of rapid cultural change occurring both locally and nationally.

The first step in constructing an Erotic City involved pornography, which was practically nonexistent in New York during the Sixties and virtually unavoidable by the mid-1970s. The mainstreaming of porn, in both New York City and throughout the nation, was set into motion at the very onset of the decade by, of all things, a presidential commission appointed by a now-defunct political administration. The summer of 1970 had dawned on a tumultuous note: President Nixon's invasion of Cambodia in May had set off massive antiwar demonstrations on college campuses nationwide, culminating in the slaying of four protesters by National Guardsmen at Kent State University. The nation had no sooner begun to absorb the aftereffects of this turmoil when the Nixon administration was rocked by a second political bombshell in August 1970, this time of the domestic variety. In 1967, President Lyndon Johnson had appointed the Commission on Obscenity and Pornography to study the problem of pornography and recommend solutions; the following year, Johnson's political career effectively ended, a casualty of the Vietnam War stalemate, when he decided not to seek re-election in 1968. It was a surprise to the nation at large, and the Nixon administration in particular, when the by-now-forgotten commission issued its preliminary report in late-summer 1970.

The commission's report was controversial, to say the least. It determined that "erotic materials do not contribute to the development of character deficits, nor operate as a significant factor in antisocial behavior or in crime and delinquency causation." Instead, finding "no evidence that exposure to pornography operates as a cause of misconduct in either youths or adults," the panel opted for what was called the "Danish solution" to pornography: it advocated the repeal of all federal, state, and local laws against showing and selling pornographic films, books, and other material to adults.[1] The final draft of the report, issued in September, went even further, insisting that "a massive sex education effort should be launched . . . aimed at achieving an acceptance of sex as a normal and natural part of life and of oneself as a sexual being. It should not aim for orthodoxy; rather, it should be designed to allow for a pluralism of values." Although the commission recommended retaining provisions shielding pornography from minors, it expressly validated the need for an adults-only cultural realm, stating "we do not believe that the objective of protecting youth may justifiably be achieved at the expense of denying adults materials of their choice. It seems to us wholly inappropriate to adjust the level of adult communication to that considered suitable for children."[2]

After recovering from its initial shock and revulsion at the report, the Nixon administration quickly went into damage-control mode, making sure the American public understood that this was *Another President*'s Commission on Pornography and Obscenity, not Nixon's. Rejecting the commission's conclusions as "morally bankrupt," Nixon insisted, "[s]o long as I am in the White House, there will be no relaxation of the national effort to control and eliminate smut from our national life."[3] The president promised to direct the Supreme Court to a redefinition of some of its earlier decisions regarding pornography through new test cases, in the hope that his two new appointees—Chief Justice Warren E. Burger and Associate Justice Harry A. Blackmun—would impose stricter views of obscenity.[4] Nixon's efforts were joined by dissenting members of the commission itself, who repudiated the majority report as "a *magna carta* for the pornographer."[5] Polemics aside, there is evidence that the commission report was greeted with celebration by the porn community: Greenleaf Classics, a publisher of adult books, put out an X-rated version of the government report containing sex photographs that retailed at 42nd Street shops for twelve dollars.[6]

The commission's advocacy of an unrepentant adults-only culture was bolstered by a newly emboldened Hollywood, which saw more explicit fare as a solution to its sluggish box-office performance during the Sixties. The revolution in what Americans could expect to see on their movie screens was set in motion in 1968, when the Motion Picture Association of America (MPAA) instituted the current ratings system. Instead of the status quo ante, where all MPAA-approved films were considered family-oriented and "adults only" fare was relegated to a deviant substatus, the new ratings system ("G," "R," "X," as well as "M" for "Mature," which became "PG" in 1972) acknowledged the existence of both an exclusively adult film audience as well as an adult-oriented one, creating child-oriented categories to shield children from mature content. The adults-only "X" rating was devised by the MPAA but never copyrighted: as a result, while mainstream Hollywood filmmakers dodged the "X" rating like a bullet, soft- and hardcore filmmakers self-imposed the "X" and used it as a branding device ("XXX") for marketing and identity.[7]

As a creatively liberated Hollywood struggled to define and categorize the outer limits of permissible content (*Midnight Cowboy* was accorded an "X," won the 1970 Academy Award for Best Picture anyway, then had its rating revised to an "R" by the MPAA), and as the requisite test cases played their way out in the system (the Danish softcore film *I Am Curious [Yellow]* was originally seized by U.S. customs, but an appeals court held that the film "falls within the ambit of intellectual effort that First Amendment was designed to protect"[8]), New York movie houses began showcasing an eye-popping smorgasbord of explicit films ranging from hardcore Danish porn to sex-and-violence-drenched Italian crime thrillers. This soft- and hardcore fare raised the bar for a new wave of radical mainstream Hollywood cinema enlivened by the deregulation of content. After initial ambivalence about the new ratings system, Hollywood embraced its adult-oriented rating, "R," and rode it through the Seventies. The number of films released with "R" ratings skyrocketed from 25 in 1968 to 276 in 1973; over the course of the decade, consistently fewer films were released with the family-oriented "PG" rating.[9]

Late-Sixties innovations in technology worked in tandem with these porn-permissive cultural and political milestones to extend the frontiers of the Erotic City through the now-common feature of all red-light districts, the peep show. The central feature was the "loop," devised in 1966. "Loops," Super 8 porn films typically ten minutes long, were viewed in coin-operated peep-show booths installed in adult bookstores and sex shops. Essentially a nickelodeon for the horny, the peep show proved a revolutionary sexual innovation for the masturbation-oriented male consumer, the first pay-per-porn format deployed on a massive scale in the Erotic City's expanding red-light districts by the early Seventies.[10] "Loops were the tough, heartless training ground for the first generation of porn stars, a fifteen-year phenomenon made obsolete by video," recounted Josh Alan Friedman in the cult chronicle *Tales of Times Square.* "This was pornography's strongest medium, in which one could pick his favorite female creature, crystallized into a perfect 8mm, ten-minute rhapsody, and pop one's cookies."[11] The earliest peep-show loops of the late Sixties were by and large shackled by relatively tame content—say, G-stringed dancing girls—but all prudery was tossed aside by the early Seventies when "peeps" began to brazenly explore all the sundry fetishes and subfetishes of the day, including bestiality, kiddie porn, explicit gay sex, and S&M. Consumers responded avidly to the new fare: A 1970 New York State Investigation Commission of alleged racketeer infiltration into the city's porn business concluded that peeps "are now found in most of nearly 70 so-called bookstores and are the stores' largest source of income." One man, who leased several stores on 42nd Street, claimed to have owned twenty peep-show machines that took in roughly one thousand dollars a week.[12]

In cultural memory, Times Square was never sleazier than in the Seventies, but the fact is that the untamed sector had been a headache for mayors, reformers, and municipal authorities for at least a century before then. As early as 1905, when the *New York Times* building conferred upon the area its name,[13] Times Square had already established a trademark dialectic of risqué adult entertainment on the one hand and on the other countervailing social reform initiatives aimed at "cleaning up" the sector. As historian Laurence Selenick points out, "Times Square did not gradually change from the Great White Way to the City of Dreadful Night; rather, its veneer rubbed off to reveal the economic realities that had always been present."[14] Prostitution flourished during the first two decades of the twentieth century, purveyed not simply by "pros" but by chorus girls and kept women who used area hotel bars to meet their clients; hotels catering to the trade lined the side streets of Broadway, despite the recurring attempts of social reformers in 1905 and 1912 to curb the illicit goings-on. The Prohibition Twenties produced a boom in after hours, supposedly nonalcoholic cabarets where, for fifty dollars, customers were regaled by chorus girls and walk-on actresses and worked side deals on an individual basis. During the Depression, cleanup crusades launched by such organizations as the Society for the Suppression of Vice did not prevent a nationwide surge in burlesque entertainment (the original "striptease") that brazenly advertised its bawdy fare. Those who imagine that the evocation of Times Square as a latter-day Sodom was a product of the Seventies need look no further than the era of Mayor Fiorello LaGuardia—a kind of proto-Giuliani in his zero-tolerance approach to vice during the Forties—where the sector was routinely described as "a cesspool of filth and obscenity."[15]

On the consumer end of the Times Square experience, two modes of engagement predominated throughout its history. "Participatory" sexual activity—involving johns paying for hustlers and prostitutes as well as assorted forms of consensual "cruising"—commingled with more voyeuristic, passive modes of adult entertainment that Selenick dubs "spectation"— a natural outgrowth of the Broadway theatergoing experience that attracted so many consumers seeking milder forms of titillation.[16] Spectation could take many forms, such as visits to burlesque houses or to Hubert's Museum, a Coney Island–like dime museum on Times Square that enticed visitors with shocking displays of deformed genitalia, wax casts of venereal ailments, and the requisite "freak show."[17] What distinguished Times Square in the Seventies from its consistently raunchy prehistory is that participation and spectation were amplified and extended to altogether new frontiers. By the early Seventies, Times Square consumers could avail themselves of a bewildering array—and unprecedented volume—of fare catering to either inclination. Sexual "spectators" more comfortable with a masturbatory, voyeuristic approach could finally view explicit, hardcore pornography, both in feature-length films or pay-per-view peeps. Persons vying for a more participatory approach to sex (that is to say, paid sex) might opt instead for massage parlors, those less-than-coy fronts for prostitution that inundated Times Square by the early 1970s. Most of these short-lived enterprises attempted to conceal their raison d'etre behind some less flagrant premise, offering customers the chance to photograph or even finger-paint a "model." Massage parlors of the era boasted price structures designed to empty the customer's wallet in fits and spurts: one place charged seventeen dollars for thirty minutes alone with the "masseuse," where "you're naked and she wears panties." In private, the woman charged ten dollars to strip to the waist and fifteen dollars more to strip completely, with an open-ended price spiral for additional services.[18]

For those seeking to unearth the collective unconscious of the sexual revolution, at least insofar as it concerned (primarily male) adult-entertainment consumers in Times Square and other red-light districts of the Erotic City, the first place to look is on celluloid. The movies and even porn loops consumed by thrill-seeking New Yorkers reveal both the utopian ambitions and desultory limitations of sex cinema in its golden age. Generally speaking, adults-only movies fall into three broad categories: eros-ideology films filled with sex-positive messages about the virtues of sexual liberation; sadoerotica films, many emanating from Europe, that reveled in the new freedom of depicting nudity and extreme violence while subtly or overtly condemning the very sexually liberated climate that enabled this type of cinema to flourish; and finally, genital-oriented, almost clinical porn films with minimal plot and no narrative "message."

A perfect example of the eros-ideology film is *Emmanuelle* (1974, directed by Just Jaeckin), an influential softcore porn movie that, until recently, reigned as the highest-grossing film in French history. It was released in the United States on the heels of the box-office and critical success of *Deep Throat* (1972, directed by Gerard Damiano), which opened the floodgates for imitators in both the soft- and hardcore arenas.[19] *Emmanuelle* chronicles the exploits of a young woman (Sylvia Kristel) whose sexually liberated husband encourages her to sleep with other men and women, assuring her that their love is completely compatible with such extramarital indulgences. The film laces its erotic content with near-constant, evangelical preachiness about the evolved nature of sexual liberation values. In an early scene set in Thailand (a locale favored by softcore productions because of Asia's imputed compatibility with sexual primitivism, experimentation, and erotica), Emmanuelle's husband, Jean, explains to a sexually unenlightened male friend, "I didn't marry Emmanuelle to keep her to myself or in some sort of cage. I married her because no woman I know loves making love more, or does it as well. Jealousy went out with primitive man." Emmanuelle is initially presented as a sexual acolyte who requires a hedonistically evolved male guide to navigate her through the treacherous straits of sexual liberation. In one scene, Jean, whom Emmanuelle calls her "professor," tells her, "We can even be closer through pleasure. Pleasure can be an absolute." Emmanuelle eventually adopts a toney, somewhat discriminating sexual freedom lined with arcane caveats—she decides, for instance, that she can never cheat on Jean in Paris, but she has no problem engaging in two separate sexual encounters on a Pan Am flight to the Orient.

The box-office success of *Emmanuelle* in the United States and Europe spawned an eponymous softcore franchise, including innumerable authorized or bootleg sequels and a cable-television erotic serial. But during the heyday of the more propagandistic *Emmanuelle* films made in the 1970s, one mantra was constantly invoked: there is no shame in sexual freedom. Or, to quote the tagline of *Emmanuelle: The Joys of a Woman* (1975), "Nothing is wrong if it feels good." Vanquishing the shame nascent among consumers of raunchy entertainment in the Erotic City was a tall order and proved one of the more chimerical ambitions of the age. The majority of Seventies exploitation and porn film producers, far from contesting a shame-based sexuality, understood that most of the men consuming their product were plagued by sundry sexual hang-ups. Rather than trying to deflect the issue of shame, most exploited it for maximum lure. Take this ad for the 1969 film *Very Friendly Neighbors*, a supposed expose of sexual liberation in suburbia. "They try extramarital affairs. They try wife swapping. They try many partners. They try communal marriages. They are a generation of young adults who are dedicated to pleasure seeking. Is theirs a NEW MORALITY? Or is it as immoral and decadent as the critics and censors say? NOW the Supreme Court has ruled in your favor . . . NOW YOU can be the JUDGE."[20]

At least *Very Friendly Neighbors* purported to let audiences decide whether their viewing pleasures were sinful; other productions were much more heavy-handedly critical of the sexual revolution. Commingling sadism and erotica, sadoerotica films centered on the notion of pleasure-at-a-cost, signifying pleasure as something that can be reached only by running a gauntlet of pain, violence, and resistance. Italian *giallo* films, which routinely played at "grindhouses" (adults-only movie theaters) in the Erotic City, provide a case in point. ("Giallo" means "yellow" in Italian, the color of the pages in the sex-and-violence-drenched pulp-fiction books on which the films were based.) Pioneered by Italian director Mario Bava in the Sixties and perfected by Bava protégé Dario Argento in the Seventies, giallo films typically involve a fetishistic, leather-clad maniac who brutally kills women (and, occasionally, men) in a plot laden with gratuitous nudity and graphic violence. While exploring the limits of adult content, giallo films also contain highly conservative, counterrevolutionary messages reflecting the filmmakers' ambivalence about sexual freedom. A representative example is *The Slasher Is a Sex Maniac* (1972, directed by Roberto Bianchi Montero). This giallo stars a debauched Farley Granger as a detective pursuing a masked, leather-clad killer who is eliminating the wives of rich cuckolds. Replete with sex, violence, and gore, the film ends when the detective, discovering his own wife's infidelities, lets the killer dispatch her as well. Hardcore scenes featuring Kim Pope and Harry Reems were added for the U.S. release of this giallo, which appeared on the adult circuit as *Penetration* (1976). An even more twisted take on sexual libertinism is served up in *What Are Those Strange Drops of Blood Doing On the Body of Jennifer?* aka *Case of the Bloody Iris* (1972, directed by Giuliano Carmineo). In this classic of the genre, the leather-clad masked murderer knocking off models in a high-rise condominium turns out to be an old man terrified that his attractive daughter will be lured into lesbianism by her eros-obsessed neighbors, even though none of the model-victims is engaged in a homosexual relationship.[21] Prototypes of American "slasher" films like *Friday the 13th* (1980), in which sexually active characters are all killed off and only the virgin survives, giallo films relentlessly reinscribed the sex-equals-death equation in the viewer's mind—an ultimately sex-negative message.[22]

Other adult movies of the era defy all categorization but nonetheless testify to the strange sexual predilections of Seventies grindhouse filmmakers and consumers. Two adult cult genres that enjoyed a vogue during the 1970s were Nazi sex films and cannibal movies. The Nazi sex genre, derived from sadism-tinged men's pulp magazines of the 1960s, took root in such films as *Ilsa: She Wolf of the SS* (1974, directed by Don Edmonds). The tale of a sexually depraved concentration-camp warden (Dyanne Thorne) who tortures and has weird sex with her inmates, *Ilsa* (shot on the set of the 1960s television comedy *Hogan's Heroes*) features castration, a drunken gang rape, a victim impaled on a dildo, nipple clamps, and the agonizing hanging of a nude woman made to stand on a melting block of ice. In true exploitation fashion, the film was "dedicated to the hope that these atrocities never happen again."[23] The success of the *Ilsa* formula spawned three sequels. An equally debauched adult cult genre was the erotic cannibal film, in which the inclination to devour took its sexual, and then ultimate, form. It is significant that films like *Emmanuelle and the Last Cannibals* (1977, directed by Joe D'Amato), *Cannibal Holocaust* (1979, directed by Ruggero Deodato), *Zombie* (1979, directed by Lucio Fulci), and *Dawn of the Dead* (1978, directed by George Romero) were made in the scarcity-plagued Seventies economic landscape of recession, a bear market, and the energy crisis. The various R- or X-rated films commingling sex and cannibalism can be interpreted as scarcity nightmare fantasies that illustrate the stagflation Seventies cultural equation: when money, gas, and national prestige are scarce, rely on other currencies—flesh and bodily fluids.

Although many of these darker exploitation and porn films flew in the face of the more positivist aspects of the sexual revolution, in so many ways these filmmakers were preaching to the converted. They had successfully tapped into the conflict-ridden subconscious Pandora's box of straight-male sex-film aficionados. *Emmanuelle* notwithstanding, the average 42nd Street sex shop was not a convivial meeting ground for evolved sexual liberationists who group-hugged and addressed each other as "brother" and "sister." A more common sight was the commuter-businessman exiting nervously from the peep-show booth after having jerked off, rushing to the door and studiously avoiding eye contact with anyone else in the store. French director Catherine Breillat, who had a small role in the softcore art film *Last Tango in Paris* (1972, directed by Bernardo Bertolucci) and whose directorial debut (*Une vraie jeune fille,* 1976) was declared too explicit and banned in France for twenty-five years, explained how the institutionalization of pornography, paradoxically, reinscribed the association between pleasure and shame:

Films in the 1970s began to scare governments. Sex is a question of power, and even the liberal or somewhat liberated regimes became scared by what was happening. At the very beginning, before the porn industry really became institutionalized, there were a lot of experimental films—like Art and Jim Mitchell's *Behind the Green Door* [1972]. These films were both pornographic and artistic, and you sensed an interest in dealing with sexuality. The governments became scared, and imposed laws and taxes to institutionalize the porn industry, making it functional . . . genital. In doing so, governments restricted our sexuality as well. The pretext was the protection of children, but with the masses of porno videotapes and sexually explicit TV programs available, that's clearly not what's at issue. The porn industry puts us in the role of shamed consumers of sex, and makes sex into something shameful. Sex can be something pure, something sacred, a moment of transfiguration. Sexual taboo in and of itself isn't obscenity, but rather a rite of initiation, a doorway, a manner of transcendence. But the governments don't want us to see sex as a transfiguration; they want us to remain prisoners of our sense of degradation. Anything can be made obscene. The obscene is, in fact, an aesthetic order that's constantly fluctuating, like fashion. I agree completely with [director David] Cronenberg, who says that we have to completely change our notion of aesthetics. We have to stop our censors, who want to keep entire countries from becoming adult. If it were up to them, censors would keep us in a perpetual state of preadolescence. If they really believe that our sense of judgment is so imperiled, if they believe that they must protect us from emotions that we may find disturbing, then what is the purpose of allowing us to vote?[24]

In fact, adult-oriented entertainment in Paris during the 1970s initially produced an eroticization of public space not unlike New York City's, but comparisons with Paris ultimately underscore the untrammeled ease with which New York embraced adults-only culture. In the first half of the Seventies, Paris—like New York—felt the cultural weight of the burgeoning adult sector amid the mainstreaming of pornography: in a two-week period in 1972, only six films in Paris could be classified "adult," but by 1975 this figure had risen to seventy-five. Beginning with director Roger Vadim's risqué "art films" of the Fifties and Sixties, French filmmakers soon distinguished themselves as innovators and architects of softcore (*Emmanuelle*) as well as "statement" porn films that mixed sex and politics, like *Shocking* (1976), a XXX-rated film in which seven people indulge in a night of sexual depravity during a nuclear showdown between the superpowers. In the mid-1970s, however, the French abruptly changed course and relinquished their frontrunner role in the porn arena. Fearing that family-oriented cinema would all but disappear under the onslaught of adult films, the liberal government of Giscard d'Estaing, which ironically professed an anticensorship position regarding the arts, passed the so-called X Law in October 1976: a finance bill that made adult films exempt from government subsidies and limited their exhibition to specially designated cinemas where outside advertising would be reduced to a minimum.[25]

The Erotic City, by contrast, abided no such limitations. Soon after President Nixon grafted the war against "smut" onto his broader "law and order" campaign against "the permissive society," Mayor John Lindsay devoted the waning years of his second term (1969–1973) to a largely unsuccessful attempt to rid Times Square and other red-light districts of the porn glut. But Lindsay was dealt a crushing blow in 1973, ironically, through the very vessel that

Nixon had hoped would rid the nation of obscenity. In June, the Supreme Court issued its landmark ruling amending the 1957 *Roth* decision regarding obscenity. In a five-to-four decision, the Burger court ruled that local community and not national standards be used to determine what is obscene.[26] Buoyed by the high court's decision, New York legislators wasted no time in passing a civil statute that would have outlawed much of New York City's flourishing porn fare on grounds of obscenity. The porn lobby disputed the statute, and the case wound up in New York State Supreme Court. There, presiding judge Abraham Gelinoff screened several porn films and declared them "obscene," but proceeded to overturn the state legislation anyway. The basis of his decision was that "there is no evidence before this court, at this stage of the case, to enable the court to gauge the community standards of this community." In other words, the Erotic City had no "community standards." Obscenity law attorney Herbert Kassner, when asked his opinion of the ruling, responded, "New York has no penal or civil obscenity law: that's what it means."[27]

In dizzying tandem with the revolution in pornography, gay-male (and, to a lesser extent, gay-female) pleasure seeking in New York City underwent a rapid metamorphosis between the late 1960s and the early 1970s. As late as the Stonewall Rebellion in 1969, gay life in New York City remained shrouded in quasi-anonymity. In his landmark study *Gay New York,* historian George Chauncey describes the hidden gay city that lasted into the Sixties, where gay clubs and cruising sites were known only by word of mouth. Newly arrived gay refugees in Manhattan "discovered the gay world almost by chance," writes Chauncey,

> through the contacts they made in their rooming houses or in the streets; others found it by looking for places such as the Life Cafeteria (or the Village in general) they had heard their heterosexual associates mention scornfully. Whatever the route by which men made their initial contact with New York's gay world, they usually needed guidance in their exploration of it. They often received the counsel of men they met in their first forays into gay clubs or neighborhoods. Those men, often older and better established in both the straight and gay worlds, became their mentors—and in some cases their lovers as well.[28]

Even during these subterranean days, however, gay men had already established a trademark pattern of inventively reappropriating urban spaces for their own purposes, quite often for sex deemed illicit. Barton Benesh, an artist born in 1942 who moved to Manhattan at the age of fifteen and began exploring his gay identity, described the camouflaged gay habitation of Greenwich Village. "Everything was sneaky back then," recalled Benesh.

> After school I'd go sit in Washington Square Park, and that used to be the pickup place. There was a fence that went from Waverly Place to MacDougal, and all the guys would just sit on the fence, and then people would walk by, and then walk back and forth. Another great place was Howard Johnson's, which used to be on 6th Avenue and 8th Street. They used to have toilets in the basement, and that was the hot spot. In fact, that was the big pickup place in the Sixties—subway toilets.[29]

The gay Erotic City's transition from nebula to neon began, not surprisingly, with the Stonewall Rebellion of July 1969. Descriptions of the famed event are legion, but suffice it to say that the police picked the wrong moment—the day after Judy Garland's funeral—to raid the the Stonewall, a dive, in their routine pattern of shaking down Mafia-run gay clubs. Although it has since been endowed with lofty and multifaceted political significance, the Stonewall Rebellion was foundationally about the gay right to party, a proclamation of gay urban territoriality, and a claim to sanctioned public space for adult purposes. It is difficult to understate the degree to which an unfettered nightlife helped forge an affirmative gay urban identity in the early 1970s. While "gay pride" would subsequently attach itself to the health crisis (AIDS) in the 1980s or political issues (gays in the military) in the 1990s, an immediate and ongoing goal of the generation infused by the spirit of Stonewall was to make the Erotic City safe for an openly gay club scene.[30]

One of the mavericks in spotlighting the heretofore-invisible gay city was Michael Giammetta, who wrote about gay club life for Al Goldstein's raunchy *Screw* and *Gay* magazines. Like virtually everyone who has ever worked for Goldstein, Giammetta fled as soon as he got the chance ("Goldstein was impossible") and forged his own journalistic course by launching a gay club guide called *Michael's Thing*, which debuted in 1970. "Stonewall was a turning point for me," asserted Giammetta. "Before me and the magazine, people didn't know where to go. From then on a lot of gay people started reading my magazine like crazy—I couldn't print them fast enough—and that helped open up the door for gay people to own their own bars and clubs." Giammetta used the clout associated with his magazine, the *HX* of its era, to forge an association between gay pride and the right to an unconstricted nightlife. "I cleared out a lot of places that were owned by the Mafia," he recalled. "One was this place called the Roundtable on 50th Street. There were always these bullies at the door and they treated gay people like shit. So I wrote about this gay place that opened only a few blocks away, the Tambourine, owned by gay people. The Mafia eventually paid me a visit and asked me what they could do to remedy the situation, and I told them, 'Get those mugs off the door, hire gay bartenders, gay waiters, and start treating us like human beings.' "[31]

The shrine of an emergent, celebratory, hedonistic gay consciousness was the disco. Discotheques—basically small, intimate bars with dancing and a deejay—had been introduced to New York in the early 1960s from France and underwent a dizzying metamorphosis during the mid-1960s as discos like the Cheetah and the Electric Circus became bigger, flashier, and more technofetishist and psychedelic. By 1969, however, outdoor festivals like Woodstock captivated the countercultural imagination, while urban discotheques fell out of favor with the "smart set." It was during this lull in discotheque culture, from 1969 to 1972, that hedonistic gay men took over these ambient party sites and converted disco into what amounted to gay urban property for the first half of the 1970s.[32]

Debate continues to rage over New York's first openly gay discotheque, or the first nongay disco to "go gay": some say it was the Ice Palace on Fire Island, others nominate the Gay Activist Alliance Firehouse, still others identify the Manhattan restaurant-discotheque Aux Puce. If not the first, then surely the most notorious openly gay disco was the Sanctuary, which opened its doors in 1969. Located in a former German Baptist church on West 43rd Street, the Sanctuary was positioned just behind the Port Authority Bus Terminal, that terminus of shattered dreams that served as a focal point for pushers, hustlers, pimps, and transients of all stripes.[33] "I think the Sanctuary was a secret, but it couldn't have been that secret when gay men and lesbians can come out of a church from midnight till sunrise," recalled Leigh Lee, a Seventies disco habitué who went on to model for artist Robert Mapplethorpe. "The Sanctuary was the first time I was in a room full of homosexuals."[34]

Giammetta, who routinely covered the Sanctuary in *Michael's Thing*, chronicled its transformation into an openly gay dance club. "The Sanctuary was owned by this strange guy, Seymour Siden," noted Giammetta. "Gay, of course. His belief was to mix gay and straights together. There were banquettes, the deejay was where the altar used to be. Then Siden finally advertised with me because he wanted more gay people. And that started the trend of straight discos, years later, inviting gay people in to dance. The minute a straight disco opened, they would want a mailing list of gays."[35] By the time the Sanctuary closed in 1972, it had become pretty much the exclusive enclave of gay men. The Sanctuary was so overwhelmingly gay male that when Jane Fonda shot the club scenes for *Klute* (1971, directed by Alan Pakula) at the infamous disco, she complained about the lack of other women on the premises. Deep within a burgeoning feminist consciousness at the time (Fonda would go on to win the Academy Award for her performance in the movie), she suggested that the club at least throw some lesbians into the mix, for color if nothing else.[36]

Gay men involved in reclaiming urban discotheque culture during the first half of the 1970s also benefited from a revolution in dance music. During the Sixties, disco was an incomplete form, as discotheques played music not optimized for dancing. The play-list staple of famous New York City Sixties discotheques like Sybil Burton's Arthur or Le Club was the two-minute "45" single. Although these quick-shot tracks suited the hyperfrenetic dances of the Kennedy era, like the Chickenback and the Boogaloo, the laid-back Seventies demanded longer songs that allowed dancers to get their groove on. The solution came in the form of early Seventies up-tempo rhythm and blues: the "Philly Sound" of Gamble & Huff epitomized by tracks like the O'Jays' "Love Train," as well as languorous dance hits by Barry White ("Never, Never Gonna Give You Up"), Donna Summer ("Love to Love You Baby"), and George McCrae ("Rock Your Baby"). For the first time in its history, the discotheque had found music that suited its fundamental purpose, becoming the comprehensive form known as "disco": a term encompassing both the physical venue and the type of music created expressly for it.[37]

What came to be known as the Disco Lifestyle, as excavated, rearticulated, and lived by gay men in the Erotic City, is best described by Andrew Holleran in his landmark gay novel *Dancer from the Dance*, published in 1978. Describing the club party circuit, Holleran chronicled the euphoria, abandon, and overwhelming loss of self occasioned by disco life:

> They formed a group of people who had danced with each other over the years, gone to the same parties, the same beaches on the same trains, yet, in some cases, never even nodded at each other. They were bound together by a common love of a certain kind of music, physical beauty,

style—all the things one shouldn't throw away an ounce of energy pursuing, and sometimes throw away a life pursuing. . . . [In the disco they] passed one another without a word in the elevator, like silent shades in hell, hell-bent on their next look from a handsome stranger. Their next rush from a popper. The next song that turned their bones to jelly and left them all on the dance floor with heads back, eyes nearly closed, in the ecstasy of saints receiving the stigmata. They pursued these things with such devotion that they acquired, after a few seasons, a haggard look, a look of deadly seriousness. Some wiped everything they could off their faces and reduced themselves to blanks.

Holleran went on to reveal the extent to which the once-invisible gay city was itself disappearing. "[A]nd [after the disco closed] they would walk up Broadway together, exhausted, ecstatic, their bones light as a bird's, a flotilla of doomed queens on their way to the Everard Baths because they could not come down from the joy and happiness."[38]

The largest gay pleasure hub in the Erotic City was a particular stretch of gay "property" running from 14th Street and the Hudson River to Seventh Avenue and Sheridan Square: an area known as the West Village but incorporating the adjacent Meatpacking District, which was elevated to double-entendre status. The real action took place on the two thoroughfares of Washington and West streets, which early on became the geographic headquarters of gay club life. One of the most popular gay discos of the early-to-mid-Seventies was 12 West, located at West and 12th. In a 1976 overview of the gay disco scene, *After Dark* magazine described 12 West's interior as "a dance floor constructed like a Roman arena, in carpeted bleachers looking down on frenzied dancers while skylights let in the morning sun on those who disco till dawn."[39] The club burned down in its heyday and was supplanted by the now legendary Paradise Garage, located at 84 King Street. Both discos were conveniently located near the decaying piers along the Hudson River, which served as gay trysting sites for postdisco sexual encounters.

The gay propensity for creatively reappropriating public space for sexual purposes is best illustrated by a Seventies phenomenon known, to most of its participants, simply as "the trucks." Barton Benesh, who lived in the artists' complex Westbeth at West and Bethune streets, was an active participant in the scene. "All along Washington Street there used to be an elevated train, and all these trailer trucks were parked along here repairing it," Benesh recalled.

"And in the backs of those trucks, in the dark, you wouldn't *believe* what went on. Huge orgies. All day, all night. And it was all the time. So I'd be here working and then I couldn't stand it, I kept thinking 'I gotta go out there, I gotta go out there.' And I'd go into the trucks, do it, come back, work, then go back to the trucks again."[40]

Aside from its iconic discos and fuck-trucks, gay property in the West Village and Meatpacking District sector housed a veritable barracks of hardcore underground S&M clubs, including the Anvil (14th Street and 11th Avenue), the Ramrod (394 West Street), and the Cockring (180 Christopher Street). The Seventies hardcore gay club that has garnered the lion's share of folklore, however, is the Mineshaft, which opened in 1976 at 83 Washington Street, near the piers. Part erotic paradise and part open wound, the Mineshaft, on an average night, showcased the absolute gamut of unrepentant sexual exhibitionism, ranging from public fisting to "golden shower" fetishism, self-debasement being the leitmotif of most of the sexual activity. Devotee Leo Cardini in *Mineshaft Nights* described the no-nonsense ethos that pervaded all aspects of the club. "You knew then and there whether or not this was the place for you. It was not for all people and all fantasies, but if it was for you, you were at the threshold of a heaven that understudied as a hell." The Mineshaft's reputation as a sexual frontier and netherworld attracted some highbrow cultural figures who moonlighted as sexual explorers, among them French philosopher Michel Foucault and German filmmaker Rainer Werner Fassbinder. Others never saw the inside of the place. The predatory vibe and exclusionary xenophobia of the Mineshaft made it less than congenial space for gay disco fans. The prominently displayed dress code at the club's entrance provides a glimpse into the sometimes rigid politics of gay hardcore fashion circa 1978: "APPROVED ARE CYCLE & WESTERN GEAR, LEVI'S T-SHIRTS, UNIFORMS, JOCK STRAPS, PLAID & PLAIN SHIRTS, CUT OFFS, CLUB PATCHES, OVERLAYS & SWEAT. *NO* COLOGNE OR PERFUME OR DESIGNER SWEATERS. *NO* SUITS, TIES, DRESS PANTS OR JACKETS. *NO RUGBY-STYLED* SHIRTS OR *DISCO DRAG. NO COATS* IN THE PLAYGROUND. *NO LACOST* [sic] *ALLIGATOR SHIRTS*" (all emphasis in original). Cardini explained the implications of the no-cologne rule: "To be a Mineshaft doorman, you had to have a highly developed sense of smell. And the only acceptable odor was sweat."[41]

At the time of the Stonewall Rebellion, Allen Ginsberg remarked that the rioting gays had lost that "wounded look that fags all had."[42] Which look would characterize the Seventies? Was it "wounded" or was it what Holleran called "haggard," from the relentless, stern pursuit of that triumvirate of orgasms—music, drugs, and sex—enshrined at gay discos and the Erotic City's multiplying gay pleasure nodes of trucks, baths, and no-hold's-barred clubs like the Mineshaft? In fact, both looks continued to predominate in the decade as gay men, swept up in drugs, dance, and sexual delirium, attempted to numb or transcend the shame-imbued pasts they had so recently repudiated.

Whether at underground nightclubs like the Mineshaft or in peep-show booths on the "Deuce" (the nickname for Manhattan's 42nd Street), the prevalence of furtive, immediate, anonymous, one-shot sexual encounters could involve what Catherine Breillat calls "transcendence." But disco-era euphoria could also fuel a dramatic, anomic loss of personal identity. Sexual explorer and cult author Marco Vassi, who sampled both gay bathhouses and straight sex emporiums during the decadent decade, coined a term for this immolation of self in the furnace of carnality: "metasexuality," a multifaceted concept illustrated during a night spent with a female lover at New York sex palace Plato's Retreat soon after it opened in 1976. Observing his date's face while she was making love to another man, and noting that her facial expression was the same as when he made love to her, Vassi realized that sexual revelry eclipsed the individual and destroyed "the myth of specialness." He concluded that jealousy was petty and futile because "it was obvious that all of us were merely variations on a major theme. She was just another creature. I was just another creature."[43]

The flip side, or perhaps concomitant, of Vassi's metasexuality or Breillat's transfiguration could be an erasure of self, and countless cultural narratives of the era depicted people lured by the siren song of sex and "sleaze" into self-destruction. Losing one's soul—and identity—in the Erotic City was a prominent theme in such mainstream films as *Looking for Mr. Goodbar* (1977, directed by Richard Brooks), *Cruising* (1980, directed by William Friedkin), and, most important, *Taxi Driver* (1976, directed by Martin Scorcese). This landmark film about urban alienation is based on a screenplay by Paul Schrader, who lived the gutter-level lifestyle of his antihero cab driver Travis Bickle (Robert De Niro) during much of 1975.[44] In the film, insomniac cabbie Bickle has an affinity for cruising New York's red-light districts, especially Times Square, all the while decrying the decadence and sleaze around him. "All the animals come out at night—whores, skunk pussies, buggers, queens, fairies, dopers, junkies, sick, venal," he spits, prophesying that "[s]omeday a real rain will come and wash all this scum off the streets." The film constantly invokes the inescapability of the lurid metropolis engulfing and imprisoning him, as exemplified by this slice of dialogue from early in the film:

CAB DISPATCHER: So whaddya want to hack for, Bickle?
BICKLE: I can't sleep nights.
DISPATCHER: There's porn theaters for that.
BICKLE: Yeah, I know, I tried that.

Somnambulist-with-a-death-wish Bickle soon develops an obsessive crush on election campaign worker Betsy (Cybill Shepherd), whom he considers "pure." "She appeared like an angel," the demented Bickle confides to his diary. "Out of this filthy mess, she is alone. They . . . cannot . . . touch . . . her." Despite these lofty sentiments, on their first date he takes his "angel" to a porn movie at the Lyric theater on 42nd Street, which is playing a double bill of *Sometime Sweet Susan* and *Swedish Marriage Manual*. "This is a dirty movie," remarks the stunned Betsy, to which Bickle responds, "This is a movie that a lot of couples come to. I see them all the time." Repulsed by the subject matter and the theater's clientele, and now wary of his motives, Betsy bolts from the venue. "Taking me to a place like this is about as exciting as saying to me 'let's fuck,' " she rails, prompting a nonplussed Bickle to mutter, "I don't know much about movies." By the end of *Taxi Driver*, he metamorphoses into an accidental hero after killing a pimp and "freeing" teen prostitute Iris (Jodie Foster). Yet he remains to the end a split personality (Betsy calls him "a walking contradiction"): a true casualty of the Erotic City, he mindlessly dwells in and consumes the very "scum" he wants to eradicate.

Another flash point in the Erotic City during the latter 1970s was disco, which remained controversial even in the wake of abject commercialization. For the first half of the Seventies, disco had been an ongoing dialogue between black female vocalists and gay male dancers; its subsequent popularization posed problems to discophiles and discophobes alike. Pinpointing the date of disco mainstreaming is hazardous, but a decent milestone is the *Brady Bunch Variety Hour* (aired November 28, 1976, on ABC), which featured the surreal spectacle of the all-American family from the canceled television show singing "The Hustle" and "Shake Your Booty." The following year, the culturally iconic box-office smash *Saturday Night Fever* made disco safe, and proprietary, for hypermacho straight men. That same year, a writer in *Harper's* magazine described the incursion of straights into gay disco terrain. "I had only recently become aware myself that men and women who did not consider themselves homosexuals were routinely spending time at discos where most of the clientele was gay. . . . [T]heir presence had about it an ambiguity of purpose, for while they might say they were there only as watchers, only as voyeurs, they were also becoming participants, regulars in a scene which could never be theirs, outlaws in what had always been an outlaw world."[45]

Gay disco-era veterans recalled other adverse effects of the heterosexualization of disco: the loss of early disco culture's whiff of gay exclusivity and conspiracy. Steve Sukman, who ran the club Private Eyes in Manhattan in the early 1980s, remarked that "pleasure and being around your own people was the gay metaphor for disco; simple pleasure was its straight application."[46] It was the difference, essentially, between Diana Ross's "Love Hangover" and Rod Stewart's "Do Ya Think I'm Sexy?" Another complaint about the degaying of disco was that, quite simply, the songs changed. As Kevin Kaufman, a gay disco deejay in the late 1970s, said, "If you were in any gay bar worth its salt back in 1977 or '78—when the Bee Gees were hot—you would never, ever, ever have heard ["Stayin' Alive"] in a gay bar. Never."[47] By the late disco era of the early Eighties, disco songs had become parodies of the pleasure principle that early Seventies sexual acolytes had loftily embraced.

Laments about disco mainstreaming from its foundational gay contingent were minute compared with the overt, politicized disco bashing emanating from embattled fans of rock music. Sixties rock had reveled in an antiestablishment ethos, and the premature deaths of rock stars Brian Jones, Janis Joplin, Jim Morrison, and Jimi Hendrix had established a heroic rock mythology based on excess. While Seventies rockers like Led Zeppelin and AC/DC continued to mine this mythology, rock music was now the Establishment itself, in many cases more cliché than counterculture. Disco emerged over the course of the Seventies as the insurgent musical form, one that rivaled and called into question rock's outlaw pretensions. At the same time, disco showcased demographics—gay men, black female disco divas, black men and women—traditionally neglected by "classic" rock while it studiously ignored that fulcrum of the white rock-music world—the straight white male. Elevated to deity status by Bic lighter–brandishing rock fans chanting "Freebird!" white male heterosexuals found themselves radically decentered in the disco pecking order. Faced with castration anxiety stemming from disco's sexual politics, and musically outgunned by its cultural insurgency and connection with the dancing masses, rockers responded in one of two ways. Rock musicians sometimes "defected" to disco, as did Blondie with "Heart of Glass" (1978), the Rolling Stones with "Miss You" (1978) and the entire *Emotional Rescue* (1980) album, and even punk heroes the Clash with "The Magnificent Seven" and other tracks off the *Sandinista!* album (1980).

Rock fans took another route: they sought to annihilate disco. As I have argued elsewhere, the disco backlash was the first cry of the angry white male.[48] A lot of the animus was directed at the gay or feminine components of disco but coded as disdain for disco music itself, which was characteristically reviled by rockers as "synthetic," "plastic" (read: effeminate), and "mindless." The misogynist overtones of disco-hating were apparent in the lyrics to prankster deejay Steve Dahl's "Do You Think I'm Disco?" a venomous parody of the Rod Stewart hit:

> I like to dance with girls in sleazy dresses
> Lipstick, nail charms, and make-up in excesses
> Buy them a drink and try to get their number
> Usually they are as cold as a cucumber

The song concludes with the narrator repudiating disco:

> Some people call me scum because I don't have a realistic set of values
> And you know what
> I'm beginning to think they're right.

Throwing himself back into the arms of rock, the singer, in an act of contrition, resolves to melt down all his gold disco jewelry into a Led Zeppelin belt buckle.[49]

Other rhetoric of the rock-versus-disco wars, which began in earnest in 1977, was explicitly violent: from the none-too-subtle homophobia of "Disco Sucks!" to more precise instructions like "Shoot the Bee Gees!" and that old standby "Death to Disco!" The killing ritual was enacted at the infamous Comiskey Park "Disco Demolition" rally in July 1979, an event widely interpreted as disco's Waterloo. Chicago White Sox fans converged to witness the detonation of disco albums during intermission between a doubleheader, but the discophobe bonfire incited the fans to riot and tear up the stadium. Occurring exactly ten years after the Stonewall Rebellion, Comiskey has been interpreted as a composite-coded gay bashing / lynching / wife beating, because it brought to the surface all the misogyny, racism, and homophobia that fueled antidisco animus among white rock fans. But the violence at Comiskey was also simpler, less coded, and more idiotic. It was the revenge of every Seventies stoner who spent the past few years sulking at sweet-sixteen parties for "snooty" girls in his class who would never go out with him (and who liked disco), the same stoner who cringed to songs like "Boogie Oogie Oogie" and conspired with his burnout buddies to beat up the deejay and make him play Aerosmith. All that teen peer-group angst, that oppositional identity that grafts itself onto musical tastes, welled up at Comiskey Park in a vast, frightening catharsis of destruction.[50]

No one hated disco more than Son of Sam, and no one struck back more violently at the erotic manifestations of disco's world-is-my-bedroom attitude in the Erotic City. On June 26, 1977, attractive, young Judy Placido was leaving the Elephas disco in Queens with her date, Sal Lupo. The crowd at the club had been pretty thin that night: the .44-caliber killer had already struck six times and murdered five people. "This Son of Sam is really scary," Judy told Sal. "The way that guy comes out of nowhere. You never know when he'll hit next." That very instant, Son of Sam drew at the young couple and fired four times, wounding them both but leaving them alive. Although this was serial killer David Berkowitz's only attack on an actual disco, he had been implicitly warring on the disco lifestyle since his first attack a year earlier. Over the course of his rampage, Berkowitz consistently targeted the public sexual overflow in the Erotic City, his favored victims being young couples making out in cars. Although clearly a woman hater in the discophobe mold (in one of his letters to *New York Daily News* journalist Jimmy Breslin, Berkowitz called himself "John Wheaties, rapist and suffocator of young girls"), his behavior was simply an extreme version of the revulsion, confusion, and pained attraction to public promiscuity felt by many prisoners of the Erotic City.[51] In this sense, his "mission" was to destabilize the sexual colonization of New York City in the Seventies. Berkowitz's antidisco credentials were confirmed the night of his capture in August 1977. When news of Son of Sam's arrest arrived at Studio 54, Steve Rubell interrupted the disco Star Wars theme and hysterically screamed into the public-address system, "They got him! They got Sam!" The crowd cheered, and observer Albert Goldman subsequently remarked that Berkowitz, one of those "bridge and tunnel" people, would never have been let into Studio 54 anyway.[52]

Even though the late Seventies ushered in the last days of disco, they did not mark the end of the Erotic City. The factors that gutted the disco movement—the collapse in the dance-music market, the election of neoconservative Ronald Reagan in 1980, the encroaching AIDS pandemic—did not imme-diately rend the seedy erotic fiber that New York had acquired in the Seven-ties. AIDS, in particular, had contradictory effects on the eroticization of public space consolidated during the Seventies. On the one hand, gay club life—along with its overflow effect—was reduced by the AIDS pandemic; on the other hand, the Eighties did see their share of vibrant new gay discos, like the legendary Saint, but gay club life soon acquired a desperation and paranoia. By 1985 and the onset of what was called "The Fear" in gay circles, gay club life—of the disco or underground variety—had become a shadow of its former self, with remaining clubs handicapped by panic and AIDS-related paranoia.[53] During this same period, gay bathhouses, those preemi-nent sites of promiscuity during the Seventies, were padlocked by the city in an attempt to curtail the spread of AIDS.

Sex shops geared to straight people proved more resilient. By catering to the voyeuristic tendencies exacerbated during the AIDS era, video porn blos-somed and diversified in the 1980s. Although the invention of the Betamax in 1976 and the subsequent video revolution in porn privatized much of the activity, porn videos before the introduction of the Internet still had to be bought somewhere, often in sex shops that enticed the masturbatory audi-ence with peep and "live sex" shows. By the end of the Seventies, 40 percent of all VCR owners polled claimed to have bought or rented an X-rated tape, and more than fifteen million hardcore videos were being rented per week, with an annual gross of more than one billion dollars.[54] The AIDS era cur-tailed promiscuity, all the while instilling the desire for safe fantasies in the neorepressed male consumer. This cultural blowback occasioned, paradox-ically, a new wave of sexual colonization of public space in the form of strip clubs. Cultural historian Katherine Liepe-Levinson argues that the period 1990 to 1993 "coincided with the historical apex of the second major strip-tease boom in America." According to one report, strip clubs across the United States more than doubled from 1987 to 1992.[55]

The Erotic City, in other words, was by no means predestined for extinc-tion. Instead, its demise in the 1990s owed to two interlocking factors. The first was New York mayor Rudolph Giuliani's crusade against the legal sex trades, set in motion in 1994 with the development of a new zoning code that, in Liepe-Levinson's estimation, "was aimed at forever changing the Big Apple's infamous map of sexual desire." In the course of his eight-year tenure and legally emboldened by a 1991 Supreme Court ruling that raised harmful-secondary-effects and quality-of-life issues related to live nude adult entertainment, Giuliani converted the raunchy Times Square area to a family-oriented Disney zone, forced adult-book and -video stores to adopt a 60/40 rule (whereby 60 percent of the inventory must be nonporn), and curbed overt advertisements of adult entertainment (topless bars had to rename themselves "stopless").[56] Coinciding with Giuliani's successful war against the Erotic City was the mainstreaming of Internet adult entertainment, abetted in the late 1990s by the widespread deployment of broadband access enabling video pay-for-porn, live nude chat, streaming videos, and other adult fare that makes the Internet the new century's Deuce.[57]

During the Seventies, most of the nation—and a fair share of New York's own inhabitants—regarded the Big Apple not as an Erotic City but as a lawless metropolis on the brink of destruction amid ballooning crime rates, impending fiscal collapse, serial killers, racial strife, and rampant public indecency. It was a pervasive perspective aptly conveyed in the Rolling Stones' hit "Shattered" (1978):

> Don't you know the crime rate's going up, up, up, up, up
> To live in this town you must be tough, tough, tough, tough, tough!
> You got rats on the West Side
> Bed bugs uptown
> What a mess
> This town's in tatters
> I've been shattered.

True to form, however, Mick Jagger is careful to qualify this downbeat assessment:

> Pride and joy and greed and sex
> That's what makes our town the best
> Pride and joy and dirty dreams and still surviving on the street
> And look at me, I'm in tatters, yeah
> I've been battered
> What does it matter?

The song's evocation of "dirty dreams," of rapture amid squalor, underscores the fact that the Seventies urban apocalypse of low rents and high murder rates provided for New York's more hedonistically inclined citizens a suitably lurid backdrop for an unprecedented mass experiment in hedonism. In the Sixties, a contingent of urban hippies centered in Manhattan's East Village had attempted to forge a countercultural community rooted in geographical space, but their somewhat inchoate efforts foundered in short order. By contrast, the participants in New York's revolution in sexual mores and adult entertainment fared much better during the Seventies in consolidating sizable sectors of the city for the purposes of pleasure, from the Hudson Piers to Times Square, from Central Park's Rambles to the nexus of discos, after-hours clubs, and sex emporiums. For gay men in particular, the Seventies has taken on a kind of debauched innocence as an island in time wedged between the Stonewall Rebellion and AIDS—an era of sexual libertinism that has been both reviled and extolled in gay cultural memory. For others, particularly those living in a latter-day New York where restrictions on adult entertainment rival those of small midwestern cities, the Seventies seem like the "anything goes" salad days of unbridled libido. What both critics and fans of New York in the Seventies often overlook is the stern nature of this hedonic pursuit, the fact that sexual adventurism could lead to both transfiguration and debasement, and the heroic overtones of this pioneering mass experiment in pleasure seeking.

Notes

1. "Concern on Smut Held Unfounded," *New York Times,* August 8, 1970; "Panel's Draft Urges Liberal Pornography Laws," *New York Times,* August 9, 1970.

2. Richard Halloran, "A Federal Panel Asks Relaxation of Curbs on Smut," *New York Times,* October 1, 1970.

3. Warren Weaver Jr., "Nixon Repudiates Obscenity Report as Morally Void," *New York Times,* October 25, 1970.

4. Murray Schumach, "Ironical Obscenity Issue," *New York Times,* July 16, 1971.

5. Ibid.

6. Ibid.

7. The MPAA ratings system instituted in 1968 and the X rating are treated in Eddie Muller and Daniel Faris, *Grindhouse: The Forbidden World of "Adults Only" Cinema* (New York: St. Martin's, 1996), 118.

8. For the controversy surrounding the didactic porn film *I Am Curious (Yellow),* see Muller and Faris, *Grindhouse,* 117–122. See also John Heidenry, *What Wild Ecstasy: The Rise and Fall of the Sexual Revolution* (New York: Simon and Schuster, 1997), 52–53.

9. MPAA data.

10. Heidenry, *What Wild Ecstasy,* 55; see also Laurence Senelick, "Private Parts in Public Places," in *Inventing Times Square: Commerce and Culture at the Crossroads of the World,* ed. William Taylor (Baltimore: Johns Hopkins Press, 1991), 341.

11. Josh Alan Friedman, *Tales of Times Square* (Portland, OR: Feral Press, 1993), 77–78.

12. Eleanor Blau, "3 Balk at Hearing on Rackets and Sex Exploitation," *New York Times,* October 20, 1970.

13. William Taylor, "Introduction," *Inventing Times Square,* xii.

14. Selenick, "Private Parts," 330.

15. Ibid., 331–337.

16. Ibid., 332.

17. Ibid.

18. Murray Schumach, "Sex Exploitation Spreading Here," *New York Times,* July 1971.

19. For the making and success of *Deep Throat,* see Heidenry, *What Wild Ecstasy,* 149–153.

20. Muller and Faris, *Grindhouse,* 123.

21. *What Are Those Strange Drops of Blood Doing On the Body of Jennifer?* aka *Case of the Bloody Iris* is part of a foundational giallo trilogy showcasing Italian sex-film icon Edwige Fenech. The other features include *Next Victim,* aka *The Strange Vice of Signora Ward* (1971, directed by Sergio Martino), in which a leather-clad mass murderer kills sexually promiscuous women in Vienna, and *Day of the Maniac* (1972, directed by Sergio Martino), in which the murders involve occultists who have weird sex with their kidnapee-acolytes. All three gialli were released theatrically in the United States, and *Next Victim* played on local New York television into the 1980s.

22. Craig Ledbetter, "The Color of Fear: Giallo," *European Trash Cinema* 2, no. 6 (1991): 27.

23. Muller and Faris, *Grindhouse,* 103.

24. Catherine Breillat, interview by Peter Braunstein, September 1999. See also Peter Braunstein, "Scandalous! *Romance* Director Has Tongues Wagging," *Getting It,* September 16, 1999, http://www.gettingit.com/article/54.

25. Cathal Tohill and Pete Tombs, *Immoral Tales: Sex and Horror Cinema in Europe 1956–1984* (London: Titan Books, 1995), 53–55.

26. Warren Weaver Jr., "Supreme Court Tightens Rule Covering Obscenity, Gives States New Power," *New York Times,* June 20, 1973.

27. C. Gerald Fraser, "State Court Upsets Civil Obscenity Law," *New York Times,* August 15, 1973.

28. George Chauncey, *Gay New York: Gender, Urban Culture, and the Making of the Gay Male World, 1890–1940* (New York: Basic Books, 1997), 277.

29. Barton Benesh, interview by Peter Braunstein, August 21, 1997.

30. A description and interpretation of the Stonewall riots can be found in Ian Young, *The Stonewall Experiment: A Gay Psychohistory* (London: Cassell, 1995),

54–56. Young's account was part of a wave of self-flagellating gay literature that flourished in the mid-1990s that implanted the Seventies experience within a gay declension narrative culminating in AIDS. Young's argument is that gay men during the 1970s lived out a fatal self-fulfilling prophecy, caving into their culturally encoded self-sacrificial impulses and accepting straight society's depiction of them as "walking sex acts" (51).

31. Michael Giammetta, interview by Peter Braunstein, May 25, 1997.

32. For a chronicle of the history of the discotheque from its French origins to its transplantation to the United States in the 1960s, see Peter Braunstein, "Disco," *American Heritage,* November 1999, 43–57. See also Albert Goldman, *Disco* (New York: Hawthorn, 1978).

33. Speculation on New York's first openly gay disco also appears in Peter Braunstein, "The Last Days of Gay Disco," *Village Voice,* June 30, 1998, 54–58. Craig Scott Druckman argues that "for the first time, boys danced with boys in public" at the restaurant-disco Aux Puce in "Disco History: From Peppermint to Poppers," *After Dark,* November 1976, 40, 42.

34. Leigh Lee, interview by Peter Braunstein, February 15, 1997.

35. Giammetta, interview.

36. The Fonda anecdote, as well as a lively history of the notorious Sanctuary disco, can be found in Goldman, *Disco,* 112–118.

37. Braunstein, "Disco," 53–55.

38. Andrew Holleran, *Dancer from the Dance* (New York: Morrow, 1978), 38–40.

39. Druckman, "Peppermint to Poppers," 44.

40. Benesh, interview.

41. A photo of the Mineshaft dress-code sign appears in Leo Cardini, *Mineshaft Nights* (Teaneck, NJ: Firsthand Books, 1990), iii.

42. Allen Ginsberg quoted in Young, *Stonewall Experiment,* 56.

43. Marco Vassi quoted in Heidenry, *What Wild Ecstasy,* 212.

44. For the back story on the making of *Taxi Driver,* and how Scorcese paradoxically avoided an "X" rating by making the film look even sleazier, see Peter Biskind, *Easy Riders, Raging Bulls: How the Sex-Drugs-and-Rock 'n' Roll Generation Saved Hollywood* (New York: Simon and Schuster, 1998), 299–307.

45. Sally Helgesen, "Disco," *Harper's,* October 1977, 20.

46. Steve Sukman, interview by Peter Braunstein, September 13, 1997.

47. Kevin Kauffman, interview by Peter Braunstein, March 30, 1997.

48. Braunstein, "Last Days of Gay Disco," 54–58.

49. "Do You Think I'm Disco?" lyrics by Steve Dahl, Rod Stewart, and Carmine Appice, Ovation Records, 1979.

50. The antidisco movement's homophobic, misogynist, and sexist components are assessed in Peter Braunstein, "The Killing of Sister Disco," *CUPS Magazine,* no. 91, (1998–99): 12–13. See also Alice Echols, "Ball of Confusion," *L.A. Weekly,* April 29–May 5, 1994, 24–30.

51. See Son of Sam archive at the Crime Library, http://www.crimelibrary.com/serial/son/sonfinal.htm.

52. Goldman, *Disco,* 20. Goldman dubbed Son of Sam "the Grendel of the disco world."

53. For gay New York during the Fear, see Young, *Stonewall Experiment,* 5.

54. Heidenry, *What Wild Ecstasy,* 213.

55. Katherine Liepe-Levinson, *Strip Show: Performances of Gender and Desire* (New York: Routledge, 2002), 3–4.

56. Ibid., 5, 19–20.

57. The subject of Internet porn and the online adult entertainment gold rush is treated in Frederick Lane III, *Obscene Profits: The Entrepreneurs of Pornography in the Cyber Age* (New York: Routledge, 2000).

7

America's *Poseidon Adventure*

A Nation in Existential Despair

WILLIAM GRAEBNER

On July 15, 1979, President Jimmy Carter addressed the American people. Exasperated by the nation's failure to arrive at a solution to the energy crisis, he had spent the previous week at the presidential retreat at Camp David, searching for the source of the problem with a series of illustrious guests. The speech was in one respect quite ordinary; it was a call, not unlike that made by other presidents, for Americans to overcome "fragmentation and self-interest" to forge a unified, national political response to a specific problem of undeniable importance. Yet as Carter spoke, it became clear that solving the energy crisis had become a means to a greater end: energy, he vowed, would be the "immediate test of our ability to unite this nation," and the process of winning the energy war would "rebuild the unity and confidence of America."[1]

It was a tall order, especially given what the president claimed to have learned at Camp David. As Carter explained (and not always with consistency or coherence), America suffered from a "crisis of confidence," a loss of faith in the future that was at least in part rooted in the "wounds" of the past: the defeat in Vietnam; the spectacle of Watergate; the inflation of the currency; the Arab oil boycott with its lesson of dependency; and, reaching back to the 1960s, the assassinations of John Kennedy, Robert Kennedy, and Martin Luther King Jr. Beyond this familiar litany of shocks and traumas, Carter's speech was laced with passages that reflected a different sort of analysis, one less dependent on discrete events of the past and more steeped in a generalized analysis of American culture. The crisis of confidence, he said, was a crisis of "heart and soul and spirit," apparent in the "growing doubt about the meaning of our own lives" and in eroding confidence in the future, in the idea of progress. Too many Americans, he argued, were empty and without purpose, given to "self-indulgence and consumption," locating identity in "what one owns" and "unable to satisfy our longing for meaning." Probing the American psyche, Carter had found collective, existential despair.

As politics, the address was a mistake. Even assuming that people could identify with Carter's sweeping critique of the American spirit, the proposed remedy—a national energy policy—hardly seemed adequate to the task, and it seemed unlikely that Carter could inspire the Kierkegaardian "leap of faith" that his vision of change seemed to require.[2] As cultural analysis, the address fares better. Carter had identified a real if somewhat shapeless problem; he understood that its historical origins were complex, predating not only his presidency and the severe economic dislocation of the 1970s, but the decade; and, in phrases such as "longing for meaning," he revealed his concern that the problem was, indeed, beyond economics and beyond politics—certainly beyond the therapeutic power of a national energy policy—and framed by the existential dread of modern humanity.

What he might have added had he had more time (and even less political savvy) was that many Americans experienced the 1970s in psychic shutdown and withdrawal, understanding themselves as emotionless and affectless—the nation of soulless zombies depicted in George Romero's film trilogy—and, like the passengers on the inverted *Poseidon* in *The Poseidon Adventure* (1972), carrying on as if life itself was something one had to be convinced to value. To be sure, this perspective was not universal. There were communities and groups—gays, feminists, African Americans, and environmentalists among them—that experienced the 1970s as an exhilarating moment of possibility and progressive change. Yet for most of the white middle class, and for a great many others, the events and developments of the decade seemed to coalesce to mock one's dreams and ambitions and to deflate expectations. Time and again, Americans lamented the decline of heroism and the heroic, defining themselves instead as survivors—of incest, of cancer, of the Vietnam War, and of the sinking ships, burning buildings, shark attacks, zombie invasions, and other disasters and tragedies that reflected the siege mentality and were staples of Hollywood in the era. At bottom, they perceived and talked about themselves as bored—not bored with the little things, or min-imally bored, but bored big time. They were bored by what they saw as the collapse of meaning and values; bored by the absence of meaningful work; bored by a new definition and understanding of humanity seen emerging in the late 1960s and early 1970s from genetics, genetic engineering, ethol-ogy (the study of animal behavior), robotic technologies, and the God-is-dead movement; bored, and more than a little frightened, by the blank face in the mirror.

The state of the nation's psyche was discussed and debated everywhere in the 1970s—in publications that catered to elites, such as the *New York Times* and *Saturday Review;* in journals of science and social science, where PhDs read about the implications of new work in genetic engineering or weighed in on psychologist B. F. Skinner's latest book (appropriately titled *Beyond Freedom and Dignity*); or in *Time, National Review, Seventeen,* and dozens of other popular magazines that carried one story after another about the "end of the American hero." For a president to speak about the issue was almost unprecedented, but Carter and his advisers had been reading Christopher Lasch's *The Culture of Narcissism,* a favorite in the college classroom and a book whose argument underpinned many lighter and more superficial treat-ments. And one could learn about all this and more, albeit filtered for mass consumption, simply by watching television, listening to popular music, or going to the movies.[3]

Carter's "crisis of confidence" was on-screen in 1972 (before most of the events mentioned in the speech) when *The Poseidon Adventure,* the first of the decade's "disaster" films, played to packed movie houses across the land.[4] In a noir-like flourish at the beginning of the film, we are given notice of the tragedy to come: "At midnight on New Year's Eve,[5] the S.S. *Poseidon,* en route from New York to Athens [from the overcivilized West to its mythic origins], met with disaster and was lost. There were only a handful of survivors. This is their story. . . ." Like other disaster films of the period, *The Poseidon Adven-ture* implicates an irresponsible elite, in this case the ship's owners, whose profit-driven operating decisions render the *Poseidon* vulnerable. On that fate-ful midnight, an earthquake-produced tidal wave swamps and inverts the ship while it remains afloat, making rescue possible only through the hull of the ship, exposed above the waterline. Those that make the journey upward include the Rogos (Ernest Borgnine and Stella Stevens), a working-class cou-ple; Martin (Red Buttons), a lonely jogger; Belle and Manny Rosen (Shelley Winters and Jack Albertson), a New York Jewish couple on their way to

Israel; Acres (Roddy McDowall), a steward; Nonnie (Carol Lynley), the ship's blond and bland vocalist; Susan (Pamela Sue Martin), a sexy teen; and Reverend Scott (Gene Hackman), the hero/leader.

Every Hollywood film solves (or purports to solve) a problem. In this case, the problem is existential despair. Indeed, the hero/leader's central function is to convince the ship's passengers and crew to take personal responsibility for a life worth living. This process begins before the ship capsizes, when Scott, a semi-defrocked Catholic priest being punished for past indiscretions with an assignment in Africa, delivers an on-deck sermon. Having identified something akin to a victim mentality among those on board, Scott enjoins those assembled to "have the guts to fight for yourself." He continues, "God wants brave souls, he wants winners, not quitters. If you can't win, at least try to win. God loves tryers. . . . Resolve to fight for yourselves, and others. . . ." Later, with the ship upside down and filling with water, Scott learns from the ship's chaplain that most passengers have chosen to stay where they are to wait for help to arrive, a course that can lead only to death. "That's the way out," Scott says, pointing upward while addressing them. "That's the only chance. . . . There's nobody alive but us, and nobody's gonna help us except ourselves. It's up to each one of you—it's up to all of us. . . . If you stay here you'll certainly die" (and minutes later, they do).

Even those who choose to work their way through the ship's decks to possible rescue have to be coaxed, cajoled, implored, and persuaded to do so, as if they were empty of desire—the living dead. When Belle Rosen, fearful that she cannot climb the Christmas tree[6] that offers the only access to the deck above, resigns herself to waiting with the others, Scott must function as the life force. Belle asks, "There's something different up there than there is from down here?" Scott replies, "Yes. Life. Life is up there. And life always matters very much, doesn't it?" Later, when Belle is dying after saving Scott from drowning, she confirms the lesson learned. "That's the sign of life," she says, showing Scott the pendant she wishes to pass on to her grandchildren. "Life always matters very much." Others who must be convinced of the value of life—life as a survivor—include Manny Rosen (after Belle's death) and Nonnie (after her brother dies), whose rather tepid commitment to life, and to life after disaster (that is, survival), is revealed in Lynley's low-affect portrayal and in the morose lyrics and dreary pace of the film's Academy Award–winning song, "The Morning After."[7]

Scott's project, and the cultural work of the film, might best be understood as an effort to deal with boredom. Boredom's history runs through Hamlet, the weary, bored intellectual; Charles Dickens, whose *Bleak House* (1852) was the first literary work to make mention of it; turn-of-the-century social scientists, among them Emile Durkheim, who remarked on the bored as those engaged with "novelties, unfamiliar pleasures, [and] nameless sensations"; Samuel Beckett's existential classic *Waiting for Godot* (1952); the conceptualization, by psychologists in the mid-1950s, of boredom as a "pathology"; and, in 1975, the first convention of Boredom Anonymous.[8] By the mid-1970s, critiques of boredom were ubiquitous, appearing in *Ladies' Home Journal,* *Harper's, Smithsonian, Mademoiselle, Psychology Today,* and many other publications. The first book-length analyses would appear in the 1980s.[9]

Although Americans spent most of the 1970s in the throes of a serious economic downturn, most analysts of boredom ignored the dislocations and wounds of a postindustrial economy and instead emphasized a set of national cultural and social characteristics—affluence, consumerism, a surfeit of leisure, "enforced idleness," the absence of "primal hunger" and other "survival needs," the relentless pursuit of pleasure—for which the cruise ship *Poseidon* was an apt metaphor. "It is absurd to speak of the intellectual boredom of a starving woman or man," wrote Estelle Ramey in *Harper's,* adding, "[I]t takes a lot of ingenuity to stay viable in the face of total leisure."[10] Even Jimmy Carter, presiding over an economy with 7 percent unemployment and 13 percent inflation, felt compelled to use his 1979 address to register his concern that too many Americans "worship self-indulgence and consumption."[11]

Yet Carter and Scott (Carter's equivalent on the *Poseidon*) and other critics/therapists of boredom ultimately turned elsewhere for the source of the problem or took the affluence argument in new directions. Sociologist Robert Nisbet did the latter, arguing that boredom was a product of mismatch between man's "central nervous system," which had evolved to produce qualities such as aggressiveness that were essential to survival, and a leisured and secure twentieth-century existence in which those qualities were largely if not wholly irrelevant. Others argued that Freud, Marx, Darwin, and, most recently, psychologist B. F. Skinner had made boredom inevitable by conceptualizing the human being in ways that put determinism in the foreground and left little room for autonomy and agency.[12]

Like Carter and Scott, however, most analyses underscored boredom's roots in a profound and elemental crisis of meaning, values, standards, purposes, and ideals, a crisis reflected in the position and posture of boredom in which nothing mattered, one could not and did not care, and the emotions shut down—a "world ruled by the logic of death," wrote Sam Keen. Caught up in that crisis, adrift in a sea of uncertainty and relativism (the postmodern condition), the *Poseidon*'s passengers exist in what Sean Desmond Healy has described as a state of "hyperboredom," involving a "more or less complete withholding of assent to existence, positively or negatively"—until, that is, Scott persuades a handful of the bored to reject the "logic of death" and, miraculously, to value life.[13]

"Catastrophe alone," wrote Nisbet in 1982, "would appear to be the surest, and, in today's world, the most likely of liberations from boredom." Exactly. When the *Poseidon* flips over, its passengers are invited —as was the movie's audience in 1972—to experience that liberation, to feel the blood rush that comes from a commitment to risking life and courting death, to exist within a curiously pleasurable space—a space of emotion, of decision, of action, of caring, of sacrificing, of agency—in which one's survival is truly in doubt and in one's own hands. (Of course, much the same could be said of any of a dozen disaster films.)[14]

A second option to relieve boredom was to find a way to tap into the primordial residue that was assumed to exist beneath the civilized, rationalistic, atheistic, and genetically perfected veneer of modern humanity. This is the theme of *Altered States* (1980). Set in April 1967, the film examines the effort of physiologist Eddie Jessup (William Hurt) to resolve a crisis of religious belief triggered by the death of his father. Using a Mexican potion concocted of mushrooms and blood and water-tank sensory deprivation, Eddie feels himself shot back into time through genetic regression, becoming a "proto-human" in touch with his primitive self, consuming the blood and "hot flesh" of a goat. Another trip into the tank, this one without assistance, yields further regression into a potentially murderous ape-man. "I was utterly primordial," Eddie recalls. "I consisted of nothing more than the will to survive. To live through the night. To eat. To drink. To sleep. It was the most supremely satisfying time of my life."

The third antidote to boredom involved overcoming or transcending the crisis of belief that underpinned the phenomenon, that is, getting people to believe that there was some meaning to existence that went beyond the self and its preservation. For some, that meant a worldwide revival of religion—a direct attack on the death-of-God theology, an appeal to faith—to which the lay preacher Carter and the priest Scott might both be said to have contributed.[15] Others relied on myth and ritual rather than traditional religion to reinvest the cosmos with a sense of unity and purpose and to prevail over boredom. The 1976 founding of the journal *Parabola*—devoted to "Myth and the Quest for Meaning"—took place in that context. Writing in the first issue, which contained essays on heroes and quests and other topics dear to mythologists, and which anticipated the Joseph Campbell–centered popular enthusiasm for mythology a decade later, publisher D. M. Dooling grounded the new publication in the "conviction . . . that human existence is significant, that life essentially makes sense in spite of our confusions, that man is not here on earth by accident but for a purpose. . . ." That was Carter's message and Scott's, too. After all, the ship was the *Poseidon,* and it was headed for the epicenter of mythology: Greece.[16]

Bruce Springsteen's rise to rock-and-roll stardom and national acclaim in the 1970s—he was featured on the covers of both *Time* and *Newsweek* in October 1975—was due in some substantial way to the direct and credible way his music and lyrics address the issue of existential despair. Born to working-class parents (his father drove a bus, his mother was a secretary), Springsteen was raised in Freehold, New Jersey, a nondescript town about fifteen miles west of the dismal beach community of Asbury Park, where he developed a local following at the Upstage club. Although neither Freehold nor Asbury Park was a typical industrial site, Springsteen's experience in eastern-shore communities that had seen better days allowed him to understand and represent the world of millions of working-class and middle-class men and women who were bored, limited, and made desperate by the sameness and repetition of their jobs as factory workers or, as the 1970s wore on, by virulent deindustrialization and high rates of unemployment and inflation.[17] No less important, because he had experienced his own moment of transcendence of boredom ("I was dead until I was thirteen," he said) through the guitar and rock-and-roll, he was able to use his own reawakening to imagine and to explain how others might confront the demons of despair.[18]

Springsteen explored these issues in four albums released in the 1970s: *Greetings from Asbury Park, New Jersey* and *The Wild, The Innocent and the E Street Shuffle* (both 1973); *Born to Run* (1975); and *Darkness on the Edge of Town* (1978). In classic existential fashion, the characters in his songs confront and measure the hopelessness of their lives, the crushing sameness of their work, the improbability of change or success; a few contemplate death and even suicide. Yet despite the odds against them, they have the courage to believe in the possibilities of redemption and transcendence. That is, in classic existential fashion, they refuse to accept life's "sentence," or, having accepted it, they refuse to be governed by its terms. Even so, Springsteen's space of hope and passion and faith is a remarkably limited one, set apart from the workplace and even the family, accessible only at night and only on the "back-streets," where the speed and power of a 1969 Chevy and the passionate embrace of lovers might yield a moment of ecstatic escape or a glimpse of a different future.

Although the tension between limits and possibilities was a hallmark of Springsteen's work in the 1970s, the balance between the two was not always the same. "Show a little faith, there's magic in the night," he sings on the 1975 release "Thunder Road"; it may be a "town full of losers," he concludes, but he's "pulling out of here to win." In contrast, *Darkness on the Edge of Town,* released months before Carter's address and in a less hospitable economic climate, presents fewer options. The hot rods and fast cars are still present, but the prospects of the "backstreets" have been replaced by bleaker scenarios scripted in the "darkness on the edge of town." In *Darkness,* Springsteen emphasizes the burden of the working life; the way in which that burden and the limits of social class that it imposes are transferred from father to son; and a new, more "religious" (though not especially efficacious) language of sin, prayer, and apocalypse. Two of the pieces that deal with fast cars, "Something in the Night" and "Racing in the Street," are marked by funereal drumbeats.[19]

Although Springsteen, like Scott on the *Poseidon,* functions as something of an existential hero—showing the unbelieving a way out, offering the defeated a way to understand their lives as meaningful—he was less confident in that role in 1978 than he had been only a few years earlier. Indeed, *Darkness* contains only one reference to heroes (there are three on *Born to Run*), and it is disconcerting: "In Candy's room, there are pictures of her heroes on the wall/But to get to Candy's room, you gotta walk the darkness of Candy's hall."[20] David Bowie's 1977 anthem "Heroes" is equally cautious about claiming too much for the heroic stance. The song was recorded in Berlin, Germany, a worldwide symbol of decadence that Bowie described as a "city made up of bars for sad, disillusioned people to get drunk in." Explanations for the song's lyrics vary, but it seems clear that the piece deals with a moment Bowie had witnessed: two lovers, standing at the wall that divided East from West Berlin, beneath a tower manned by armed soldiers, contemplating the meaning of the structure for their relationship and for themselves as human beings. Although the song's refrain, "We can be heroes/Just for one day," can be read as an affirmation of the possibilities of the heroic, its bleak, plaintive tone and repetitive chord structure and backbeat contain and make ironic the heroic impulse. "Maybe," Bowie suggested to an American reporter, "[the lovers] felt guilty about their affair and were drawn to the spot for that reason, to cause the affair to be an act of heroism. It seemed a very 70's incident and their personal survival by self-rule—that's my only positive thought on society today." The use of lines that suggest a permanent resolution—"we can beat them forever and ever" and "we can meet there forever and ever"—might even be read as a suggestion that the act of heroism being contemplated is, indeed, suicide.[21]

At least some of Springsteen's followers, and some of the *Poseidon's* passengers, could be saved; that is, they somehow are made to appreciate the value of existence and are brought back to life. This is not so with the zombie—the soulless "living dead" of George Romero's zombie trilogy of *Night of the Living Dead* (1968), *Dawn of the Dead* (1978), and *Day of the Dead* (1985)—who roams the landscape, gnawing on the remaining living, utterly beyond the therapeutic. Although the genre dates to 1932 and the appearance of *White Zombie*, its heyday began in the mid-1960s with *Plague of the Zombies* (1964) and *War of the Zombies* (1965) and continues through the late 1980s and early 1990s, when the subject was presented in camp films such as *Hardrock Zombies* (1988) and *My Boyfriend's Back* (1993).[22]

The opening scene in the critically acclaimed *Night of the Living Dead*—perhaps the most famous scene in all of zombie film—offers some clues about the meaning of the zombie and of zombie films. Barbra and Johnny, brother and sister, have driven for three hours from Pittsburgh to a rural hilltop cemetery to put a cross and flowers on their father's grave. While Barbra approaches the task with what is understood to be an appropriate sense of obligation and respect, Johnny's appearance and rhetoric suggest that he is unable to understand or appreciate the sacred. His thick glasses imply not only a myopic inability to "see," to understand, but also an excessive, calculating, utilitarian rationalism, confirmed by the pens and pencils in his shirt pocket and his incessant complaining about the length of the trip, its purpose, and the cost of the "little cross" that must be purchased anew each year from the cemetery. His driving gloves—an unnecessary yet intentional layer between his hands and the steering wheel—suggest a man removed and insulated from the sensations of his world.

Worse still, Johnny lives in his selfish present, dismissive of the past and its claims (Carter had admonished that "just as we are losing our confidence in the future, we are also beginning to close the door on our past"). He has forgotten his father. "We still remember," Johnny says sarcastically, as he reads from a small cross he and Barbra are to place on the grave. "I don't. You know, I don't even remember what the man looks like." As Barbra tends to the gravesite, Johnny's impatience spills over into a sharp critique of religious ritual. "Hey, come on Barb, church was this morning, huh? I mean, praying's for church, huh? Not much sense in my going to church." As Johnny observes a figure walking toward them—a zombie, as it turns out—Johnny's mocking tone reveals his dismissal of the mysterious: "They're coming to get you, Barbra." Nor is Johnny the only one lacking a sense of the sacred. Later, when the crisis has taken on a public character, an expert, interviewed by television, says, "The bodies [of those recently killed by the zombies] must be . . . burned . . . immediately. The bereaved will have to forego the dubious comforts that a funeral service will give. They're just dead flesh."[23]

And what are the zombies? What sorts of anxieties and fears do they represent? Above all else, perhaps, the zombie is an ugly reminder that we are all the living dead, all living persons in the process of becoming "just dead flesh." Ben, the movie's protagonist, valiantly tries to save himself and others from the zombie attack on the farmhouse in which the "survivors" have taken refuge. However, in the end, when Ben's body is placed on the pile of corpses to be burned, "he does not," as film scholar Gregory Waller observes, "look much different from the other corpses; the dead are the undead." And even the sheriff's men have the sunken eyes and corpselike look of the living dead.[24] Barbra and Johnny embody different strategies for dealing with that knowledge—religious ritual on the one hand, denial on the other—but neither strategy is of much use in keeping the knowledge of one's finiteness from rising to the surface.[25] In that context, the prominence of the zombie marked by the Romero trilogy signifies just how difficult it had become to hide humanity's dirty secret.

Writing in 1965, when the zombie phenomenon was in its infancy, Susan Sontag described the qualities of "emotionlessness, of impersonality, of regimentation" that characterized the alien, "zombie-like" invaders common to science-fiction films of the 1950s and early 1960s.[26] The moblike, undisciplined zombies of Romero's films could hardly be described as threatening "regimentation"—perhaps reflecting the easing of the standard cold-war tensions in the 1960s and 1970s. Indeed, early scenes in *Dawn of the Dead* work visually to conflate zombies with African Americans and Puerto Ricans, but the other qualities Sontag mentioned—emotionlessness, and impersonality—are carried over and emphasized in the figure of the zombie.[27]

This emotionlessness is referenced in a variety of ways. In the opening scene of *Dawn of the Dead*, the zombie is equated with, and comes to represent, the unsympathetic "rational" scientist, who rants, "If we'd dealt with this phenomenon properly, without emotion, without emotion [the phrase is repeated in the original], it wouldn't have come to this." Science, understood as reason carried to an absurd conclusion, is again pilloried later in the film when a scientist uses television to suggest the (racist) idea of ending the zombie threat by dropping nuclear bombs on all the big cities. "We've got to remain rational," he adds, "logical, logical [more repetition]—it's that or the end." Later, when the zombies invade a large shopping mall, that same emotionlessness is described as akin to some sort of thoughtless, knee-jerk "instinct." One of the characters, Stephen, explains their presence: "[They're doing] what they used to do. This was an important place in their lives." Inside the mall, the presence of Muzak and intercut shots of zombies and store mannequins emphasize the zombie's lack of "human" agency.

Bereft of a meaningful past and a future that went beyond the programmed quest for human flesh, the zombie might be understood as the ideal postmodern subject, trapped in a shallow, media present. Unlike Klaatu, the hyperrational alien of *The Day the Earth Stood Still* (1951) who actually comes from somewhere and bears a message he hopes to share with the backward earthlings, the zombie (at least the zombie of the 1960s and 1970s) is a placeless, history-less creature. Indeed, the zombies of *Night of Living Dead* originate from an idiosyncratic event: radiation from a space probe activates the brains of people who are dead but not yet buried. *Dawn of the Dead* does better, grounding that film's zombies in Trinidadian Mokumbo (Voodoo). "When there's no more room in hell," says one of the protagonists, Peter, "the dead will walk the earth." But neither film grants the zombie any thoughtful relationship to a motivating past or an imagined future, perhaps because the creature is so closely identified with "us." "They're us, that's all," confirms Peter. "There's no more room in hell."

The figure of the zombie might also be understood as a comment on the nature of humanity, a subject very much at issue in the late 1960s and 1970s. In what Kenan Malik presents as the modern struggle between evolutionary psychology and cognitive science to define that nature, the zombie represents the idea—and the threat, one should add—of humanity understood as a being lacking consciousness (prefiguring the cyborg). This conception of humanity is far removed from an alternative, humanistic vision that emphasizes man's evolution into a higher animal of remarkable imaginative and creative talents. Although Malik insists that the zombie he describes is not the "living dead" of horror films, his definition of the zombie as a "human being who seems perfectly natural, normal and alert but is in reality not conscious at all, but is rather some sort of automaton" invokes the near absence of consciousness that all Romero's zombies possess. The zombies of *Night of the Living Dead* and *Dawn of the Living Dead* lack the attributes of consciousness, including self-awareness, language, and the social awareness that one's existence is defined by a community of others. They arrive at the mall but without consciousness of why they have come or what they might do there. And they show no emotion, because to do so would betray an inner existence they do not possess.[28] Lacking emotion and affect, living and dead, locked in a present bereft of past and future, consumed with hunger to the point of cannibalism, driven by the most primitive instincts of survival—the list of zombie characteristics bears an eerie resemblance to the Jewish victims of the Nazi concentration camps.

By about 1970, the idea of survival, so prominent in the zombie films and central to most accounts of the Holocaust, was emerging as an important cultural concept, articulating the sense that many Americans had that they were survivors of one disaster or another—even, one might say, the sense that they were living through a disastrous era that defined life as survivorship. A search of one university's computer catalog for references to "survivors" reveals an average of 1.3 references per year between 1946 and 1964; 4.2 between 1965 and 1969; 11.7 for the 1970s; and 22.6 for the 1980s. The PsychLIT database for 1974–1990 lists 246 articles under the term "survival," with incest, the Holocaust, suicide, child molestation, cancer, the Vietnam War, and the 1972 Buffalo Creek (West Virginia) flood heading the list of problems and events most often presented as requiring a survival stance or inducing a survival mentality.[29]

As Christopher Lasch pointed out in his treatment of the phenomenon in *The Minimal Self* (1984), the language of survival was everywhere in the 1970s, describing and labeling problems as disparate as the coming apocalypse and the need to "survive" final exams or as different as the survival of lung cancer and Gloria Gaynor's exuberant "I Will Survive" (1979), a feminist anthem featuring a woman frightened at the prospect of living without her companion but also courageously committed to making a go of it. According to Lasch, one result of the proliferation of ideas of survival was to trivialize the concept itself and hence to encourage a curious indifference to genuine crises—an indifference akin, perhaps, to what Carter found when he tried to rally Americans to a solution to the energy "crisis" of the late 1970s.[30] For Lasch, that indifference or sense of helplessness derived from the unfortunate tendency, apparent from the mid-1960s onward, to generalize from the Holocaust to the ordinary events of everyday life, with Auschwitz as the "consummate mythology of victimization and survival." Without denying the horrors of the Holocaust—without denying, even, that it had profoundly shaped the perception of the species and its potential for doing harm—Lasch implied that Americans in the 1970s would have been better off had they eschewed the Holocaust metaphor for a more sensible system for evaluating life's problems, both minor and serious.[31] Had they done so, one is left to imagine, energy might have been more easily understood as a problem amenable to ordinary politics, and Carter might have been signing a bill into law rather than lamenting the failure of the national will.

Whatever its origins and impact, the idea of survival proved compelling and useful for 1970s Americans in their efforts to locate and fix a guide to moral conduct. Although Holocaust texts such as Lina Wertmuller's concentration-camp film *Seven Beauties* (1976) served that purpose admirably, so did texts that had no apparent relationship to the Holocaust or no relationship to it at all. Consider, for example, *The Towering Inferno*, a 1974 film featuring a 140-story building—the world's tallest—that goes up in smoke and flames, killing more than one hundred people. Among those who share some responsibility for the tragedy are Doug Roberts (Paul Newman), the building's architect, who lacks the necessary concentration on the project and fails to seek the guidance of practical firefighters in how a safe tower might be built; Jim Duncan (William Holden), whose company, Duncan Enterprises ("We Build for Life"), builds the tower with cheap circuit breakers that fail; and Roger Simmons (Richard Chamberlain), Duncan's son-in-law and an employee of Duncan Enterprises, who takes money in exchange for allowing slipshod work. If the film has a central metaphoric referent, it is the Vietnam War rather than the Holocaust. Led by Chief O'Hallorhan (Steve McQueen), the firefighters function as Vietnam grunts, battling a blaze that would not have happened had the best and the brightest done their jobs. The helicopter is a basic image, at first as a symbol of transcendence as Roberts scouts the coast for a retreat from the city and its perils, then, when a helicopter crashes on the roof of the burning building, as a symbol of failed rescue technology with echoes of Vietnam. Body bags and the term "body count" complete the Vietnam imagery.

Simmons's guilt is confirmed and fused with the film's treatment of survival when the fire traps him and many other guests at the building's grand-opening celebration in a vast lounge on the 135th floor. Because the fire has cut off escape and rescue from the floors below, rescue by a complex and time-consuming "chair" utilizing two nearby buildings is the remaining hope. To determine the order of rescue (with women and children first), the guests draw numbers. When it becomes clear that many will die before they can be evacuated, Simmons tears up his number and insists that he and two others will be the next to ride the chair and escape. Marked by this effort as a man who values survival too much, Simmons fights his way to the chair, only to die in the latest of the explosions to rock the building. Duncan achieves partial redemption for his efforts to stop Simmons from violating the rescue queue and especially for announcing that he and Simmons will be the last to leave the building (that is, for saying that he will refuse to value his own survival over that of others). The film also privileges the position of the firefighters, who are understood, in the Christian rhetoric that opens the film, "to have given their lives so that others might live," that is, to have purposefully and knowingly risked their own lives for others.

For perhaps most Americans, surviving the 1970s meant hunkering down to somehow cope with waves of factory closings, skyrocketing gasoline prices and home heating bills, a stagnant stock market (for the few who had something invested in it), and rising rates of divorce and single parenting. In the popular culture of the era, the most attractive figures—one is tempted to call them "heroes," but they do not reach that stature—were ordinary folk with ordinary jobs who came to learn that the good life required more than getting by. This was true of Bruce Springsteen's protagonists, whose daily labors purchase nighttime transcendence ("And somehow you survive/ Till the night," he sings). Hollywood's equivalent can be found in Tony Manero and Bud Davis, the rather unremarkable characters played by John Travolta in *Saturday Night Fever* (1977) and *Urban Cowboy* (1980). Like their Springsteen counterparts, Manero and Davis work by day for a modicum of nighttime glory, playing the game of survival while cautiously exploring a netherworld of moderate risk.

As a meditation on the theme of survival, *Saturday Night Fever* offers three settings, each representing a stance on the idea of survival. At one end of the spectrum is Bay Ridge, a working-class community in Brooklyn where Tony clerks in a paint store, cavorts with his Italian buddies, and lives with his unhappy parents. At the other end is the space beneath the Brooklyn Bridge, where Tony "daydreams" about what it might be like to go for the brass ring in the big city across the East River, where his ambitious, working-class girlfriend Stephanie (Karen Lynn Gorney) is employed. In the middle is the colorful, magical, and sometimes troubling world of 2001 Odyssey, a 1970s-style discotheque where Tony dances in the film's most memorable scenes.

The first two of these spaces are spaces of survival. Bay Ridge is survival as security, or so it seems. Tony has friends, a community of people who know him, evenings at the disco, a local girl full of adoration, and a tolerable job that he seems not to dislike and that appears to offer the prospect of "a future" should he give himself to ten or twenty years selling paint. Yet problems abound. His father is out of work, suddenly unemployed after twenty-five years in construction; the family members yell and hit each other at the dinner table. Tony often seems ill at ease with his friends, who relish pack sex and revenge rumbles and appear to have given up on life. And he does not reciprocate Annette's (Donna Pescow) affection. In short, the best that Bay Ridge has to offer is the possible security that comes from keeping one's nose to the grindstone, and to get to it Tony will have to wade through layers of dysfunctional kin and companions.

In an early scene with his boss, Tony rejects this form of survival. It is Friday, and Tony asks for a salary advance so he can buy a shirt for that evening's disco activities. Their conversation pits Tony's presentism against his employer's advocacy of planning for the future:

BOSS: You can save a little, build a future [by getting paid on Monday].
TONY: Fuck the future!
BOSS: No, Tony. You can't fuck the future. The future fucks you. It catches up with you, and it fucks you if you ain't planned for it.

For Tony's boss, the future is a source of concern and anxiety, something from which one must protect oneself; security is everything, survival is the only goal. For Tony, whose heroes are strong and aggressive risk takers—Farah Fawcett Majors (of the television series *Charlie's Angels* and the most widely admired media figure of the late 1970s),[32] the mythic Rocky, Al Pacino, Bruce Lee—mere survival is not enough.

In the film's narrative, the discotheque occupies a transitional position between the unsavory survival of Bay Ridge and the challenge of a new life in Manhattan. Unlike the paint store, the disco is in part a highly competitive space, where one's skills are compared with those of others, and where one's style and technique are subject to scrutiny. There are dance contests with money at stake. Like Manhattan, it is a space where one can win or lose. Tony understands this aspect of the disco; he practices as if he were studying for the bar exam or preparing for a meeting with a business client. "If you're not gonna take this seriously," he says to his partner Annette, "I don't wanna dance." Yet for Tony the disco is also something of a womb, interior and sheltering, glowing with warmth, a stage for his obvious talents, a projection, perhaps, of his deep need for security and acceptance—all in all, a space of narcissistic survival. On the dance floor—especially in the film's first big dance scene—there is unity and grace, order and discipline, line and flow, men and women united in dance. In this aspect, the disco is less about competition than the harmony that comes when everything is right. "The high I get at 2001 is just dancing," Tony tells Stephanie. "It's not being the best or nothin' like that. The thing is, I would like to get that high someplace else in my life."

The disco's zone of comfort and protection is disrupted in the second major dance scene, the dance contest, when Tony, observing the skills of a Hispanic couple, realizes that his victory in the competition has more to do with popularity and the disco's mostly Italian patrons than with ability. "If spics are good," Tony comments, "they deserve [to win]." Significantly, his revelation takes place over the film's blockbuster hit, the Bee Gees' survival anthem "Stayin' Alive," which we have not heard since the opening credits when Tony struts through the neighborhood with a can of paint, ogling the girls. The words underscore the disco-as-survival perspective:

> Got the wings of heaven on my shoes
> I'm a dancin' man and I just can't lose
> You know it's all right, it's OK
> I'll live to see another day[33]

Used in this negative context, the song suggests that Tony now understands what survival in Bay Ridge will mean: Italians will survive at the expense of Puerto Ricans, men at the expense of women, and that the disco is insufficient compensation. It is not all right, and it is not enough to live to see another day.

This revelation reflects Tony's migration from one set of values and positions to another: from ethnicity to universalism, from working class to middle class, from a corrupt survival to merit, and, in the film's narrative trajectory, from Bay Ridge to the beneath-the-bridge daydreams that project him outward. At the film's end, Tony is with Stephanie in a trendy apartment in Manhattan, where one imagines that he will encounter a meritocracy he can handle, achieve the success he presumably wants, and find happiness with the upwardly mobile Stephanie. But this Hollywood ending lacks credibility; we have heard too little of Tony's daydreams and have seen too little of Manhattan to believe that he would choose to live there or enjoy life as, say, a stockbroker. The film's heart, and what is true about Tony, is in the warmth and flow of that first disco scene, where we learn how he—and thousands of other guys like him—survived the 1970s.

The Towering Inferno assumes that everyone wants to survive, and even that some value life too much, but other accounts located and relished situations in which the choice of life appeared remarkable. One such story involved the crash of a Fairchild F-227 on October 13, 1972, in the cold and snow of the Andes Mountains, with forty-five persons on board, many of them members of the Uruguayan rugby team. When rescuers located the plane's fuselage ten weeks later, it became clear that the sixteen survivors had quickly run out of food and, after some soul searching, had taken to eating the well-preserved bodies of the dead. "No one suggested that God might want them to choose to die," wrote Piers Paul Read in his best-selling account of the ordeal, *Alive* (1974). "They all believed that virtue lay in survival and that eating their dead friends would in no way endanger their souls, but it was one thing to decide and another to act." The reviews on the book's cover suggest the lesson that many readers no doubt took from the story. The *Detroit Free Press,* insisting that a genuine choice had been made, called the episode a "testimonial to the durability and determination of young men who might have chosen to die and simply would not." The *New Republic* opined, "There is no way of reading *Alive* without a heightened sense of one's own life and its value"—as if life and its value were a murky issue, as yet unsettled.[34] The sentiments are familiar, reprising Scott's call to life on the *Poseidon,* Ben's efforts to save a frightened and confused humanity in *Night of the Living Dead,* and the decision of Stephen, Fran, and Peter in *Dawn of the Dead* to choose life over a comfortable but purposeless "slow death" inside the mall.[35]

The basic concept seemed clear enough: value life but not to excess. However, amid the complex of ideas about life that swirled through the decade, another idea loomed large. Those who survived, whether by chance or deep commitment to life, might have regrets about being alive when others were not. Known as survival guilt, this perverse concept, which seemed designed only to punish the fortunate, has been appropriately contextualized by Lasch as an aspect of the intense debates over the impact of the Holocaust that absorbed Bruno Bettelheim, Viktor Frankl, Terrence Des Pres, Robert J. Lifton, and other Holocaust scholars in the 1960s and 1970s.[36] Yet it was not so much the Holocaust that elevated survivor guilt to prominence at this moment, though the emergence of that event was undoubtedly significant. Rather, the qualities demanded of a Holocaust survivor—especially the extreme repression of emotion, resulting in a paralysis of the will—were those that President Carter had identified as troubling in his 1979 address, precisely because Americans had found them so useful. Told and retold in the 1970s, the survivor-guilt story was a story about emotional repression and its therapeutic release.[37]

Among its best-known retellings is the story of the Incredible Hulk—first a Marvel Comics character, then the subject of a 1977 feature film, and, from 1978 through 1982, a popular television series.[38] The film version opens with a long montage of childless, domestic bliss and introduces Dr. David Banner (Bill Bixby), who is a research scientist, and Laura, his wife. A car accident intervenes, trapping Laura inside the burning vehicle. David, thrown free but unable to open the door to save Laura's life, screams his frustration. Later, at the Culver Institute, he joins with fellow scientist Elaine Marx (Susan Sullivan) in an effort to ascertain why some people are able to summon a "reserve of human strength" that normally goes unused. They conduct a series of interviews with ordinary people who had accomplished extraordinary things—a man who battered down a fire door; a Vietnam veteran who saved a friend despite being hit by seventeen bullets; an earthquake victim, trapped in her home and smelling gas (and reminded of her parents' death in the Holocaust), who found the strength to free herself—all of them, David concludes, sharing "extreme emotional commitment," and all of them, he finds, sharing a DNA deviation triggered by high levels of gamma-ray radiation. A self-administered dose of radiation allows his frustration to vent itself in anger. A flat tire on a dark, rainy night (a moment when men are supposed to act like men) provides the spark. He cracks and is transformed into the Hulk (Lou Ferrigno)—the primordial beast, to be sure, and hence capable of that "extreme emotional commitment" that will save lives and help others survive but who is also, somehow, inexplicably, in control. A second fire, this one at the lab with Elaine trapped inside, again brings forth the Hulk, who pulls Elaine from the blaze, only to have her die in his arms. Twice abandoned, both times by women who had ministered to his needs (the second one coded by pants and occupation as something of a feminist), David emerges as a signifier of the abandoned and damaged male survivor of the 1970s, now freed to express his resentment and to feel good doing it.[39]

The crisis of the spirit that hung over the 1970s had no single solution or easy resolution; indeed, it had no resolution at all, because its source ran deeper than energy dependence, stagflation, the Iran hostage crisis, or the nation's deteriorating industrial plant. Its source even ran deeper than the unseemly events of Watergate, the national humiliation in Vietnam, or the sense (for some, at least) that the epochal moment of the 1960s, when all things seemed possible, had come and gone. The earthquake that flips the *Poseidon* and reveals its passengers to be in existential despair is itself the product of forces of long gestation: a religious declension, captured by the slogan "God is dead"[40]; a revolution in genetics that threatened the autonomy of the self and the efficacy of the social environment[41]; the continued popularity of behaviorist psychology, with all that implied for what Skinner called "freedom and dignity"; memories of the Holocaust, seeping into consciousness; the postmodern turn, calling into question the possibility of knowing the truth[42]; and boredom, that complex amalgam of the affluent, leisured society and existential doubt.

To struggle against this matrix of ideas was to tilt with windmills, but Americans made the effort. In the search for absolutes, they mounted a fundamentalist religious revival, made abortion a moral touchstone, and mocked the intellectuals of postmodernism. Americans sought out and valued experiences that could take one beyond boredom, or least beyond the look of boredom (i.e., the zombie's trance). Hence, the Incredible Hulk advocates and takes pleasure in the cathartic expression of anger, Reverend Scott bullies and shouts, Tony Manero finds momentary bliss in the pulse and flow of the disco, and *Altered States* offers a critique of Faustian rationalism and revels in the idea of human salvation through contact with the primordial and the primitive. Skinnerian psychology and genetic engineering—the most threatening of social-scientific and scientific developments—were the objects of vitriolic attack through the decade.[43] Eventually, elements of an unwelcome history would be rewritten, recasting the idealism of the 1960s as drug-induced disorder and, in the Rambo films of the 1980s, reinterpreting the defeat in Vietnam as a conspiracy against the common soldier. By far, the most widespread and public effort to deal with the psychic withdrawal of the 1970s was to probe the decline of the hero and to imagine how heroism might be revived, reconstituted, and reinvigorated.[44] Holden's Duncan, Hurt's Jessup, Travolta's Manero, Ferrigno's Hulk, the flesh-eating survivors of the Andes plane crash, Springsteen, Bowie, and even Jimmy Carter were all part of that act of imagining, of that willful effort to fashion a hero that could take the measure of humanity's despair and, in the words of Reverend Scott, find "the way out."

Notes

1. *New York Times,* July 16, 1979; reprinted in *A History of Our Time: Readings on Postwar America,* 4th ed., ed. William H. Chafe and Harvard Sitkoff (New York: Oxford University Press, 1995), 435–440.

2. See Alastair Hannay, *Kierkegaard* (London: Routledge and Kegan Paul, 1982), 97–101.

3. B. F. Skinner, *Beyond Freedom and Dignity* (New York: Knopf, 1971); Christopher Lasch, *The Culture of Narcissism: American Life in an Age of Diminishing Expectations* (New York: Norton, 1978).

4. *The Poseidon Adventure* (Twentieth-Century Fox, 1972).

5. For Mircea Eliade, every New Year is a moment of restoration and renewal, of "repetition of the mythical moment of the passage from chaos to cosmos" and, curiously, a moment that "permits the return of the dead to life." Mircea Eliade, "The Eternal Return," *Parabola* 13 (Summer 1988): 13. The essay was first published in 1949.

6. For a possible reading of the tree as the Cosmic Tree, whose climbing symbolizes one's ascension to heaven, see Mircea Eliade, "Nostalgic for Paradise: Symbolism of the Center and the Ritual Approach to Immortality," *Parabola* 1 (Winter 1976): 9–11.

7. In a comparison of the lyrics and "emotional tone" of popular songs from 1964, 1967, and 1971, Gary Burns gave the 1971 songs the label "dream is over," and he argued that only in that year did songs abandon hopeful themes for a message of despair, anger, and defeat. In 1964 and 1967, song lyrics were "unusually happy"; in 1971, they were "unusually unhappy." The 1971 artists include James Taylor, Joni Mitchell, Elton John, Cat Stevens, and Janis Joplin. Gary Burns, "Trends in Lyrics in the Annual Top Twenty Songs in the United States, 1963–1972," *Popular Music and Society* 9, no. 1 (1983): 25–39.

8. Robert Nisbet, "Boredom," *Commentary,* September 1982, 49 (Hamlet); Seán Desmond Healy, *Boredom, Self, and Culture* (London: Associated University Presses, 1984), 24–25, 27 (Dickens), 32 (Durkheim), 35 (Beckett); Peter T. Chew, "Ten Ways You Can Cheat Boredom," *Science Digest,* December 1972, 40–42; "Bores Meet for a Bit of Dull Fun," *New York Times,* July 18, 1979.

9. Theodore I. Rubin, "How to Fight Boredom," *Ladies' Home Journal,* January 1974, 36; Patrick Ryan, "There's No Such Thing as a Little Boredom," *Smithsonian,* July 1977, 104; Dr. Ann Frisch and Dianne Partie, "How to Know If You're

in a Rut and How to Get Out of It," *Mademoiselle*, May 1978, 204–205; Sam Keen, "Chasing the Blahs Away: Boredom and How to Beat It," *Psychology Today*, May 1977, 78–84; Estelle R. Ramey, "Boredom: The Most Prevalent American Disease," *Harper's*, November 1974, 12–22. The books include Healy, *Boredom, Self, and Culture* (1984); Orrin E. Klapp, *Overload and Boredom: Essays on the Quality of Life in the Information Society* (Westport, CT: Greenwood Press, 1986); and Patricia Meyer Spacks, *Boredom: A Literary History of a State of Mind* (Chicago: University of Chicago Press, 1995).

10. Nisbet, "Boredom," 48 ("enforced idleness"); Ramey, "Boredom," 20 ("primal hunger," "starving woman"), 22 ("total leisure"); Keen, "Chasing the Blahs," 78 ("survival needs"); Spacks, *Boredom*, 23 (pleasure).

11. Chafe and Sitkoff, *A History of Our Time*, 438.

12. Nisbet, "Boredom," 48; Healy, *Boredom, Self, and Culture*, 91–92, 113; Skinner, *Beyond Freedom and Dignity*.

13. Keen, "Chasing the Blahs," 84; Healy, *Boredom, Self, and Culture*, 28. On boredom's relationship to the emotions, see "Psychiatric Chore: Analyzing a Bore," *Newsweek*, May 3, 1982, 84; Rubin, "How to Fight Boredom"; Healy, *Boredom, Self, and Culture*, 49; and Keen, "Chasing the Blahs," 80.

14. Nisbet, "Boredom," 50; "Adventure: Into Outlaw Territory," *Harper's*, November 1974, 3. Donald Barthelme's short story "Subpoena" features a man who relies on a friend, Charles, to validate his stance of noninvolvement and aversion to risk. "Without Charles, without his example, his exemplary attitude, I run the risk of acting, the risk of risk. I must participate, I must leave the house and walk about." Donald Barthelme, *Sadness* (New York: Farrar, Straus, and Giroux, 1972), 116.

The disaster films of the 1970s include *Earthquake* (1972), *The Hindenburg* (1975), *The Big Bus* (1976), *Fire!* (1977 [TV]), *Avalanche* (1978), and *The Swarm* (1978). *Airplane!* came out in 1980. Daniel Lopez, *Films by Genre* (London: McFarland and Company, 1998), 75–76.

15. Nisbet, "Boredom," 50; Spacks, *Boredom*, 21.

16. D. M. Dooling, "Focus," *Parabola* 1 (Winter 1976): 2; Healy, *Boredom, Self, and Culture*, 63–64, 93, 98n76 (Joseph Campbell), 84 (on Mircea Eliade), 104. On Poseidon, God of the Sea, see Richard Carlyon, *A Guide to the Gods* (New York: William Morrow, 1982), 180–181; Jan Bremmer, "Poseidon," in *The Encyclopedia of Religion*, ed. Mircea Eliade (New York: Macmillan, 1987), 11:457–458; William Sherwood Fox, in *The Mythology of All Races*, ed. Louis Herbert Gray, vol. 1, *Greek and Roman* (New York: Cooper Square Publishers, 1964), 210–212.

17. Dave Marsh, *Born to Run: The Bruce Springsteen Story* (Garden City, NY: Doubleday, 1979), 12, 26, 44 (Springsteen on boredom).

18. Ibid., 16 ("dead"), 62.

19. Bruce Springsteen, "Thunder Road," on *Born to Run*, CBS CK 33795 (1975); Bruce Springsteen, "Factory," "The Promised Land" (fathers and sons), "Adam Raised a Cain" (fathers and sons), "Bandlands" (prayer), "Racing in the Street"

(sin), "Streets of Fire" (apocalypse), "Something in the Night" (funereal drum-beats), "Racing in the Street" (funereal drumbeats), all on *Darkness on the Edge of Town*, Columbia CK 35318 (1978).

20. Bruce Springsteen, "Candy's Room" (heroes), on *Darkness on the Edge of Town*.

21. The lyrics used here are from the single version of "Heroes" on *Best of Bowie*, EMI/Virgin 7243 5 41930 2 6 (2002). Bowie's comment on Berlin is from Robert Hilburn, "Which Way David Bowie?" *Los Angeles Times*, November 8, 1977, Internet version at www.up-to-date.com/bowie/heroes/latimes.html. Bowie's discussion of the song, and other views of its origins, are at www.up-to-date.com/bowie/heroes/heroes.html.

22. Lopez, *Films by Genre*, 391–392; Richard B. Armstrong and Mary Williams Armstrong, *The Movie List Book* (Cincinnati, OH: Betterway Books, 1994), 413.

23. Robert J. Lifton argues that the function of funeral ceremonies is to produce a rite of passage for the dead, at once honoring and embracing them and push-ing them away, speeding them "on their 'journey' to another 'plane of existence.' " With that in mind, Barbra and Johnny might be understood as, together, em-bodying that ambivalence. Robert J. Lifton, *Death in Life: Survivors of Hiroshima* (New York: Random House, 1967), 493.

24. Gregory Waller, *The Living and the Undead: From Stoker's* Dracula *to Romero's* Dawn of the Dead (Urbana: University of Illinois Press, 1986), 296.

25. The zombie also carries the meaning of death as a contagion. Lifton notes that many cultures, fearing the contagious dead, remove the near-dead to places of isolation. *Dawn of the Dead* contains this fear of the near-dead. See also David Chidester's description of the treatment given the contagious bodies returned from the 1978 Jonestown massacre, in *Salvation and Suicide: An Interpretation of Jim Jones, the Peoples Temple, and Jonestown* (Bloomington: Indiana University Press, 1988), 12–24.

26. Susan Sontag, "The Imagination of Disaster," in *Film Theory and Criticism: Introductory Readings*, 2nd ed., ed. Gerald Mast and Marshall Cohen (New York: Oxford University Press, 1979), 499. The essay was first published in *Against Interpretation* (1965).

27. Waller offers the suggestion that the living dead "are our version of what in the past was called the 'rabble.' " *Living and the Undead*, 278 (quotation), 279–280.

28. Kenan Malik, *Man, Beast and Zombie: What Science Can and Cannot Tell Us about Human Nature* (London: Weidenfeld and Nicholson, 2000), 13, 25, 219–220 (definition of zombie).

29. Author search of SUNY/Buffalo catalog (1996); PsychLIT database, CD-ROM version (a WinSPIRS database). On the Buffalo Creek flood that killed 125 persons, see Robert Jay Lifton and Eric Olson, "The Human Meaning of Total Disaster: The Buffalo Creek Experience," *Psychiatry* 1 (February 1976): 1–18.

30. Christopher Lasch, *The Minimal Self: Psychic Survival in Troubled Times* (New York: Norton, 1984), 60–64.

31. Lasch, *Minimal Self*, 112 ("consummate mythology").

32. See Denise Lowe, *Women and American Television: An Encyclopedia* (Santa Barbara, CA: ABC-CLIO, 1999), s.v. "Fawcett, Farah" (116) and *Charlie's Angels* (63); and "The Farah Factor," *Ladies' Home Journal,* June 1977, 34, 36, 38, 151.

33. http://display.lyrics.astraweb.com:2000/display.cgi?the_bee_gees..staying_alive..staying_alive.

34. Piers Paul Read, *Alive* (1974; New York: Avon Books, 1975), 78, cover.

35. Waller, *Living and the Undead,* 314, 315 ("slow death"), 320, 321.

36. Lasch, *Minimal Self,* 119–122; Robert J. Lifton, *Death in Life: Survivors of Hiroshima* (New York: Random House, 1967), 482–539.

37. On the theme of survivor guilt in 1980s Vietnam films, see William J. Palmer, *The Films of the Eighties* (Carbondale: Southern Illinois University Press, 1993), 87–102. See also Carol Zisowitz Stearns and Peter N. Stearns, *Anger: The Struggle for Emotional Control in America's History* (Chicago: University of Chicago Press, 1986), 200–214.

38. Vincent Terrace, *Fifty Years of Television: A Guide to Series and Plots, 1937–1988* (New York: Cornwall Books, 1991), 326–327.

39. *The Incredible Hulk* (1977; GoodTimes Home Video Corp., 1996). For *The Incredible Hulk* interpreted as an adolescent fantasy, see Timothy H. Wright, "Life on TV as Perceived from the Inside," *Christian Century* 96 (October 31, 1979): 1064–1065. The theme of repression and release is central to the Kenny Rogers song "Coward of the County" (1979).

A similar survivor-guilt story of emotional repression and release is told in the Judith Guest novel *Ordinary People* (1976) and the 1980 film version, which won the Academy Award for Best Picture. In the novel, Conrad Jarrett suffers from emotional withdrawal, triggered by the death of his brother in a boating accident that Conrad survived. In a trope more suited to the Freudian 1950s than the 1970s, a Jewish psychiatrist locates the problem and allows Conrad to get in touch with his feelings. Like David Banner in *The Incredible Hulk,* Conrad is victimized by a woman—in this case, his mother, an uptight supermom—suggesting the possibility of a gendered reading of some of these texts. Judith Guest, *Ordinary People* (New York: Viking Press, 1976); Trisha Curran, review of *Ordinary People* (movie), *Film in Review* 31 (November 1980): 565.

40. The death-of-God movement took its name from a 1961 book by Gabriel Valhanian. The idea captured the general public's attention in 1966, when *Time* featured the question, "Is God Dead?" on its cover in red letters on a solid black background—the first time that the magazine had run a cover with words only. George Alfred James, "Atheism," in *The Encyclopedia of Religion,* ed. Mircea Eliade (New York: Macmillan Publishing, 1987), 1:489–490; *Time,* April 8, 1966, cover, 21. See also Thomas W. Ogletree, *The Death of God Controversy* (New York: Abingdon Press, 1966); Billy Graham, Bernard Ramm, Vernon C. Grounds, and David Hubbard, *Is God "Dead"?* (symposium, Grand Rapids, MI: Zondervan Publishing, 1966); and John Warwick Montgomery, *The 'Is God Dead?' Controversy: A Philosophical-Theological Critique of the Death of God Movement* (Grand Rapids, MI: Zondervan Publishing, 1966), 22–39, 60–61.

41. The best analysis of the impact of genetics on recent American culture is Dorothy Nelkin and M. Susan Lindee, *The DNA Mystique: The Gene as a Cultural Icon* (New York: W. H. Freeman, 1995). See also "Intelligence: Genes or Environment?" *Intellect: The National Review of Professional Thought* 103 (April 1975): 422–423; Eugenia Keller, "Genetic Engineering—PANDORA's Box?" *Intellect* 106 (February 1978): 327–328; Jeremy Rifkin and Ted Howard, "Who Should Play God?" *The Progressive,* December 1977, 16–22; and Gene Bylinsky, "A New Power to Predict—and Prevent—Disease," *Fortune,* September 25, 1978, 108–110, 114–115.

42. J. David Hoeveler Jr., *The Postmodern Turn: American Thought and Culture in the 1970s* (New York: Twayne Publishers, 1996), 15–34.

43. For critiques of the perspective developed in Skinner's *Beyond Freedom and Dignity* (1971), see the Arnold Walter review in *Saturday Review,* October 9, 1971, 47–48, 52; Paul F. Boller Jr., "Conditional Man in a Behaviorist Universe," *Southwest Review* 57 (Winter 1972): 80–82; Peter Caws, "Psychology without a Psyche," *New Republic,* October 16, 1971, 32–34; Harold Kaplan, "Life in the Cage," *Commentary,* February 1972, 82–86; and Spencer Klaw, "B. F. Skinner's Brave New World," *Natural History,* January 1972, 81–86.

44. See, for example, Robert Penn Warren, "A Dearth of Heroes," *American Heritage,* October 1972, 4–7, 95–99; "Of War and Heroes," *Time,* June 14, 1971, 12; "The Vanishing American Hero," *U.S. News & World Report,* July 21, 1975, 16–18; William J. Bennett, "Let's Bring Back Heroes," *Reader's Digest,* December 1977, 91–94; "Where Have All Our Heroes Gone?" *Sr. Scholastic,* April 6, 1978, 15–16; and a special section on heroes in *Saturday Review,* December 1978.

8

Cutback

Skate and Punk at the Far End of the American Century

MICHAEL NEVIN WILLARD

In the late 1970s, Eric Boucher left his suburban Denver home, moved to northern California, changed his name, and started the punk-rock band the Dead Kennedys.[1] In their very name, the Dead Kennedys (like the Sex Pistols, with their 1977 antianthem "God Save the Queen") expressed an extreme disrespect for authority. Jello Biafra, Boucher's new name, bore a more complex relation to contemporary culture: "Jello" referred to a mass-marketed form of gelatin, an odorless, colorless, tasteless "food" with no nutritional value but a very high silliness factor in its fun-to-wiggle state; and "Biafra" referred to the short-lived African nation where a 1968 famine caused by the Nigeria-Biafra war (1966–1970) had produced unspeakable human tragedy. Jello Biafra was a shorthand combination of meaningless consumerism and overwhelming catastrophe, of banality and anger. What better way to symbolize the nihilism of the 1970s?

But more was happening in Eric Boucher's new name than a nihilistic rejection of the belief that one could make a difference. Nihilism was part of it, of course. But we tend to overplay that claim because we continue to see the 1970s as the betrayal of the 1960s, as the time when America lost its innocence, or faith, or passion. During the 1960s, the usual story goes, people came together to work for a better world. But by the 1970s, the fires that had fueled the movements for social change had burned out, and what remained was a core—and dangerous—belief in the primacy of individual freedom and personal fulfillment. Christopher Lasch attacked what he called "the culture of narcissism" in his 1979 best-seller, *The Culture of Narcissism: American Life in an Age of Diminishing Expectation.* Lasch blamed the monotonous rationalization and bureaucracy of modern life for the turn to a therapeutic culture focused on personal fulfillment and self-realization. "The atrophy of older traditions of self-help," he wrote, "has eroded everyday competence, in one area after another, and has made the individual dependent on the state, the corporation, and other bureaucracies."[2] The result, he claimed, was an "ironic detachment" and "asocial individualism" that pervaded American life and culture.[3]

Other historians have made similar, and persuasive, arguments that support Lasch's assessment of the late 1960s and 1970s.[4] Key to 1970s culture is this desire for personal fulfillment and self-realization, core values of a therapeutic "consciousness revolution" that reached from the pages of the *New York Times* to school curricula and even into Jello Biafra's oppositional subculture.[5] But critiques that portray the 1970s as intentionally apolitical because Americans retreated from mass-movement politics to personal and individual concerns are not sufficient. As a historical problem, the difficulty lies in figuring out how to take Seventies culture seriously.

Describing Seventies culture as apolitical is incorrect; it was immersed in conflict. If the culture seems anti- or nonpolitical to us now, it is because the 1970s were not only a decade in which Americans reacted against the 1960s, but because they were also a decade when Americans responded to major and difficult historical changes. During the 1970s, the system of political accountability and the administrative intervention in (and oversight of) the economic and social institutions that make industrial society possible were taken apart and reassembled: Before Nixon had betrayed the Constitution in his failed attempts to hide illegal actions from the American people, he had begun to dismantle the ability and responsibility of the federal government to foster and administer social change. Ford was perceived as entirely ineffectual. And Carter was sincere, but his sincerity seemed to undercut his presidential authority; he, too, had begun to explore and promote policies of economic deregulation. In different ways, all three presidents furthered the decline of industrial society and Americans' faith in the ability and willingness of government, whether federal or local, to implement any ameliorative reforms.

During the 1970s, major transformations in the American economy—transformations experienced simply as economic decline but now understood as the beginnings of a postindustrial economy—caused great upheaval and privation (economic, emotional, familial, and community) for millions of Americans. Industrial workers felt the cutback when American corporations disinvested from their manufacturing interests, diversified their activities away from basic industry, and reinvested in labor-intensive industries (e.g., textiles, apparel, electronics assembly) abroad.[6] American factories closed as a result, sending a shockwave through local and regional economies and devastating entire communities. The combined impact of a stagnant economy and rapid inflation—stagflation—reached into the middle class as well, contributing to a sense of frustration and hopelessness, especially among youth.

In 1976, Americans found collective expression for their frustrations in the character of Howard Beale, a disaffected news reporter in Paddy Chayefsky's screenplay *Network*. One evening, when Beale can no longer stand the meaningless information he must foist as news on the American public, he breaks from his newscast and, staring directly at the camera, issues a long tirade against all that is wrong with American society. Raving about economic decline, social chaos, consumerism, and the media itself, Beale ends his rant imploring his audience to "get up right now and go to the window, open it, and stick your head out, and yell, 'I'm as mad as hell, and I'm not going to take it anymore!'"[7] His tirade reveals the contradictions of a culture grappling with the transition from one social order to the next.

The pervasive banality one finds in 1970s culture—such as Jello Biafra's first name—might thus be explained as a recognition of the futility of electoral or even social movement politics; the pervasive anger of 1970s culture—reflected by Jello Biafra's last name—might be explained both as resentment that government (the state) is no longer representative and no longer serves the average American's interests and as hostility toward the forces of historical change (including multinational corporations and the pervasive, increasingly global mass media). Awareness of this shift from an industrial society to an information world became widespread in the 1970s.

If the conflicted sentiments found in Seventies culture—from Hollywood movies and mainstream television to countercultural punk rock—can be taken as evidence of the prevailing attitude toward society, they differ markedly from the predominately utopian opposition of Sixties counterculture, the mainstream optimism and conformity of postwar American culture, and the purposeful moral outrage used by mid-twentieth-century rights movements to demand institutional reforms through legislation. Rather than emphasizing politics, the culture of the decade reveals a pervasive belief that politics no longer work, coupled with a frustrated search for a mode of collective action that might replace politics. The culture of the 1970s is simultaneously defeatist and oppositional, banal (the oxymoronic leisure suit, the fad of pet rocks, or Jimmy Carter's less-than-presidential "aww-shucks" smile) and angry (suggested in the ritualized violence and defiance of danger in everything from disaster and horror movies to the fascination with daredevil motorcycle jumping to the lyrics, visual graphics, and performance style of punk-rock and heavy-metal music).[8] In this banal-angry culture of the late 1970s and early 1980s, situated in a moment of political mistrust and social-economic decline, a range of subcultures developed: the appropriate technology movement, networks of organic food production and distribution, and spectacular youth cultures such as heavy metal, disco, goth, rap, graffiti, break dancing, punk, and skateboarding.[9]

These subcultures, though in some ways built on the countercultures and youth cultures of the 1960s, were shaped by the conditions of an emerging postindustrial society during a time of political and economic decline. Late-Seventies subcultures, unlike the Sixties counterculture, rarely aspired to live completely outside modern society. Nor did they fully embrace an anticonsumerist ethic, unlike many of the bohemian and avant-garde cultural undergrounds of the first half of the twentieth century. Living in cities in economic decline, in which social-welfare provisions were inadequate, subcultures based in economic practices made both sense and cents. The subcultures of the Seventies developed as a logical way to interact with the material conditions of a postindustrial world. They did not absolutely oppose consumerism, nor did they try to create communities outside society. Precisely because they often emerged in postindustrial places that had already been abandoned or dismantled by politicians who sought to transform the state into a tool of business rather than of the people, they chose cultural ideals and socioeconomic practices that directly engaged—as well as critiqued—the problems of postindustrial life. Like previous countercultures, the new subcultures developed styles that emphasized cultural opposition. But they also formed "translocal" microeconomic communities of small-scale craft production and micromedia.[10]

This essay analyzes two related subcultures of the 1970s: skateboarding and punk rock. In these important subcultures I do not find Lasch's asocial individualism and narcissism or a nihilistic apolitical apathy. Those who identified themselves as skaters or punks were engaged in forms of social activity or cultural production, but they did not direct their attention to the political reform of the nation's society or institutions. Instead, they adopted both a belief in what came to be called "D-I-Y" (do it yourself) and an oppositional style fusing consumerist and anticonsumerist principles and embodying the complex combination of banality and anger that seemed to suffuse the larger society. Complicating 1970s tendencies toward ideals of self-realization and personal fulfillment is skaters' and punks' direct interaction with (as opposed to retreat from) the postindustrial conditions in which they lived.

My discussion of skate and punk centers around the subcultural careers of skater Tony Alva and punk performer Darby Crash. Alva and Crash are significant because they achieved their respective successes early in the history of skateboarding and punk rock, when each subculture was becoming distinct. Both men came from neglected places in Southern California where social and economic discontent were magnified. Rather than trying to transcend their psychological preconceptions, as therapeutic self-help programs asked their adherents to do, each called attention to his circumstances with a snarling "fuck you" attitude. Acting not by themselves, but as important figures who crystallized a widespread social ethos, Alva and Crash reconfigured youth rebellion to fit new world-historical circumstances, formulating strategies useful for living in an increasingly stateless, less political, more economic world.

❖ ❖ ❖

PAVE MEANT MOVE MEANT

Skaters by their very nature are urban guerillas: they make everyday use of the useless artifacts of the technological burden, and employ the handiwork of the government/corporate structure in a thousand ways that the original architects could never dream of.
—Craig Stecyk, 1976

SKATEBOARDER: *Do you like skating around cameras?*
TONY ALVA: *It's fun; you draw the lines and come really close, playing hit and miss with them. It's double timing, yours and the photographers. If they are fast, there's no problem; if they're slow, well (laughing) then you bang their heads. The good photographers don't really get in the way though.*
—Tony Alva, 1977

One need only watch *Dogtown and the Z-Boys,* the recent documentary about the early history of skateboarding, to see that the oppositional style of aggression and anger that has come to dominate skateboarders' cultural expressions began in Venice, California, in the mid-to-late 1970s. The *Dogtown* skaters' style was a response to the economic decline that turned the beach town into what Skip Engblom, one of the documentary's interviewees, calls a "seaside slum."[11] The documentary does not explain that Venice suffered from the repercussions of state-subsidized suburbanization—the start of the deindustrialization that would culminate during the 1970s. Beginning in the late 1940s and early 1950s, the federal government implemented programs that subsidized interstate highways and community-scale housing developments (such as Lakewood in south Los Angeles County or farther-flung communities in Orange County). This allowed homeowners to live greater distances from their jobs but still commute easily between home and work. Such funding priorities caused massive migration from central Los Angeles and left little money for urban-development priorities in older neighborhoods. Such shifts in urban development caused a shift in the Southern California tourist industry, as amusement followed suburbanization to Orange County when Disneyland opened in 1955, leading to the demise of the tourist economy at Venice Beach.[12] Amusement piers that had supplied customers for local retailers and restaurant owners began failing by the mid-1960s, and Los Angeles (of which Venice was a part) consistently overlooked residents' requests for improvements in infrastructure and education. The small beach town went into decline.[13]

The radical skateboard style developed by Jay Adams, Tony Alva, Shogo Kubo, Nathan Pratt, Stacy Peralta, Wentzl Ruml, Paul Constantineau, Bob Biniak, Allen Sarlo, Jim Muir, Chris Cahill, Peggy Oki, and others in collaboration with photographer Craig Stecyk, surfboard shaper Jeff Ho, and surf-shop owner Skip Engblom was a direct response to the economic demise visible in what they called Dogtown—the neighborhoods of South Santa Monica, Ocean Park, and Venice. These neighborhoods had already been similarly characterized. In 1965, KNXT News in Los Angeles produced a one-hour documentary titled *Appalachia by the Sea,* in which newsman Joseph Benti identified Venice as a "pocket of poverty . . . with congested and dilapidated housing; a population with one-third of the families earning less than four thousand dollars . . . [and] two thousand families receiving public assistance; illiteracy and a high rate of school dropouts; crime and juvenile delinquency."[14] Such decline reached its nadir during the late 1960s and early

1970s. In *Dogtown and the Z-Boys,* Engblom explains Dogtown skaters' aggressive style as a response to the economic decline of their neighborhoods: "Because of the financial insecurity of the area, people looked at this [skateboarding and surfing] and went, 'Man I gotta make it *now.'* "[15] Rather than make it by escaping, Dogtown skaters made it by directly engaging their surroundings.

LINES OF FLIGHT, GROUNDS FOR OPPOSITION

When skateboarders talk about what they do, they often talk about drawing lines. Tony Alva was known for the lines he drew on concrete and, so to speak, in the sand. According to lore, upon receiving his five-hundred-dollar paycheck for winning an event at the 1975 Hang Ten World Pro/Am Skateboard Championships, Alva issued a one-liner, "Take the money and run, son!" and promptly departed for Hawaii.[16] Whether his statement is a legend—promoted in a magazine article by skateboarding's first scene maker, artist-photographer-writer Craig Stecyk—or a fact, it is a declaration of principles and a straightening of priorities, a calculated punch line that outlines the oppositional cultural style and D-I-Y work ethic of this local group of skaters.

Craig Stecyk's 1976 article "Fisheyed Freaks and Long Dogs with Short Tales," in which Alva's statement appears, shows aspects of the style and D-I-Y ethic of the emergent skateboarding subculture that distinguish it as an example of Seventies subcultural formation. The article features several Dogtown skaters in a series of quasi-nonfiction vignettes, each of which offers a variation on the theme of getting paid. In the first, Nathan Pratt and his "manager," Skip Engblom, convince movie executives at Universal Studios to pay them for the right to film Pratt riding his skateboard off a roof. Engblom stipulates that the roof must be at least twelve-feet high and that they will be paid more than three hundred dollars per foot. After Pratt completes the stunt, he and Engblom laugh like hell as they ride home in the limousine provided by the studio. Engblom takes his share of their score to the racetrack and Pratt takes his share to "the tropics."[17]

Another vignette focuses on Stacy Peralta. Only eight months after entering his first contest "on a lark," and already one of the best freestyle skateboarders in the world, Peralta quits competing, drops out of college, accepts an invitation for an "all expenses paid" trip to Australia to put on exhibitions, and takes "the next flight out" of town. In the final sketch, Stecyk recounts a " 'non-contest' contest," a downhill race for one thousand dollars in which the winner takes all but has to spend the money on a postrace party for all the contestants. Stecyk concludes the piece by considering the advantages of making up the rules on the fly: "By holding it [the race] themselves, they sidestepped the tremendous amount of red tape and financial, legal, organizational, insurance, supervisory and other hassles inherent to the 'official' contest situation. . . . [I]f organized contests, per se, don't measure up to your dictates . . . who needs them? Just hold your own. Gather up your friends and equipment, venture up into the hills, put your money down and get on it."[18]

Tony Alva goes to Hawaii. Skip Engblom goes to the track. Nathan Pratt goes to the tropics. Stacy Peralta goes to Australia. Hawaii, the tropics, and Australia are more fulfilling than the "Establishment" (to use a Sixties word), which, in this case, is competitive, professional skateboarding. With its consistent theme of escape to nature, Stecyk's vignettes can be read as a classic statement of Sixties countercultural ideals: nature as the place (real or metaphorical) where rejecting materialism and consumerism becomes possible. But none of the skaters in Stecyk's article reject materialism: all of them take the money and run.

One could also regard Stecyk's portrayals of skateboarders interested in their own pleasure and success as confirming the mass sentiment that Christopher Lasch would define as narcissism. However, Stecyk emphasizes a group ethos. His final vignette about the noncontest contest emphasizes not simply individual skill but shared financial success. Stecyk and the Dogtown skaters champion informal organization, custom, and tradition, in which fame is found in local lore, not mass-media publicity. Stecyk's portrayals of skaters who reject competition, commercialism, and the mass media are an affirmation of an early form of D-I-Y: local control and the promotion of a subcultural competitive ethic of mutually recognized prowess of the moment.

When Stecyk's "Fisheyed Freaks" appeared in *Skateboarder* magazine in June 1976, not all skateboarders shared the aggressive ethic he promoted. Editors, writers, advertisers, photographers, and skateboarders sought appropriate ways of defining an activity that amounted to an anomalous combination of physical performance and artistic expression. From 1975 to 1978, the pages of *Skateboarder* revealed their search for metaphors. Advertisements and articles made comparisons with other physical activities and sports, such as surfing, skiing, ice skating, auto racing, ballet, gymnastics, track-and-field high jumping, and ice hockey. But the articles, advertising copy, graphics and design, photos, and physical movements also drew both upon Sixties countercultural ideals of nature and upon Seventies ideals of self-liberation and statements of extreme aggression. By the end of the 1970s, however, the extreme aggression of Dogtown skaters like Tony Alva and Jay Adams would become the dominant imagery and social ethos that defined skateboarding not just a mere sport, but as an oppositional subculture.

Editors select magazine cover photos for their drama and spectacle, and as such the photos project concentrated, culturally constructed meanings. Serving as the subculture's public face and designed to attract new believers, skateboarding cover photos have less to do with their informational content than with social meanings. In 1975 and 1976, *Skateboarder* magazine covers featured skaters riding swimming pools. They showed young men with flowing locks, some riding barefoot, arms outstretched in metaphors of flight, but inwardly engrossed in personal explorations and soulful emulation of surf maneuvers, performing for magazine readers the abstract ideals of freedom and nature. Photographers reinforced such performed meanings by shooting from below, most often framing skaters in vertical terrain, within the boundless, context-free expanses of blue sky.

Eventually, vertical terrain would become the place where new meanings for skateboarding were created. The earlier cover photos, though, seldom defined vertical terrain in urban terms or as images of specific places; rather, they most often portrayed the terrain in terms of nature, a refuge from the urban. Skaters rode pools as if riding a wave down the line, bodies arched backward in expressions of soulful flow. Photographers pressed their shutter release when a skater was at the height of his carve, arms outstretched, soaring weightless. Magazine editors selected these and not other photos for publication. Each step in this selection process, from skaters to photographers to editors, reinforced a consistent set of meanings and visual conventions. The result was a consistent pattern in which images repeatedly emphasized the very same combination of metaphors of self-liberation and personal transformation that expressed the core values of the 1970s "consciousness revolution."[19]

Skaters draw lines. Out of the many efforts to define skateboarding that one finds in *Skateboarder* magazine, Dogtown skaters would ultimately provide a new vector when they turned away from (or at least revised) the Seventies rhetoric of personal transformation. The meaning they offered would be the only one adequate to the pervasive experience of postindustrial transformation that wracked everyday life in 1970s America. When riding concrete, they emulated the radical cutback turns innovated by surfer Larry Bertleman.[20] The surfing style the Dogtown skaters emulated was not down-the-line carves that expressed soulful flow—being at one with the wave was far less important than radically redirecting, slashing, and displacing water to take as much speed from the wave as one could get. If, as theorist Dick Hebdige argues in *Subculture: The Meaning of Style,*[21] every aspect of a subculture must make coherent sense and convey the same meaning as all others, the obvious aggression communicated through the cutback style that Dogtowners incorporated into their skateboard repertoire jibed with the imperative to "make it *now*" that Craig Stecyk celebrated in his sketches of skaters getting paid and that Skip Engblom attributed to the trying economic circumstances of Venice, California, in decline.

Images of a skater executing kick turns—pivoting on one or both of the rear wheels while elevating the front wheels—at the top edge of banked or vertical walls had already appeared inside the pages of the magazine. It was not until the October 1976 *Skateboarder,* however, that vertical skating first appeared as the cover image. As skaters refined vertical technique, photographers began to emphasize realism, portraying skateboarding as part of urban environments, its meaning ensuing from specific (as opposed to abstract), contingent (as opposed to universal), and local (as opposed to transcendent) circumstances. The old convention of shooting from below to erase immediate context was replaced by the new convention: shooting from above to establish specific context and thus link that context to the meaning of skating.

The cover for the December 1976 *Skateboarder* marks a new emphasis on "radical" skating.[22] Shot at Carlsbad Skatepark, the image shows a young Jay Adams—who would come to be known for his endorsement of "fly away" helmets—crouched on and holding both ends of his board as he flies out of the bowl. This is quite a different performance and framing of "flight," however. Although shot from below against a boundless sky, the photo was taken at night. The expanse of black sky does not evoke limitlessness and freedom so much as it directs the viewer's attention back to Adams's maneuver and his spectacular relationship to the concrete below him. Rather than approach a concrete wall as a wave—a context-free metaphor of freedom and personal transcendence —skaters such as Adams collaborated with photographers to emphasize the particular and dangerous qualities of the pavement itself. It is significant that the photo features a Dogtown skater who developed his aggressive skate techniques within the socioeconomic imperatives of his immediate, postindustrial urban surroundings in Venice, California. The photographer whose visual framings most consistently created such meanings was Craig Stecyk.

In his artistic expression, Stecyk developed a set of photographic conventions that conveyed grounded (as opposed to transcendent) social meaning connected to, rather than in flight from, real circumstances. Framed from above, paying equal attention to the surrounding environment and the skater, Stecyk's photos create direct links between skateboarders and their chosen terrain to emphasize not only the extreme risk but also the structural forces that produce such terrain. That risk gains larger meaning through direct links to urban decay and the historical conditions of postindustrial decline. In this context, anger and aggression, bravado and risk are appropriate to refusing and overcoming the conditions of decline in which Dogtown skaters developed their style. For example, an early Stecyk photo of Stacy Peralta emphasizes urban decay. Shot from above and behind the rim of a steeply sloped reservoir wall, the photo takes the viewer through the foreground past an angular jumble of cracked and broken asphalt and haphazardly discarded rubber traffic cones. One-wheeling on the thin edge is Peralta, board and feet at the top of the bowl, body extended and head leaning down into the concrete crater, hands planted on the wall and executing a sprawling, perhaps Bertlemanesque kick turn.

Dogtown skaters cultivated a set of stylized physical gestures consistent with their urban surroundings. When Dogtown photographers Stecyk or Glen Friedman used their viewfinders to frame the skaters, they also became directly linked to specific places and circumstances. "Style was like the most important thing," recalls Tony Alva. "Style was everything," reiterates Skip Engblom.[23] Facial expressions were very important. In magazine photos, most skaters appear calm with their eyes in deep focus and gaze turned inward as they let their muscle memory carry them through a turn. Early on, the dominant visual convention had photographers and writers playing up such inward focus as "insight" and self-realization. If skaters are not lost in the kinesthetics of the moment, their faces are usually grimaces of intense concentration. More often concerned with the immediacy of their precarious positions and the split-second timing required to ride back down safely, skaters in vertical situations rarely have the presence of mind to interact with the camera. Dogtown skaters, however, show a consistent and deliberately performed interaction with the camera, more so than do other skaters appearing in the pages of *Skateboarder*.

A 1976 *Skateboarder* "Who's Hot!" profile of eighteen-year-old Alva at the beginning of his career includes photos of him ripping frontside and back-side kick turns at Carlsbad Skatepark. He makes direct eye contact with and sneers at the camera, which stops his motion to emphasize the incisive way he attacks and thrusts through the turn. The captions read "Terror tactics in the beginner's bowl" and "Tony likes to freak out photographers by seeing how close he can come to their lens."[24] A June 1977 photo taken by Glen Friedman freezes a crouching Alva in a backside kick turn on the edge of only one wheel, perched on the coping of a ten-foot swimming pool just before he must redirect and control his fall back down the wall. Staring directly at the camera and demonstrating supreme mastery of his dangerous position, and perhaps intending to position himself as dangerous, he flips the bird with his free hand.[25]

In an early-1977 conversation focused on organized competition and the sport aspects of skating, interviewer Craig Stecyk asked Tony Alva, "Do you consider yourself a professional?" He replied, "Yes, I do. Totally professional . . . thoroughly. . . . I don't do anything for free." Alva expressed confidence that the sport would grow: "Once they start making bigger, more demand-ing tracks [skate parks], you'll start drawing more people. As things start to get hairy instead of lightweight and piddly, people will start to notice." But when asked about making money as a skateboarder, Alva answered that he believed he had been exploited. "Now I've got a lawyer and an agent to back me up. Before, people took advantage of me and of a lot of other kids 'cause we didn't know any better. Times are changing; we are learning fast. If I'm the first one to do something about it, then that's going to further the sport."[26]

After winning the world championship in 1977, Alva's competitive efforts diminished. Always ambivalent about organized competition, he chose not to participate in a major contest in 1978 at the Pipeline Skatepark in Upland, California, later commenting that the contest favored local skaters who had the time to fine tune their skating to the contours of the park. "A good skater is someone who can go to *any* good skate spot and just rip the first day—take a half an hour to feel it out, then just rip," he said. "The Dogtown guys have hit every skate park and ripped it; then, they've split, cuz they take it to the limit and then get burned out on a spot. I know it for a fact, because that's what I do. . . . That's why I don't go back. It's the same old thing, and I don't want to ride the same old thing cuz there's only so much you can do. I'm finding new things."[27] Thus, one's ability to find new places defines skating as much as one's ability to create new maneuvers. Rather than accepting structures provided by others, Alva applied the creative ethic of D-I-Y not only to skateboarding as a physical activity but also to skateboarding as a means of economic survival.

Alva's interest in making money and in finding new things would be realized on the cultural (as opposed to competitive) side of skateboarding, where public image was at a premium. "I'm investing in my company. The more money I put into my company the bigger percentage I get. My company is really right on right now. . . . That's what I'm really into because it's *my* name. . . . If I wanted to I could make Tony Alva jock straps. . . . That's what's good about having your own company."[28] Although all Dogtown skaters were looking to get paid, Alva was one of the first to cross over to the other side to management, ownership, and control of his own company.

Throughout the world of skateboarding, as skaters, photographers, editors, and advertisers searched for a vocabulary consistent with vertical skating, ads for Alva Skates stood out because of their connotations of danger and urbanism. The first ad in the October 1977 *Skateboarder* emphasizes Alva's in-your-face attitude. Looking off camera, he stands in a pool, staunch, arms crossed in a sleeveless red T-shirt with a "D-Town" logo that accentuates his muscular biceps. A nearby skateboard hanging from the pool's coping prominently features the red, graffiti-like Alva logo cut into the black grip tape on top of the board. A dog stands on the deck above and peers out from behind the board. The ad copy reads "Alva Skates" and "My 4 models/ Will Blaze/ Anywhere."[29] In a subsequent issue of *Skateboarder,* an interior shot of a parking garage bathed in an eerie green fluorescent light fills the entire frame. To the side of the frame, nearly invisible in the darkness, Alva sits on a parking block, his board at his feet. The only text reads "Alva Skates."[30] In another ad, amid steel and concrete connotations of an industrial setting, he sits calmly in a stairwell on the flat section of a purple-hued metal handrail angling upward to the left. He is cornered, surrounded by sheer walls of gray concrete and the metal girders of the overhead stairway landing.[31]

Closely associated with the cold, stark, hard, and gray reality of such urban imagery was Alva's use of horror imagery. His June 1978 ad reads "Dominate Alva Skates" and shows a bare-chested Alva, board held before him, grinning evilly at the camera. Smears of red paint bloody his chest and splatter his face and headband.[32] For its time, the violent implications of such graphic imagery caused alarm among parents and generated controversy among other skaters.[33]

Musicologist Robert Walser explains that horrific imagery in contemporaraenous heavy-metal music engaged social anxieties about power, history, and morality, allowing fans—especially young white men who found their expectations of upward mobility frustrated by the prospect of low-paid service jobs in a stagnant economy—to critique the inequities of the social order in which they found themselves.[34] Michael Ryan and Douglas Kellner make similar points about horror films, one of the most popular film genres during the 1970s and early 1980s: "During times of social crisis, several sorts of cultural representations tend to emerge. Some idealize solutions or alternatives to the distressing actuality, some project the worst fears and anxieties induced by the critical situation into metaphors that allow those fears to be absolved or played out, and some evoke a nihilistic vision of a world without hope or remedy."[35] It is not surprising that Tony Alva was a heavy-metal fan, proudly claiming allegiance to Led Zeppelin and Ted Nugent and even skateboarding with Craig Chaquico of Jefferson Starship.[36]

Alva's skating and business acumen suggest that Dogtown skaters may have evoked a nihilist vision, but their solution was to turn this vision into a style that, both as a marker of difference and as a business, defined their subculture.[37] Their radical cutback from pure narcissism, nihilism, and personal transcendence quickly came to dominate the pages of *Skateboarder*. Shortly after Alva Skates ads began to appear in the magazine, one could find an ad for Independent Trucks that reads "They're #*X!! Hot!"[38] Dogtown skaters' concrete style, grounded in their experiences of deindustrial Venice, California, had become the standard and defining imagery of a subculture. In their economic practices, Alva and others made an innovation more important than style: they began to turn skateboarding into a subcultural industry that provided a means of making a living in a world where political action was less possible, precisely because the state provided less oversight of business and fewer social programs to remedy socioeconomic inequalities. In a world where youth found themselves increasingly at the mercy of the market, it made sense to create a subculture that would itself be a market.

"CARBONATED FREEWAY FURY AND TERMINAL SWIMMING POOL DESPAIR"

Break on through to the other side.
—Jim Morrison, 1967

SLASH [MAGAZINE]: *Give us some titles of songs you do.*
BOBBY: *We don't have any. . . . Umm, "Sex Boy," "Death of an Immortal," "Jet Scream," which is about a guy who steals an airplane and it crashes in Lithuania. Umm . . . "Teenage Clone," and our single, which is "Forming" about breaking down the government and forming our own.*
—Bobby Pyn [Paul Beahm], lead singer of the Germs, 1978

At some point during their years (ca. 1972–1976) in the "Innovative Programs School" (IPS), an experimental "school within a school" at University High School in West Los Angeles (near Venice and Santa Monica and overlapping with Dogtown skaters' territory), Georg Ruthenberg and Paul Beahm took advantage of the option to devise their own classes.[39] Will Amato, former IPS student, remembers an exchange about creating a "sewing" class that occurred between his friends Ruthenberg and Beahm and Fred Holtby, their teacher:

> Georg and Paul announced that they had formed a class. Fred [Holtby] said, "Oh really? What's your class?" They said, "It's a sewing class." Which got a lot of laughs. So Fred said, "Okay, well, you can do whatever you want—so I guess you're going to form a sewing class. When are you going to start sewing?" And Paul said "Right now." "Well," said Fred, "How are you going to do that?" Paul looked at him and said "So?" Fred said, "What do you mean? I don't understand you." And Paul said "So?" Fred looking real puzzled said, "You do know you have to fill out this form and keep track of the work you do?" And Paul replied "So?" No matter what Fred or anyone said to them they'd say "So?" and that was their big "so-ing" class![40]

Eventually, the Future Seamsters of America were thrown out of IPS. According to Beahm, it was "for having our own religion," for renaming and referring to IPS as Inter-Planetary School, and for issuing silver stickers that read "Certified Space Case" to fellow students.[41] More than clever teenage rebellion, postmodern punk-rock provocation, or symbolic counterhegemony, Ruthenberg and Beahm's so-ing class sheds light on the history of the development of the D-I-Y work ethic that eventually informed many Seventies subcultures.

Ruthenberg and Beahm's so-what wordplay was the source of the profane "fuck you" rhetoric they would later espouse as punk rockers. The wordplay also may have been inspired by "free speech" opposition proclaimed by Sixties counterculture adherents who used obscenity to challenge moral uniformity and the enforced conformity of social institutions.[42] But Ruthenberg and Beahm were not challenging the conformity of a typical "institution." IPS was a school based on the values of personal fulfillment and self-discovery, the basic doctrine of the human potential movement. Two teachers, Caldwell Williams and Holtby, started IPS. Williams had gone through self-realization Erhard Seminars Training (EST), an intensive sixty-hour seminar/retreat that promised personal transformation through intense discipline and deprivation of food, sleep, and bathroom breaks. Trainers screamed at and berated trainees to break down their preconceptions.[43] Both Williams and Holtby used some of EST's precepts in combination with similar ideas from Scientology, another brand of 1970s spirituality, to reach bright but disaffected students. Williams sometimes encouraged students to undergo the intense and psychologically demanding EST training; Holtby preferred to manipulate students through cryptic, self-reflexive, performative, blunt, and personally challenging (if not abusive) verbal statements.[44] "He'd look at you and just say 'flunk' and wouldn't elaborate. He'd just say 'flunk,'" says former IPS student Will Amato.[45]

Ruthenberg and Beahm seemed to be in compliance with the tenets of such personal awareness philosophies, but their make-your-own-religion sticker campaign was not well received by Williams and Holtby. "The big thing in IPS was that the teachers were always right, you were never supposed to question anything that they said or told you to do, which of course, is exactly what we did. Our thing was, 'You're not God, not everything you say is right—fuck you!'" says Ruthenberg.[46] Clearly, IPS teachers' contradictory, passive-aggressive, antidisciplinary approach to education seemed hypocritical to Ruthenberg and Beahm. Their mocking refusal of the human potential movement allows us to gain a greater understanding of the historic significance of Seventies punk-rock and youth subcultures.

The case of the two young men illuminates a path that circumvents both traditional institutions intended to integrate the individual into society (like most high schools) and alternative institutions organized around individual fulfillment (like IPS). Ruthenberg and Beahm experienced firsthand what sociologists variously refer to as "the crisis of the bureaucratic welfare state" or, more relevant to an explanation of IPS, "the decline of institutions."[47] Consequently, they chose neither high school nor the alternative "school within a school." Instead, as Ruthenberg remembers, he and Beahm "were acting out as wannabe rock stars. It was the EST/Scientology thing—it's so creepily mind controlling! We were rebelling against *that*."[48]

The possibility of creating an identity through mass-media stardom and commercial youth culture seemed a more compelling option. After their high school tenure ended, Georg and Paul became more involved in music. First calling themselves Sophistifuck and the Revlon Spam Queens, they eventually adopted the punk-rock names of Pat Smear and Bobby Pyn (who would change his name yet again to Darby Crash in 1977) and settled on the band name "The Germs."[49] This is the kind of identity choice that Christopher Lasch would have decried as narcissism. However, as Ruthenberg and Beahm began to make a living in music, stardom quickly became part of the problem. Many youth during the 1970s found their way into punk rock because the heavily corporate music industry was regarded as impossibly closed, for it placed a high premium on beauty and musical ability.

The music industry was thus seen as inherently false. Mike Watt, who gravitated to punk in the late 1970s, recalls that he and guitarist D. Boon decided to pursue punk rock when they realized that it was a form of rock and roll that was not based on beauty and a virtuoso's ability. "See, me and D. Boon were the guys who were not supposed to be in bands. . . . We *looked* like bozos, so if we're going to be bozos, then let's go with it." After seeing punk-rock shows in Hollywood, Watt realized he could do it, too. "I saw hey, these guys are actually playing gigs. And some of them made records! . . . [G]oing to Hollywood and finding out there's other cats like this, it wasn't so lonely."[50]

Punk rockers intentionally mocked the star system of corporate rock that celebrated the rock singer as a technically skilled, individual artistic genius who makes music from his or her inspiration and achieves transcendence. As much as punk rockers cite Jim Morrison of the Doors as an early exemplar of who-cares punk attitudes for his iconoclasm, embrace of revolt and chaos, antagonistic relationship to audiences, and disregard for his physical well-being, a song like "Break on Through (To the Other Side)" still expresses a belief in the possibility of achieving transcendence somewhere else, somewhere separate from the problems, limitations, and contradictions of modern life, outside what we might call society.[51]

Ruthenberg and Beahm, rather than "work" to make it as a rock band, changed their names to Pat Smear and Bobby Pyn, teamed up with Terri Ryan and Becky Barton (who became Lorna Doom and Donna Rhia), forming the The Germs, and became a band by hanging posters around Los Angeles before they even knew how to play instruments. Their efforts were a symbolic statement of loyalty to the subcultural world they were making, a social, economic, and cultural sphere that would effectively (if not intentionally) substitute for increasingly ineffectual societal institutions like the school they had recently left.[52]

Song lyrics written by Beahm in his later persona of Darby Crash focus on unresolved pain of personal relationships, war, death, false religion, political dishonesty and futility, greed and corruption, media hypocrisy, violence, and horror. Lyrics from the song "Media Blitz" read like Christopher Lasch's assessment of modern life:

> We feed the science
> We deal in riots
> We play by ideal time
> We're a government fix
> All social convicts
> Watch the idle rhymes.

The song ends not with transcendent actualization, but with resignation and imminent failure: "Forget the truth—accept your curse."[53]

The Germs' attitude certainly went against any emphasis on ability, skill, and musicianship. "With the Germs we went out of our way to say and do things most other people would never say or do, it was a reaction to our disappointment in other rock stars—specifically finding out that Alice Cooper played *golf!* That really upset us—really freaked us out—'Alice Cooper does *what?*' " says Pat Smear. "It was like, 'We're gonna fucking start a band, and we're gonna change our names, and we're gonna fucking be this thing—we're gonna really be like that, 24-7, we're not going to fake it!' "[54] Like Mike Watt and Dennes Boon, Ruthenberg and Beahm found punk rock early—by 1977—and they liked it for the same reasons. Ruthenberg, Smear's alter-ego, remembers having the attitude that "we're gonna be the most this, or that, or whatever. . . . Whatever it is . . . we're gonna be the most—if we're gonna be punk, then we're gonna out-punk the Sex Pistols! If we're gonna be the worst band ever, then we're gonna be the fucking *worst* band ever!"[55]

Similar to Dogtown skaters who rejected organized contests (seen in Craig Stecyk's vignettes for *Skateboarder*), Ruthenberg rejected Alice Cooper and mainstream rock for their feigned rebellion when he realized that they might really be part of the mass-media and mainstream monolith. To the disillusioned Ruthenberg, no one could be more mainstream than someone who golfed. Like Dogtown skaters, Ruthenberg and Beahm and other punk musicians chose sincerity over mass culture, stressing locally defined expertise instead of a universal standard. What is most significant about the choices that Ruthenberg and Beahm made as high school students when they rejected both the social role of student and the goal of individual fulfillment through psychological liberation, and as musicians when they rejected the mass-media stardom of commercial rock, is that they chose a form of identity based on cultural loyalty. Social commentators explain that the failure of institutions—from the traditional family to schools to the workplace to government—during the 1960s and 1970s "destroyed individuals' identification with their citizenship, their professions or even their standard of living."[56] Punk rock created identity through commitment to mutual attitudes and behaviors shared by a small group of like-minded people who were responding to similar experiences of decline. They created punk subcultures by creating their own magazines, hangouts, clubs, record labels and stores (a nascent industry), and codes of behavior (regulations), all of which would replace the loss of industry, protective regulations, and social institutions of the welfare state in the shift to a postindustrial world.

Bobby Pyn/Darby Crash is most remembered for his performances. During a June 1977 show at the Whisky, the band covered the Archies song "Sugar, Sugar."[57] "It was my job to hand Bobby [Pyn] the bag of sugar on cue so he could dump it all over the place. During the rest of their set, we were opening up all these condiment packs and throwing them at the audience," remembers punk-rock journalist Gus Hudson. Pleasant Gehman was there as well: "The Germs told everyone they knew to bring some kind of food, and the results resembled a hurricane in a Safeway produce department. Sickening concoctions of salad dressings, beans, sour milk, and Campbell's soup flew from the balconies onto the stage below . . . as Pat and Bobby emptied two-pound bags of sugar over the stage and the crowd."[58]

These provocations, which defied the conventions of hero worship and invincibility that rock stars usually cultivated, placed the singer on an equal footing with audiences, rather than above them like a god. Crash's extreme disregard for his personal well-being—he was known to cut his chest with broken beer bottles—and the band's celebration of failure and incompetence contrast starkly with the ideals of personal fulfillment and self-realization of inner potential that pervaded 1970s culture. "I never felt the spirit in any Punk band the way I felt when I saw The Germs. . . . What I liked was that everything was a negative but when you put it all together it somehow made a positive," says Dez Cadena, former member of the influential hardcore band Black Flag. "A lot of times they were too fucked-up, a lot of times they didn't play well, a lot of times there was hardly any vocals because the vocalist [Crash] was too high, or the bass player [Doom] was out of tune, but somehow they embodied Punk."[59]

The Germs' erratic performances, their individual names, and their safety-pin cut-and-paste style of dress were conscious emulations of English punk rock, made famous by Sid Vicious and Johnny Rotten of the Sex Pistols.[60] Pictures of Crash show him wearing torn jeans covered with hundreds of safety pins, or ripped T-shirts with taunts like "No God" scrawled on them. Other Hollywood punks wrapped themselves in cellophane and black electrical tape, spiked and dyed their hair, and wore dog collars, fishnet stockings, and leather.[61]

Unlike other punk-rock groups such as Black Flag, the Minutemen, and, slightly later, Minor Threat, however, The Germs are not credited for emphasizing a D-I-Y ethic of record it, sell it, and tour relentlessly.[62] Instead, they are placed at the beginning of that tradition in punk-rock genealogies. The Germs also occupy a place in history as a transitional band, part of the Hollywood punk scene that more closely resembles early punk rock in New York City than the hardcore scene that would emerge in Orange County during the early 1980s. The Hollywood scene of which they were a part is often defined as more arty and aesthetic. In these accounts, the Germs' historical significance is limited to being some of the first punk rockers, forerunners of punk-rock style and ethos. When defined in terms of only the history of the music and the collective aesthetic of their "arty" Hollywood scene, their significance is diminished. A better measure of their significance can be found in a consideration of their interactions with processes of postindustrial transformation.

The Germs' legacy, a "we-don't-care" attitude, had its roots in Beahm and Ruthenberg's experiences of institutional decline and failed reform at the IPS. Similarly, many other early punk-rock bands came from places that had undergone postindustrial decline.[63] Mike Watt and Dennes Boon of the important early punk band the Minutemen grew up in the working-class port city of San Pedro. The first song the two ever wrote was "Storming Tarragona," which is about the bleak public housing development where Boon and his family resided.[64] The Orange County band Black Flag lived, practiced, and performed in a bohemian area of Hermosa Beach, where they became the target of police violence when city leaders sought to remove undesirables for the sake of property values.[65] Although interviews of Pat Smear and Darby Crash provide no evidence about when or how they encountered the conditions of postindustrial decline that so directly affected Dogtown skaters in Venice and Santa Monica, both performers spent their early lives in the very same cities.

Ruthenberg and Beahm grew up in Venice, while Watt and Boon grew up in San Pedro. Both places were on the front lines of urban decline, neglect, and abandonment caused by postindustrial transformation. All four men gravitated to Hollywood, a place very similar to the Venice that Dogtown skaters knew: both were places that had been left behind when tourists sought entertainment elsewhere. Compounding the decline of the tourist economy, Hollywood's industrial base, the film industry, abandoned mass production of movies and pursued subcontracted, small-scale filmmaking in suburban locations outside city limits.[66] Hollywood had always been defined as much by images and symbols as by the actual work of the movie industry. From the 1920s to the 1950s, Hollywood was a magnet for tourists who hoped to see a real star at work on the set or perhaps after work in a restaurant or nightclub.[67] During the 1970s, long after the stars had gone away and big-budget nightclub entertainment had relocated to Vegas, the magnetic attractions presented by the city of celluloid dreams coincided with the dismantling of the social-welfare state in significant ways: Hollywood attracted runaway and homeless youth.

In 1977, Beahm, Ruthenberg, Watt, and Boon discovered punk rock not on the Sunset Strip or Hollywood Boulevard, the traditional thoroughfares of mass entertainment, but in the alleyways, abandoned buildings, and back regions of a city at the nadir of a twenty-year economic downturn. When bands like The Germs began to receive media attention, runaway youth gravitated to the punk-rock scene. Youth from working-class neighborhoods, middle-class suburbs in the San Fernando Valley, and elite enclaves in the Hollywood hills came together with runaways to become punks in Hollywood. Not simply out of rebellion, these youth found in punk rock a coher-

ent set of images and spaces that matched their experiences of deinstitu-
tionalization (whether in failed schools as with Ruthenberg and Beahm or in
inadequate social programs for runaways for many punks in Hollywood) in
a landscape dominated by economic conservatives who labeled these youth
as "criminal" in order to achieve their goal of deregulation and greater corporate profits. Punk-rock criticism of diminished opportunities resonated
with youth who, outside the juvenile care system, had become potential
inmates for the juvenile justice system.

Punk rock, performed in back-alley clubs and celebrated in parties in
abandoned buildings, communal-living apartments, and illegal squats, provided a network of physical places and cultural space that made coherent
sense to youth facing a postindustrial landscape of neglect and a government that favored business over people. These aspects of The Germs' history show the significance of group formation and microeconomic strategies
during the 1970s.

WITHER THE STATE

The legacy of Dogtown skaters' aggressive style, the Germs' loyalty to their
world of anticelebrity, and Tony Alva's and Darby Crash's subcultural
careers have outlived the banalities of 1970s leisure suits and pet rocks that
are still celebrated on VH1. The legacy of 1970s skate and punk can be found
in the staying power of ESPN's nine-year-old *X-Games*, "extreme" sports
competitions. The success of the show has led to a partnership with Mills
Corporation, a retail real-estate developer. Mills and ESPN have arranged
for the inclusion of *X-Games* skateboard parks as anchors/major stores within
their Atlanta, Philadelphia, Dallas, and Denver shopping malls—and there
are plans for a mall near you. One could note the January 2003 launch of the
daily extreme-sports program *54321* on Fox Sports Network. Or, finally one
could follow the music career of Pat Smear from the Germs to Nirvana, the
band that made it possible to buy punk rock in Wal-Mart. All this is evidence
that spectacular and oppositional subcultures such as skateboarding and
punk rock have now become industries and economic markets unto themselves.[68] Subcultures were a definitive aspect of Seventies cultural history that
departs from our perceived wisdom about the "me decade." The predomi-

nance of subculture as a mode of social formation during the time shows that forms of collective activity that have too often been misunderstood as apolitical made sense in a context in which the transformation of the state to serve business interests had made previous forms of countercultural and political protest not only less relevant but less possible. When the the possibility of achieving ameliorative social change through politics virtually disappeared from American society, economics became the grounds for survival. Subcultural economies became appropriate—if not adequate—to a society without guarantees, a world without state oversight.

ACKNOWLEDGMENTS

For their help with this article, I would like to thank Mary Kay Van Sistine first and last, as well as Sophie Willard-Van Sistine, Dave and Jan Van Sistine, Caroline Corser, Tabby Bokovoy, Mike Logan, Jason Lavery, Deb Desjardins, Laura Belmonte, Randy Hanson, Luis Fernandez, Jeff Rangel, Omar Valerio, R. J. Smith, Stacy Takacs, Steve Waksman, Joe Austin, Thea Petchler, Jason Loviglio, Anne Wolf, Dewar MacLeod, members of the audience at a Society for the History of Childhood and Youth panel at the University of Maryland Baltimore County, where I presented a version of this essay, and the skaters of Stillwater, Oklahoma. I would like especially to thank David Farber and Beth Bailey for their editorial tact, encouragement, and patience. Beth Bailey and Matthew Bokovoy carefully read a much longer version of the essay and provided excellent suggestions for revision. Finally, this article is dedicated to Samuel David Willard-Van Sistine, future accordion player, tap dancer, skateboarder, poet, storyteller, world-cup soccer star, who, during the months when I was working on this article, was born and changed the/my world. Little S$_{too}$, you can be anything you want. I can tell. The way you do the things you do.

Notes

1. "Jello Bio," http://www.angelfire.com/punk/jello2000/bio.html.

2. Christopher Lasch, *The Culture of Narcissism: American Life in an Age of Diminishing Expectations* (New York: Norton, 1979), 10.

3. Ibid., 94–96, 31.

4. Lasch is especially critical of New Left political methods and strategies. For similar arguments, see George Lipsitz, "Who'll Stop the Rain: Youth Culture, Rock 'n' Roll, and Social Crises," in *The Sixties: From Memory to History*, ed. David Farber (Chapel Hill: University of North Carolina Press, 1994), 206–234; Maurice Isserman and Michael Kazin, "The Failure and Success of the New Radicalism," in *The Rise and Fall of the New Deal Order, 1930-1980*, ed. Steve Fraser and Gary Gerstle (Princeton, NJ: Princeton University Press, 1989), 212–242.

5. Bruce Schulman, *The Seventies: The Great Shift in American Culture, Society, and Politics* (2001; repr., New York: Da Capo Press, 2002), 96–97, elaborates on the therapeutic consciousness revolution.

6. Barry Bluestone and Bennett Harrison, *The Deindustrialization of America: Plant Closings, Community Abandonment and the Dismantling of Basic Industry* (New York: Basic Books, 1982); Katherine S. Newman, "Uncertain Seas: Cultural Turmoil and the Domestic Economy," in *America at Century's End*, ed. Alan Wolfe (Berkeley: University of California Press, 1991), 112–130.

7. Paddy Chayefsky, writer, *Network*, Metro-Goldwyn-Mayer/United Artists, 1976. Schulman, *Seventies*, 50–51, explains that college students turned the phrase "I'm mad as hell and I'm not going to take it any more!" into the acronym "IMAHAINGTTIAM," which they printed on campus flyers that instructed students to yell the phrase from their dorm windows at midnight.

8. Thanks to Randy McBee for bringing the phenomenon of motorcycle daredevils to my attention.

9. Jordan Benson Kleiman, "The Appropriate Technology Movement in American Political Culture" (PhD diss., University of Rochester, 2000); Warren Belasco, *Appetite for Change: How the Counterculture Took On the Food Industry, 1966–1988* (Ithaca, NY: Cornell University Press, 1989); Julie Harriet Guthman, "Agrarian Dreams? The Paradox of Organic Farming in California" (PhD diss., University of California, Berkeley, 2000); Robert Walser, *Running with the Devil: Power, Gender and Madness in Heavy Metal Music* (Hanover, NH: University Press of America/Wesleyan University Press, 1993); Carolyn Krasnow, "The Development of Aesthetic Ideology in Popular Music: Rock and Disco in the Nineteen Seventies" (PhD diss., University of Minnesota, 1999); Csaba Toth, " 'Like Cancer in the System': Industrial Gothic, Nine Inch Nails, and Videotape," in *Gothic: Transmutations of Horror in Late Twentieth Century Art*, ed. Cristoph Grunenberg (Boston: Institute of Contemporary Art / MIT Press, 1997); Tricia Rose, *Black Noise: Rap Music and Black Culture in Contemporary America* (Hanover, NH: University Press of America/Wesleyan University Press, 1994); Joe Austin, *Taking the Train: How Graffiti Art Became an Urban Crisis in New York City* (New York: Columbia University Press, 2001); Barry Shank, *Dissonant Identities: The Rock 'n' Roll Scene in Austin, Texas* (Hanover, NH: University Press of America/Wesleyan University Press, 1994); Susan Ruddick, *Young and Homeless in Hollywood: Mapping Social Identities* (New York: Routledge, 1996); G. Dewar MacLeod, "Kids of the Black Hole: Youth Culture in Postsuburbia" (PhD diss., City University of New York, 1998); Ryan M.

Moore, "Anarchy in the U.S.A.: Capitalism, Postmodernity, and Punk Subculture since the 1970s" (PhD diss., University of California, San Diego, 2000); Steve Waksman, "Kick Out the Jams! The MC5 and the Politics of Noise," in *Mapping the Beat: Popular Music and Contemporary Theory*, ed. Thomas Swiss, John Sloop, and Andrew Herman (Malden, MA: Blackwell Publishers, 1998); Michael Azerrad, *Our Band Could Be Your Life: Scenes from the American Indie Underground, 1981–1991* (Boston: Little Brown, 2001); Ann Powers, *Weird Like Us: My Bohemian America* (2000; repr., New York: Da Capo Press, 2001); Iain Borden, *Skateboarding, Space and the City: Architecture and the Body* (New York: Berg Publishers, 2001).

10. My use of the phrase "translocal" comes from Brenda Jo Bright, "Nightmares in the New Metropolis: The Cinematic Poetics of Lowriders," in *Generations of Youth: Youth Cultures and History in Twentieth Century America*, ed. Joe Austin and Michael Nevin Willard (New York: New York University Press, 1998).

11. Skip Engblom, quoted in *Dogtown and Z-Boys: The Birth of Extreme*, DVD, Sony Pictures Classics, 2001, chap. 2, "Dogtown," minute 5:26.

12. George Lipsitz, "Consumer Spending as State Project: Yesterday's Solutions and Today's Problems," in *Getting and Spending: European and American Consumer Society in the Twentieth Century*, ed. Susan Strasser, Charles McGovern, and Matthias Judt (Cambridge, UK: Cambridge University Press, 1998), 136–142; Ruddick, *Young and Homeless in Hollywood*, 163–168.

13. Lynn Craig Cunningham, "Venice, California: From City to Suburb" (PhD diss., University of California, Los Angeles, 1976).

14. "Appalachia by the Sea," California Digital Library, Melvyl Database Catalogue Record, http://www.dbs.cdlib.org.

15. Skip Engblom, quoted in *Dogtown and Z-Boys*, chap. 8, "Aggressive Performance Ethic," minute 18:56.

16. Tony Alva quoted in John Smythe [Craig Stecyk], "Fisheyed Freaks and Long Dogs with Short Tales," *Skateboarder*, June 1976, 56.

17. Ibid.

18. Ibid.

19. Schulman, *Seventies*, 96–97.

20. *Dogtown and Z-Boys*, chap. 13, "Devotion to Style," minute 28:56.

21. Dick Hebdige, *Subculture: The Meaning of Style* (London: Methuen, 1979), 113, as cited in Ruddick, *Young and Homeless in Hollywood*, 100.

22. The first image of this kind appeared on the cover of the October 1976 *Skateboarder*, as discussed above.

23. Tony Alva and Skip Engblom, quoted in *Dogtown and Z-Boys*, chap. 13, "Devotion to Style," minute 29:20.

24. "Who's Hot! Tony Alva," *Skateboarder*, June 1976, 100–101. The photograph is not attributed.

25. Glen E. Friedman, *Fuck You Heroes: Glen E. Friedman Photographs, 1976–1991* (New York: Burning Flags Press, 2000), n.p.

26. "Tony Alva *Skateboarder* Magazine Interview" (1977), *The Official As It Gets Tony Alva Web Pages*, http://www.angelfire.com/ca/aalva2/1977.html.

27. Tony Alva, interview by John Smythe [Craig Stecyk], *Skateboarder,* July 1978, 71–72.

28. Ibid., 80.

29. "Alva Skates," advertisement, *Skateboarder,* December 1977, 169.

30. Ibid., April 1978, 113.

31. Ibid., May 1978, 174.

32. Ibid., June 1978, 155.

33. Alva, interview by Smythe, 67.

34. Walser, *Running With the Devil,* 155, 161.

35. Michael Ryan and Douglas Kellner, *Camera Politica: The Politics and Ideology of Contemporary Hollywood Film* (Bloomington, Ind.: Indiana University Press, 1988), 168.

36. "Alva *Skateboarder* Interview," http://www.angelfire.com/ca/alva2/1977.html.

37. Alva was not the only subcultural entrepreneur. Dogtown skaters had already been associated with Z-flex skateboards, a company that grew out of their involvement with the Zephyr surf team. Also, Jim Muir and Wes Humpston started Dogtown Skates, which featured innovative graphics inspired by Chicano graffiti. Alva Skates crystallized the style of cultural opposition that he and his friends had grown up with; not surprisingly, the company's influence reverberates throughout the pages of *Skateboarder.*

38. "Independent Trucks," advertisement, *Skateboarder,* August 1978, inside front cover.

39. Thanks to Illana Nash for helping me pinpoint the location of University High School and sharing her memories of IPS.

40. Will Amato, quoted in Mullen, *Lexicon Devi: The Fast Times and Short Life of Darby Crash and the Germs* (Los Angeles: Feral House, 2002), 18.

41. Paul Beahm, quoted in Mullen, *Lexicon Devil,* 24.

42. See Kenneth Cmiel, "The Politics of Civility," in David Farber, ed., *The Sixties: From Memory to History* (Chapel Hill: University of North Carolina Press, 1994), 263–290.

43. Schulman, *Seventies,* 98.

44. Caldwell Williams, quoted in Mullen, *Lexicon Devil,* 13–14.

45. Will Amato, quoted in Mullen, *Lexicon Devil,* 16.

46. Georg Ruthenberg, quoted in Mullen, *Lexicon Devil,* 18.

47. Margit Mayer and Roland Roth, "New Social Movements and Post-Fordist Society," in *Cultural Politics and Social Movements,* ed. Marcy Damovsky, Barbara Epstein, and Richard Flacks (Philadelphia: Temple University Press, 1995), 312; Alain Touraine, *Can We Live Together: Equality and Difference* (Stanford, CA: Stanford University Press, 2000), 36–43.

48. *Lexicon Devil,* 38, 103–104.

49. George Ruthenberg, quoted in Mullen, *Lexicon Devil,* 16.

50. Azerrad, *Our Band,* 66.

51. Marc Spitz and Brendan Mullen, *We Got the Neutron Bomb: The Untold Story of L.A. Punk* (New York: Three Rivers Press, 2001), 1–5.

52. Mullen, *Lexicon Devil*, 44.

53. Darby Crash, "Media Blitz," *GI* (Slash Records, 1979). For Germs lyrics, see Mullen, *Lexicon Devil*, 273–285.

54. Pat Smear [Georg Ruthenberg], quoted in Mullen, *Lexicon Devil*, 46.

55. Ibid.

56. Touraine, *Can We Live Together*, 31.

57. Jeff Barry and Andy Kim, "Sugar, Sugar," *Everything's Archie* (Calendar KES-103, 1969). The Germs' June 1977 performance of "Sugar, Sugar" and noise from the food fight can be heard on their record *Live at the Whisky* (Reach Out International Records, RE 108CD, n.d.).

58. Gus Hudson and Pleasant Gehman, quoted in Mullen, *Lexicon Devil*, 65.

59. Dez Cadena, quoted in Steven Blush, *American Hardcore: A Tribal History* (Los Angeles: Feral House, 2001), 14.

60. Pat Smear [Georg Ruthenberg], quoted in Mullen, *Lexicon Devil*, 46.

61. Mullen, *Lexicon Devil*, 49, 52. See also Blush, *American Hardcore;* Spitz and Mullen, *We Got the Neutron Bomb.*

62. For histories of these bands, see Michael Azerrad's excellent *Our Band Could Be Your Life.*

63. For more thorough treatments that show how punk rock emerged in places that were on the front lines of postindustrial transformation/decline, see the superb scholarship by Ryan Moore ("Anarchy in the U.S.A."), Dewar Macleod ("Kids of the Black Hole"), and Steve Waksman ("Kick Out the Jams!"), sociologists and cultural historians whose gifted analyses show how punk rock was the result of young people interacting with the material conditions of a postindustrial society.

64. Watt, quoted in Azerrad, *Our Band*, 65.

65. Azerrad, *Our Band*, 20.

66. Ruddick, *Young and Homeless in Hollywood*, 93–94, 163–185.

67. Ibid.

68. "Welcome to Grapevine Mills," *Grapevine Mills*, http://www.grapevine-mills.com/index2.html; *X Games Skatepark*, http://xgamesskateparks.com; *Fox Sports*, http://www.foxsports.com.

9

Culture, Technology, and the Cult of Tech in the 1970s

TIMOTHY MOY

Oh, what a time it was. A time of hope, of excitement, and most of all, of triumph. It was a time when young visionaries searched their hearts and found the future. Wide-eyed, they remade the world as millions of Americans joined the song. It was the Seventies.

The Seventies? The *nineteen* seventies? The Seventies of Watergate, Ford, and Carter? Of malaise, stagflation, and polyester leisure suits? Those Seventies?

Yes. Although the Seventies were a cynical age for many Americans, it was a heady time for one segment of the nation: creators of new technology. During the 1970s, technologists and their handiwork successfully created a new culture for the relationship between Americans and their technology, carved out a new cultural space for American technologists, and set the nation on a social and economic trajectory that would run through the end of the century.

SNAPSHOT, 1970

By 1970, Americans who thought deeply about technology did so with great anxiety. Typical of American intellectuals during this period, Lewis Mumford journeyed from technological enthusiasm in the 1930s to technological despondency in the 1970s. Before World War II, Mumford's *Technics and Civilization* (1934) had depicted a "neotechnic" future rich in freedom and meaning, propelled by hydroelectric power and enlightened by Bakelite and aluminum.[1] By 1970, his *Pentagon of Power* described human civilization as enslaved by "megamachines"—heartless and inexorable conglomerations of technology and power that labored only for the benefit of authoritarian elites.

For Mumford, cold-war military-industrial complexes had turned technology from liberator to enslaver; it was now a tool of insanity. "I have been driven," he wrote, "by the wholesale miscarriages of megatechnics, to deal with the collective obsessions and compulsions that have misdirected our energies, and undermined our capacity to live full and spiritually satisfying lives."[2] And the future held little promise. The United States and Soviet Union, "through their dynamic expansion, their insensate rivalry, their psychotic compulsiveness," were gradually drawing the entire world into their ghastly embrace. "Ultimately," Mumford feared, "these two systems must either destroy each other or coalesce with other similar megamachines on a planetary basis. In terms of further human development, the second possibility, alas! seems hardly more promising than the first."[3] Mumford was not alone in his concern. Even the ever-optimistic Buckminster Fuller, who remained steadfast in his faith that technology would eradicate human suffering, asked in the title of a 1969 book whether technology would lead to *Utopia or Oblivion.*[4]

For the masses who decided not to brave the tomes of Mumford, Fuller, or other critics like Jacques Ellul, the prospects of an increasingly technological world likewise provided little comfort. The misery of the Vietnam War had given the lie to any equation between technological superiority and national security. Even NASA's space program, the technological darling of the 1960s, was showing signs of wear by 1970; the television ratings for the *Apollo 13* mission in April of that year had been disappointing until an inflight explosion aborted the moon landing and nearly killed the three astronauts aboard. The heroic story of the astronauts' survival was then quickly wiped from the front page by the shootings at Kent State University.

On an everyday level, technology was important but uncelebrated. The most prominent technological interface in the home—television—was well on its way to transforming American society, culture, and politics, but in ways that had fallen pathetically short of the hopes of a generation earlier. Rather than bringing a Harvard education into every living room, television had, most Americans and commentators agreed, evolved into an idiot box, a signpost not to a wondrous land of imagination but to a vast wasteland of intellectual and cultural debility. Nevertheless, such hard feelings did not prevent the average American household from partaking of over six hours of viewing per day for most of the decade.[5]

But not everyone had given up. Some intellectuals, sympathetic to the anti-technocratic critiques of the Sixties but unwilling to share their fatalism, turned the argument back on itself and looked to technology for escape from its own drear tyranny. Although technology gave the military, corporations, and other large systems of production a harder fist with which to work their will, "soft technologies" might provide individuals and small communities the means to recover their humanity in their homes and pastures. Small-scale, decentralized technology was more appropriate to "the purification of human character," according to popular British economist E. F. Schumacher, whose *Small Is Beautiful: Economics As If People Mattered* set the tone for much of this discussion.[6]

But even appropriate technologists needed a hardware store, and Stewart Brand's *Whole Earth Catalog* (1968) intended to fill the bill. Promoting "a groovy spiritual and material culture in which one's state of being was to be expressed in higher states of consciousness and well-selected tools" (as later described by Langdon Winner), *Whole Earth* followers turned to inexpensive and low-tech windmills, water pumps, spinning wheels, latrines, and solar cookers to engineer infrastructure for small, self-sustaining communities—imagine the Amish empowered by Sears Roebuck.[7] It was antiestablishment but not antitechnology; rather, it was a vision that appealed to technology, precisely and cleverly applied, to put power (literally) back into the hands of the people.

GEEK EMPOWERMENT

Such was the cultural environment for technologists at the beginning of the 1970s. By the end of the decade, these cultural imperatives would combine with emerging technical and economic opportunities to allow a relatively small group of young technology geeks (or "techies") to transform Americans' relationship with their technology. This is a story that is simultaneously well known and incomplete; the cliché of unbathed teenagers launching multibillion dollar start-ups in their parents' garages in Silicon Valley is by now a fixture in popular culture. But what is less well known is how the imperative for technological self-empowerment shaped the desires and activities of techies during the 1970s and how the technological systems they developed have influenced American culture since.

In truth, techies had always been captivated by the vision of high technology self-empowerment. After all, Buck Rogers and Commander Cody were at their niftiest not when they were piloting spaceships but when they were zooming around with jet packs strapped to their backs. William P. Lear (1902–1978), an earlier twentieth-century geek, spent much of his professional life putting technology into individual hands. Lear developed the first commercially viable automobile radio in the 1920s (thus introducing mobility to a then-static technology; his design eventually became the signature product of Motorola, short for "Motor Victrola"); he then designed miniature autopilots during World War II. After the war, Lear developed small, private jet aircraft (forming Learjet in 1962). Also in the early 1960s, he invented the 8-track tape player, designed to bring personal portability to recorded music; in the later 1960s, he contracted with Ford, General Motors, and Chrysler to make 8-track players a popular option (though later the butt of endless jokes) in American cars. At the end of his life, Lear was working on nonpolluting engines, teleportation devices, and time machines.[8]

Techies in the 1970s had similar tastes but were emboldened with the political and social vision of transformative, appropriate technology. By then, the social and cultural options opened up by counterculture critique combined with new technological possibilities to allow, within small circles, a kind of technological utopianism not prevalent since the beginning of the twentieth century.[9] So, while 1950s techies had boosters and salesmen such as Lear, 1970s techies had gurus.

Ted Nelson was (and remains) the archetype of the San Francisco Bay Area technology guru of the 1970s. The son of actress Celeste Holm, Nelson majored in philosophy in college and earned an MA in sociology at Harvard in the 1960s. While a graduate student, he took a computer course and became entranced by the prospect that emerging computer technology might reinvigorate the humanities, particularly by opening up new literary possibilities. He tried and failed to develop what we would now recognize as an early word processor (he called it a "writing system"). In addition to allowing users to compose, store, and edit their writing, the system would also enable writers to compare versions side-by-side, track changes, and backtrack through earlier versions. Typically for him, Nelson never finished writing the software and had to take an incomplete in the course.[10]

While working on this project, Nelson also became frustrated with the arcane expertise necessary to operate software and imagined an even larger literary system that could be navigated easily by non-techies. Such a system would store and index enormous amounts of information (both technical and humanistic) and permit non-experts to engage it by whatever nonhierarchical pathways they wished. "Zippered lists" would link concepts in one piece of text to similar concepts in all others, thus allowing readers (and writers) to roam through an infinitely tunneled landscape of information. He called the format "hypertext."[11]

After graduate school, Nelson wrote what has become a cult favorite—actually, two: *Computer Lib/Dream Machines*.[12] Self-published in 1974, the two books were virtually joined at the hip; after finishing one, you flipped the entire volume over and upside down and started the other. Stylistically, the books were clearly patterned after Brand's *Whole Earth Catalog*, with large, busy pages crammed with boxed text, free-standing quotations, hand-drawn illustrations, and rapidly changing typefaces.

The message of the books echoed Mumford, but as a call to arms rather than a lament: Computers are recasting politics, society, and culture, and it is up to the people to wrest control of this transformation from the corporate, militarized, technical priesthood.

> I would like to alert the reader, in no uncertain terms, that the time has come to be openly attentive and critical in observing and dealing with computer systems; and to transform criticism into action. If systems are bad, annoying and demeaning, these matters should be brought to the attention of the perpetrators. . . . [J]ust as the atmospheric pollution fostered by GM has become a matter for citizen concern and attack through legitimate channels of protest, so too should the procedural pollution of inconsiderate computer systems become a matter for the same kinds of concern. The reader should realize he can criticize and demand; THE PUBLIC DOES NOT HAVE TO TAKE WHAT'S BEING DISHED OUT.[13]

The key to empowering people, Nelson argued, was computer liberation. All people had to become familiar, comfortable, and even friendly with computers. Computers are more than useful machines; they are the creative vehicles by which we can manifest a democratic future. "They are toys, they are tools, they are glorious abstractions," Nelson enthused, but cautioned, "If you are interested in democracy and its future, you'd better understand computers."[14]

What was the goal of computer empowerment? Nothing less than a round-the-clock exploration of art and knowledge, open to all and controlled by none. In *Dream Machines,* Nelson described a supremely democratic "docuverse" that made all the world's literary material available to everyone for both consumption and production. He envisioned a universal, instantaneous, hypertext publishing network in which reader-writers could contribute their own literary products—new works, glosses, commentaries, marginalia—at will and with complete integration into the docuverse.[15] He named the system Xanadu, after the location of Kubla Khan's fabulous palace in Coleridge's poem—though Nelson's system perhaps bears greater resemblance to Charles Foster Kane's never-finished monument to himself.[16]

TINKERING

Not all geeks are visionaries, of course. Many techies are motivated less by a grandiose vision of technotopia than by the simpler joy of playing with tech toys and the desire to impress others of like tastes.

Such were the regulars in groups like the Homebrew Computer Club, the famous electronics and computer hobbyists club in the San Francisco Bay Area during the middle 1970s. If asked at the time, most Homebrewers undoubtedly would have been able to spin out visions of technological utopia; read enough science fiction and you are bound to absorb the ethos. But that was not what really motivated them.

For example, the center of attention in Homebrew meetings during the middle years of the 1970s was the MITS Altair 8800, first released in 1975 and available by mail order from Albuquerque, New Mexico. Generally regarded as the first personal computer (PC), the Altair is completely unrecognizable as a usable machine today. In addition to its internal electronics, the entire system consisted of a case and a series of toggle switches and light bulbs on the front panel—no keyboard, no screen, no disk drive. Programs had to be entered as individual binary numbers by flipping the switches on the front; the only evidence that the program had done its job was a change in which bulbs were lit. And best of all, after it arrived in the mail, you had to break out your screwdriver, pliers—and, more than likely, your ohm meter and soldering iron—and put it together yourself.[17]

It was a machine only a dedicated hobbyist could love, or even use. But it cost less than four hundred dollars, making it accessible to anyone with the expertise and devotion to tackle it. And I do mean devotion: One elated Homebrewer, Steve Dompier of Berkeley, recounted for his fellows, completely without sarcasm, how his Altair had arrived "in the mail at 10 AM, and 30 hours later it was up and running with only one bug in the memory!"[18] It only took him another six hours to track down the memory failure; one of the circuit boards was damaged, so he had to repair it.[19] But after thirty-six sleepless hours of toil, *he had his own computer.*

What could the Altair do? With no long-term storage and only 256 bytes of memory (and those are bytes, not megabytes or kilobytes), it could essentially do nothing useful; after several minutes of tediously flipping the binary switches, your Altair might successfully add, subtract, or sort a short list of numbers—things you could do more easily by hand or in your head.

But it was a computer, and it was yours. And countless Homebrew meetings were devoted to developing and exchanging trouble-shooting tips, faster algorithms, and software code for new Altair tricks. At one meeting, Dompier had his Altair perform a music recital. A few weeks earlier, he had been playing with his computer while listening to a nearby radio and had accidentally discovered that his Altair was putting out radio interference; different pitches of squeals and hisses emanated from the radio depending on what the computer was doing. For most of us, the lesson would have been to move the radio away from the computer, but not for a Homebrewer. "Well, what do ya know," Dompier enthused, "my first peripheral device!"[20] Theoretically, the interference meant that he could use the radio to allow his Altair to speak, or rather sing. He quickly (he says it took eight hours) wrote a program to turn data into musical tones that would come across as squeals of interference on a radio. He then worked out the data codes (in base 8) for the Beatles' "Fool on the Hill," programmed the song into his Altair, and bundled it all off (including the radio) to the next Homebrew meeting. The recital was a smashing success; however, he warned that "during the demanded encore, the machine did break into its own rendition of 'Daisy,' apparently genetically inherited."[21] If you have to ask why it would be important to get a computer to sing "Daisy" (or "A Bicycle Built for Two"), you are clearly not in the right state of mind.[22] Naturally, Dompier shared the hundreds of lines of data for both songs.

Personal computing would have remained a hobbyist's passion were it not for the gradual infusion of computer-liberation culture. It was an easy match. As a group, Homebrewers had a generally antiestablishment streak.

Steve Wozniak, one half of the founding duo of Apple Computer, initially became widely known within Homebrew as a maker of "blue boxes"—small electronic devices that emitted push-button telephone tones and permitted making free phone calls, breaking into existing conversations, and other phone phreaking.[23] Nelson's computer-liberation vision enjoyed a harmonic resonance.

The resonance was evident in some of the hobbyist magazines from the period. The community favorite, and one of the few such magazines to survive to the present, was *Dr. Dobb's Journal of Computer Calisthenics and Orthodontia.* Unlike its glossy and upscale competitors, like *Creative Computing* or *Byte* magazine, *Dr. Dobb's Journal* prided itself on its antiestablishment individualism. Its debut issue, in January 1976, made clear that the magazine existed solely for the edification of true hobbyists; it warned advertisers, for example, that the editors "reserve the right to refuse any advertising from companies which we feel fall short of our rather picky standards for ethical behavior and responsiveness to consumers. Also, any such commercial advertiser is herewith informed that we will not hesitate to publish harsh criticisms of their products or services, if we feel such criticisms are valid."[24]

Most of the magazine was unreadable (at least by humans). The majority of each of the early issues consisted of page after page of program listings, often in machine language, disseminating new sorting algorithms and computer language interpreters. Early on, most of the articles were devoted to tricks and tips for the Altair. But behind it all was the inviolable principle that software (like all knowledge) was power and should therefore be free. The magazine existed as "a sharing experience, intended to disseminate FREE software."[25] The only proper exchange of money among *Dr. Dobb's Journal* readers, the editors cautioned, was to charge for the cost of reproduction (software media like cassette tapes or punched paper tape), which was simply "the cost of sharing."

It is no surprise, therefore, that the computer partnership between Steve Wozniak and Steve Jobs began at Homebrew. Although they had met through a mutual friend a few years earlier, their interest in making computers together stemmed from Homebrew meetings in early 1975, the height of Altair mania.[26] Wozniak, a hobbyist at heart, was transfixed by the possibilities of owning his own computer. Jobs, four years younger than Wozniak and impatient with the "nit-picking technical debates" among Homebrewers, was a devotee of suburban Bay Area Marxism and disciple of computer liberation.[27] With visions of putting computing power into individual hands and living rooms, and confident (mistakenly, at least at first) that there was a latent market that could put it there, Jobs cajoled Wozniak into marketing a computer kit that would rival the Altair.[28] They marketed the kit under the name Apple Computer in 1976.

The original Apple, however, was still little more than a hobbyist's toy; like the Altair, it required far too much expertise in electronics to be useful to everyday folks. To bring about true computer liberation, Jobs realized that Apple needed a machine that would appeal far beyond the hobbyist community. The machine had to be a household appliance, not an electronics engineer's pet project. It would need a keyboard, a color television-like monitor, and long-term storage.[29] It also needed a self-contained case but not a hard metal box with toggle switches and lights like the Altair and its competitors. If it were going to be a friendly household appliance, it had to look and feel like one. So, after studying the European-styled toasters and mixers in the kitchen department at Macy's in San Francisco, Jobs decided that he wanted a smooth, curved, plastic case for the Apple II. The result was an elegant and inviting design that would thereafter become the artifactual signature of Apple computers.[30]

The rest, of course, is legend. To bring the vision to the waiting world, Jobs realized that Apple desperately needed real money and business expertise. Consequently, he courted Mike Markkula, a thirty-four-year-old former Silicon Valley engineer who had become a venture capitalist after hitting big with his stock options at Intel. Markkula became Apple's first major investor in 1976 after being swept off his feet in Jobs's parents' garage—not by Jobs, but by a working Apple computer kit; it "was what I had wanted since I left high school," he would later say.[31]

Markkula brought in Mike Scott, who was even more of a geek. Thirty-two years old, unmarried, and infamous for his obesity and fondness for wearing overtight T-shirts, Scott also was a Silicon Valley engineer and had worked with Markkula in earlier jobs. He became Apple's first CEO in 1977.[32]

Together, the two Steves and the two Mikes (as they became known) formed the core of the new Apple. Markkula and Jobs were the principal choreographers of the Apple II's debut in 1977 at the first West Coast Computer Faire in San Francisco. The now-storied Faire, which was organized largely by Homebrew members, had an atmosphere that was a cross between a trade show and a *Star Trek* convention; the silent "e" in "Faire" was instantly familiar to the techie aficionados of "Dungeons & Dragons" and the Bay Area Renaissance

Faire. Markkula also helped the two Steves land the Silicon Valley marketing firm of Regis McKenna to market the Apple II and inject into the campaign a vision of computer liberation for the masses. The machine's debut print ad was a two-page spread depicting a husband sitting at the kitchen table with his Apple II and a cup of coffee, his wife chopping vegetables in the background and looking over her shoulder at him with a smile. The text on the opposite page opened with the banner, "The home computer that's ready to work, play and grow with you." The copy promised, "You don't even need to know a RAM from a ROM to use and enjoy Apple II. . . . You can begin running your Apple II the first evening, entering your own instructions and watching them work, even if you've had no previous computer experience."[33]

But why own one? You could, according to the ad, use it to help your children do schoolwork, organize household finances or recipes, or "chart your biorhythms." But the ad proclaimed that "the biggest benefit—no matter *how* you use Apple II—is that you and your family increase familiarity with the computer itself." The computer-enhanced future was here, and you needed to be part of it.[34]

❖ ❖ ❖

IN SEARCH OF THE KILLER APP

In reality, the machines themselves—the Apple II and its immediate competitors, like the Commodore PET and Tandy's TRS-80—never convinced the public of their worth. Here is where the technological self-empowerment vision faltered: owning your own computer, though nirvana for the electronics hobbyist, simply did not mean much to anyone else, even if it was easy to use. Computer liberation empowered people to do what? Chart their own biorhythms?

In fact, the only clear value added in owning your own computer was to be able to play video games without lugging pocketfuls of quarters down to the arcade at the mall. The first games available for home computers were direct ports from coin-operated arcade machines; the original Apple II ad encouraged people to play "Pong" as the first step on the way to computer liberation.[35] Versions of "Tank" and "Breakout" (a game that Jobs and Wozniak had created for Atari a few years earlier in which you aim a paddle and a bouncing ball to destroy a wall of bricks) soon followed. Being able to play at home was empowerment of a sort, but it could get a little lonely. It was also the shape of things to come.

But games, even good games, were not enough to create a market. Besides, Atari and others quickly stepped into the market with stand-alone console game systems that hooked up to your television and cost a fraction of an Apple II. The real reason that the home-computer prospect turned into the PC revolution was because of the most boring of computer uses: spreadsheet calculations and word processing. In 1978, Dan Bricklin and Bob Frankson, two Harvard business students, produced VisiCalc for the Apple II. It was a spreadsheet program (*Visible Calc*ulator) and turned out to be the first killer application of the new industry. At about the same time, a forty-something programmer and computer hobbyist named Seymour Rubenstein founded MicroPro in order to sell WordMaster, a word processing program. WordMaster's successor, WordStar, quickly dominated the market when it launched in 1979.[36]

Suddenly, the machines made sense. Now, for a few thousand dollars, a business could replace its expensive financial analysis service with an Apple II and VisiCalc and have a dedicated machine on-site. And with a program like WordStar, large and small companies could realize enormous savings in staff and typing services. With this sort of software, the PC became much more than a toy; it now had the prospect of becoming a valuable, even indispensable, business tool. Apple's revenues climbed from eight hundred thousand dollars in 1977 to forty-eight million dollars by the end of 1979.[37]

By 1980, the waters of the PC market looked inviting after all, and more-established business technology corporations like IBM jumped in. If the Altair and Apple II started the technological revolution in the 1970s, the IBM PC completed it in the 1980s. Contrary to popular myth, the blue suits at Armonk were not oblivious to the tremors underfoot; in fact, aggressive market research had convinced them by the summer of 1980 that the market was real. But they also realized that almost every facet of IBM corporate culture impeded its entry into the new industry. At the time, Big Blue made most of its money on traditional office machines (like typewriters) and on leasing (not selling) large, mainframe computers; most of the profit from the computer business came from IBM's service contracts, and its greatest corporate asset was its nearly invulnerable contract network and direct sales force.[38] Selling tiny computers (and probably through retailers, no less) would undercut all of that. Recall that a fundamental motivator of computer-liberation culture had been to rail against everything that IBM represented.

In addition, IBM's production process was deeply vertically integrated, another emblem of its Steel Age roots: all the components of IBM computers, from the semiconductors to the plastic keyboards, were manufactured in-house. This desire to make everything themselves contributed to IBM's lengthy technology development cycle, which typically took three years from design to production—a hopelessly long time in this new, mercurial industry.[39]

In a story that has become a model for how to manage technological innovation at a hidebound corporation, IBM developed the PC by "boutiquing" it—creating a small, special taskforce (Codename: Project Chess) headquartered not in Armonk but in Boca Raton, Florida, and granting the taskforce special authority to work outside of IBM's traditional R&D and business models. For twelve months, the taskforce used off-the-shelf and subcontracted components; the processor came from Intel (securing Intel's dominance of the market for two decades), the power supplies from Zenith, and the printers from Epson.[40]

Although no one realized it at the time, the most momentous component that IBM outsourced for the PC was the operating system software. Even though it was one of the largest software companies in the world at the time, IBM had no experience writing software for small, stand-alone computers. In keeping with the renegade ethos within Project Chess, it therefore seemed an obvious decision to find an external supplier of the operating system.

Bill Gates thereby walked into the henhouse through the front door. When IBM came calling in 1980, Gates's company, Micro-soft (they dropped the hyphen later), was one of dozens of tiny software start-ups. Gates's geek credentials were strong but unremarkable. The son of a wealthy legal family in Seattle, Washington, Gates had become a computer hobbyist in childhood. At the age of twelve, he and a friend (later Microsoft co-founder, Paul Allen) had written a class-scheduling program for their private school that had the undocumented feature of placing Gates and Allen in classes with the best-looking girls.[41] Gates later went to Harvard with the vague expectation of a career in law but, like so many others in this story, became captivated by the MITS Altair in 1975. He therefore left Harvard a few months later (never to return), and he and Allen trekked to the MITS offices in Albuquerque, New Mexico, to explore the possibility of starting a company to write software for the Altair. Gates and Allen founded Microsoft in Albuquerque in 1975 and developed a reputation among hobbyists as one of many skilled writers of hobby software for the tiny machine.[42]

During the latter 1970s, Gates's greatest claim to fame among computer geeks was a notorious open letter he wrote to the computer-hobbyist community in 1976. Sensing the importance (and riches) that could come from setting technical software standards in the nascent industry, Gates was constantly frustrated with the hobbyist liberation ethic of copying and sharing software; the piracy made it impossible for Microsoft (or anyone) to establish proprietary standards.

His lament was characteristically efficient and imperious: "As the majority of hobbyists must be aware, most of you steal your software. Hardware must be paid for, but software is something to share."[43] But "sharing" was destroying any financial incentive to invest in development and had reduced Gates's own income on Altair software to a wage of about two dollars per hour. "Most directly," he charged, "the thing you do is theft." He urged everyone to pay for all the software they used and to hunt down and ostracize hobby-club members who were software pirates.

Most hobbyists misread the omen and dismissed Gates's letter as an annoying but meaningless rant. *Dr. Dobb's Journal,* in an editorial entitled "Copyright Mania: It's Mine, It's Mine, and You Can't Play with It," described Gates's concern as an "incredible teapot tempest" and suggested that software writers needed to realize that rules that apply to business and industrial customers need not apply to hobbyists. Hobbyists, after all, are not in it for the money.[44]

Gates moved Microsoft to Seattle in 1979, and by 1980 the company had established a sufficient reputation for operating systems to interest IBM for Project Chess; it did not hurt that IBM president John Opel knew Gates's mother (they were both serving on the national board of United Way).[45] Gates quickly understood what IBM needed and promised that he could provide it. He then bought the rights to a preexisting operating system, called QDOS (which stood for Quick and Dirty Operating System), from a local software company for fifty thousand dollars, which was a lot of money for Microsoft at the time. After a few small modifications, Gates renamed it Microsoft DOS, or MS-DOS (claiming that "DOS" now stood for the nonsensical Disk Operating System).[46] But it worked, and it was available, so IBM bought it. Or rather, at Gates's shrewd insistence, they leased it, so that a copy of MS-DOS was licensed with every IBM PC sold, with royalties (and the market dominance to set industrial standards) going back to Microsoft. As is well known, the deal was the first step in making Bill Gates the richest man on Earth.

IBM's machine was in production the following summer. With Big Blue's imprimatur on the box, demand from the business world quickly exceeded IBM's expectations. A few days after the IBM PC's launch in August 1981, the company needed to quadruple production. The machine made $43 million in its first year; by the end of 1984, along with IBM's allied products, it had netted over $4 billion.[47] By the mid-1980s, the IBM PC (or at least its Intel-Microsoft core) was the industry standard.

It is worth noting, however, that in launching its (temporarily) successful bid to take over the burgeoning PC industry, the marketing team at IBM felt compelled to sing Apple's version of the technological self-empowerment song. IBM's market research indicated that the public considered it an efficient and capable but cold and heartless organization. Jim D'Arezzo, the advertising administrator for the IBM PC development project, realized that the IBM PC would somehow have to be friendlier than the Apple, the machine that had defined warm and fuzzy technology. After several failed ad campaign concepts—including using the Muppets, Marcel Marceau, and Beverly Sills—IBM's advertising firm settled on the Tramp—the industrious, hapless, but ultimately victorious everyman portrayed by Charlie Chaplin.[48] The choice was perfect, if achingly ironic. Most consumers must have forgotten Chaplin's leftist political controversies, or the Tramp's most famous scene in *Modern Times* (in which he was literally swallowed by a monstrous industrial machine), for the image of the vulnerable, sympathetic urchin becoming empowered by the friendly and helpful machine allowed IBM to ride the bourgeois version of computer liberation that Jobs had created at Apple. A few years later, in explaining how the IBM PC had vanquished the market, *Time* magazine suggested that "[t]he Tramp, with his ever present red rose, has given IBM a human face."[49]

NERDS AND HEROES

The larger results of these techie efforts, unsurprisingly, would not be clear for another decade or so. The explosive transformation of the technology of American work and leisure would come in the later 1980s and 1990s, as computers replaced not only typewriters but also entire categories of labor, and the Internet transformed computer technology into a communications medium. The infrastructure of the computer-liberation vision of the 1970s was largely in place by the end of the century.

Socially and economically, the greatest consequence was the increasing importance of software. As the processes for designing and producing hardware stabilized quickly in the early 1980s (especially with the supremacy of the IBM PC), the greatest financial opportunities moved to the realm of software; the shift surprised everyone, even apostles of Ted Nelson. Steve Jobs had simply wanted to transform the computer from a big calculator into a cool home appliance. Instead, it became much more than that—it became a medium. And like the printing press, radio, and television before it, after the hardware was pretty much settled, what made the personal computer indispensable was the information it could carry.

Ironically, the transformation of the computer from appliance to medium came not from computer liberation renegades but from their antithesis: the Department of Defense (DoD). The DoD's Advanced Research Projects Agency had been exploring ways to allow researchers to exchange computer files and information over networks since the 1960s. The DoD's network, originally called the ARPAnet, had become popular at many universities by the late 1970s for allowing communication between their large mainframe computers. As they became more prevalent, PCs were able to plug into the same architecture, renamed the Internet, by the early 1980s; through the end of the twentieth century, they would do so by the tens of millions.[50]

Cultural transformation followed the social and economic. For example, the Eighties and Nineties saw a new role for the techie in popular culture. Earlier in the twentieth century, scientifically and technologically empowered characters in fiction usually took the form of villains. Continuing the images of Drs. Faust and Frankenstein, scientists and engineers had commonly been some combination of mad, tyrannical, or monstrous. Movies, plays, and stories centering on scientists intent on destroying the world were moderately popular after World War I and became commonplace after Hiroshima.[51] Dr. Strangelove, Professor Groeteschele (Walther Matthau's Kissingerian monster in *Fail-Safe*), and Dr. Octopus (nemesis of Spiderman), though brilliant and powerful, were not the characters you went to in time of need; and they never, ever, got the girl.

Only slightly better, techies were sometimes played for pathetic laughs. The professor stranded on *Gilligan's Island* could build a nuclear reactor out of some palm fronds and coconuts but was mysteriously unable to fix a three-foot hole in a boat. As late as the 1980s, geeks remained bumblers and weirdos in teen movies, even when they supposedly had their day in 1984's *Revenge of the Nerds.*

There was one early exception. Peter Parker was a teenage geek—socially and sexually isolated, devoted to his science classes, picked on by jocks—until the bite of a radioactive spider transmuted him into the Amazing Spiderman in 1962. Spiderman quickly became the darling of teen geeks everywhere, as well as the anchor of Marvel Comics' domination of the industry. But even here, it was not Parker's geekdom but rather the accidental and unexplained power of radioactivity that made him a hero.

This is what changed in the 1980s and 1990s. In science-fiction novels like William Gibson's *Neuromancer* (1984) and Neal Stephenson's *Snow Crash* (1992), cyberpunk heroes save the day precisely because of their technological prowess. Often set largely within computer-generated environments (Gibson coined the term "cyberspace"), cyberpunk novels allowed geek characters who were undistinguished in the "meat" (real) world to become superheroes in the virtual world. In the meat world, the protagonist of Gibson's *Neuromancer* is imprisoned within a crippled body; in cyberspace, he is a savior.

The geek hero emerged from the niche of science-fiction novels with the blockbuster movie *The Matrix* in 1999. The movie and its sequels feature a group of computer hackers who wage a war for human freedom against a tyrannical computer system. In meat-based reality, the characters are a desperate and ragtag band of human survivors. But in the virtual world, they are fetish-clad bad asses who wield a spectacular arsenal of martial arts skills and automatic weapons. Neo, the central character, ultimately finds that he is able to use the Matrix's mind-machine interface to bend the laws of nature within cyberspace and turn himself into a god—computer liberation–cum geek apotheosis.

It is easy to exaggerate the cultural importance of this geek transformation. It is true, for example, that the greatest appeal of *The Matrix* was its cinematic style, especially the slow-motion "bullet time" camera orbits and the balletic martial-arts sequences that became signatures for the movies; the celebration of techie power in the story line was a secondary draw at best. It is also true that academics probably paid more attention to cyberpunk literature than did geeks themselves; although they started showing up on course syllabi, *Neuromancer* and *Snow Crash* never reached beyond their niche markets. Nevertheless, the geek hero became a broadly recognizable role in American popular culture during the 1980s and 1990s—a development difficult to imagine without the cultural and technological transformation of the 1970s.

CONCLUSION: GEEKING ALONE WITH
THE DESIGNER SELF

Aside from raising the cultural stock of geeks themselves, however, it is not clear that the technological infrastructure of computer liberation has helped realize its cultural goals. In many ways, the social trend for computer technology has paralleled the developments of other technologies that bring greater choice to increasingly disconnected individuals. The evolution from broadcast television to cable television to VCR to TiVo has empowered individuals to tailor their television consumption more precisely (in content, scheduling, and so on) and therefore has segmented this dimension of mass culture along overwhelmingly complex lines. Similarly, the effects of computer self-empowerment have shown ever more clearly that the journey from self-empowerment to isolation can be a short one.

On the one hand, there can be little doubt that technological changes during the 1970s contributed to the oft-lamented decline in social capital in the United States in the decades that followed. For the computer empowered, both working in the office and playing at home have been increasingly typified by sitting at a computer and interacting with other humans through the thin pipe of electron exchange. People on the Internet know only thin slices of one another and may therefore develop only tenuous and haphazard political, social, and cultural bonds with the world.[52] Fun as it may be, sitting at your home computer playing "Everquest Online" with ten thousand of your closest friends is simply not a promising environment for social and cultural exchange.

On the other hand, the thinness of computer identity opens up new kinds of cultural possibilities. People can be whatever they want to be in cyberspace. In e-mail groups, chat rooms, and especially online games, participants can design their personas without regard to the constraints of physics or biology. Passing as a different ethnicity, gender, or even species can be as easy (and low risk) as a mouse click.

This is the world that geeks began building in the 1970s. In an era of political disappointment and cultural malaise, they saw the possibilities of a new and empowered future and had the wherewithal to make it with their hands.

Notes

1. Lewis Mumford, *Technics and Civilization* (1934; repr., New York: Harcourt, Brace, and World, 1963); Thomas P. Hughes, *American Genesis: A Century of Invention and Technological Enthusiasm, 1870–1970* (New York: Penguin, 1989), 300–303.

2. Lewis Mumford, *The Pentagon of Power* (New York: Harcourt Brace Jovanovich, 1970), 1.

3. Ibid., 257.

4. Buckminster Fuller, *Utopia or Oblivion: The Prospects for Humanity* (New York: Bantam Books, 1969).

5. *Nielson Report on Television 1998* (New York: Nielson, 1998); *Communications Industry Report, 1997* (New York: Vronis, Suhler and Associates, 1998); and Cobbett S. Steinberg, *TV Facts* (New York: Facts on File, 1980); quoted in Robert D. Putnam, *Bowling Alone: The Collapse and Revival of American Community* (New York: Simon and Schuster, 2000), 222.

6. E. F. Schumacher, *Small Is Beautiful: Economics As If People Mattered* (New York: Harper and Row, 1973), 52.

7. Langdon Winner, *The Whale and the Reactor: A Search for Limits in an Age of High Technology* (Chicago: University of Chicago Press, 1986), 65; Hughes, *American Genesis*, 453–454; Alan I. Marcus and Howard P. Segal, *Technology in America: A Brief History* (New York: Harcourt Brace Jovanovich, 1989), 356–358.

8. T.A. Heppenheimer, "King Lear," *American Heritage of Invention and Technology* (Spring/Summer 1989): 34–45.

9. On earlier technological utopianism, see Howard P. Segal, *Technological Utopianism in American Culture* (Chicago: University of Chicago Press, 1985).

10. Gary Wolf, "The Curse of Xanadu," *Wired,* June 1995, 141.

11. Ibid.; Martin Campbell-Kelly, and William Aspray, *Computer: A History of the Information Machine* (New York: Basic Books, 1996), 239.

12. Ted Nelson, *Computer Lib/Dream Machines,* rev. ed. (Redmond, WA: Microsoft Press, 1987).

13. Ibid., 5. Emphasis in original.

14. Ibid.

15. Nelson, *Dream Machines*, 41, 141–151; Wolf, "Curse of Xanadu," 141–143.

16. Xanadu remains, in Wolf's words, "the longest-running vaporware story in the history of the computer industry." Nevertheless, Nelson, who regards the World Wide Web as an impotent shadow of Xanadu, remains optimistic.

17. Campbell-Kelly and Aspray, *Computer,* 240–241.

18. Steve Dompier, "Music of a Sort," *Dr. Dobb's Journal of Computer Calisthenics and Orthodontia* 1, no. 2 (1976): 6.

19. Ibid.

20. Ibid.

21. Ibid.

22. "Open the pod bay doors, HAL."

23. Michael S. Malone, *Infinite Loop: How the World's Most Insanely Great Computer Company Went Insane* (New York: Doubleday, 1999), 30–33, 54.

24. Steve Dompier, *Dr. Dobb's Journal* 1, no. 1 (1976), 1.

25. Ibid., 2. Emphasis in original.

26. Campbell-Kelly and Aspray, *Computer*, 245–246; Malone, *Infinite Loop*, 26, 53–57.

27. Campbell-Kelly and Aspray, *Computer*, 246.

28. Ibid.; Malone, *Infinite Loop*, 62–70.

29. Campbell-Kelly and Aspray, *Computer*, 246.

30. Malone, *Infinite Loop*, 120–123.

31. Ibid., 113.

32. Ibid., 120.

33. Apple II's launch print ad is available at http://www.kelleyad.com/Histry.htm, and the complete text is at http://www.faqs.org/faqs/apple2/faq/part14/. See also Campbell-Kelly and Aspray, *Computer*, 248.

34. Apple II print ad, available at http://www.faqs.org/faqs/apple2/faq/part14/.

35. Ibid.

36. Campbell-Kelly and Aspray, *Computer*, 250–251.

37. James Chposky and Ted Leonsis, *Blue Magic: The People, Power, and Politics Behind the IBM Personal Computer* (New York: Facts on File, 1988), 8.

38. Campbell-Kelly and Aspray, *Computer*, 253–254.

39. Ibid.

40. Ibid., 255; Chposky and Leonsis, *Blue Magic*, 26–112.

41. Robert X. Cringely, *Accidental Empires: How the Boys of Silicon Valley Make Their Millions, Battle Foreign Competition, and Still Can't Get a Date* (New York: HarperBusiness, 1996), 97.

42. Campbell-Kelly and Aspray, *Computer*, 241–242.

43. William Henry Gates III, "Open Letter to Hobbyists," February 3, 1976. The letter was distributed through a variety of hobbyist newsletters and magazines. It can be found at many sites on the web, including http://www.blinkenlights.com/classiccmp/gateswhine.html and http://www.tranquileye.com/cyber/1976/gates open letter to hobbyists.html.

44. Jim C. Warren, "Copyright Mania: It's Mine, It's Mine, and You Can't Play with It," *Dr. Dobb's Journal of Computer Calisthenics and Orthodontia* 1, no. 5 (1976): 3.

45. Campbell-Kelly and Aspray, *Computer*, 255.

46. Cringely, *Accidental Empires*, 132–134.

47. Campbell-Kelly and Aspray, *Computer*, 257; Chposky and Leonsis, *Blue Magic*, 180–181.

48. Chposky and Leonsis, *Blue Magic*, 76–79.

49. "Softening a Starchy Image," *Time*, July 11, 1983, 54. See also Chposky and Leonsis, *Blue Magic*, 79–80.

50. Campbell-Kelly and Aspray, *Computer*, 288–300. See also Katie Hafner and Matthew Lyon, *Where Wizards Stay Up Late: The Origins of the Internet* (New York: Simon and Schuster, 1996).

51. Spencer Weart, "The Physicist as Mad Scientist," *Physics Today*, June 1988, 28–37.

52. Putnam, *Bowling Alone*, 169–180.

Contributors

Beth Bailey is a professor of American Studies and Regents Lecturer at the University of New Mexico. Her work focuses on gender and sexuality in twentieth-century American history. Her most recent monograph was *Sex in the Heartland*.

Peter Braunstein is a cultural historian whose work has appeared in such publications as the *Village Voice* and *W Magazine*. He is coeditor of *Imagine Nation: The American Counterculture of the Sixties and Seventies*. Forthcoming works include *Discotheque: Paris, New York, and the Making of Modern; Sin City: New York in the Seventies;* and an Off-Broadway play about Andy Warhol and Edie Sedgwick.

Christopher Capozzola is an assistant professor of history at the Massachusetts Institute of Technology, specializing in twentieth-century U.S. political and cultural history. He teaches classes on post-1960s America and has published essays on the period in *Radical History Review, In These Times,* and *The World the Sixties Made: Politics and Culture in Recent America* (2003).

Jefferson Cowie is an associate professor in the School of Industrial and Labor Relations, Cornell University. He is the author of *Capital Moves: RCA's Seventy-Year Quest for Cheap Labor* and coeditor of *Beyond the Ruins: De-Industrialization and the Meanings of Modern America*.

David Farber is a professor of history at the University of New Mexico. His work focuses on twentieth-century American political history. His most recent monograph was *Sloan Rules: Alfred P. Sloan and the Triumph of General Motors*.

William Graebner is a professor of history at the State University of New York, College at Fredonia. His books include *Coming of Age in Buffalo: Youth and Authority in the Postwar Era* (1990), *The Age of Doubt: American Thought and Culture in the 1940s* (1991), and an edited collection, *True Stories from the American Past* (3rd edition, 2003). He is associate editor of *American Studies*.

Timothy Moy is a historian of science and technology at the University of New Mexico. He is the author of *War Machines* (2001) and writes on the influences of institutional culture upon the historical dynamics between science, technology, and national security in the United States.

Eric Porter is an associate professor of American Studies at the University of California, Santa Cruz. His primary research areas are African American intellectual and cultural history and popular-music studies. He is the author of *What Is This Thing Called Jazz? African American Musicians as Artists, Critics, and Activists.*

Michael Nevin Willard is an assistant professor of history and director of American Studies at Oklahoma State University. He is co-editor of *Generations of Youth: Youth Cultures and History in Twentieth Century America* (1998) and *Sports Matters: Race, Recreation, and Culture* (2002).

Index

❖   ❖   ❖   ❖   ❖   ❖   ❖

Index

Keen, Sam, 161
Keitel, Harvey, 92–93
Kelley, Robin D.G., 62
Kellner, Douglas, 194
Kennedy, image of, 13, 14
Kennedy, John F., 9, 10, 11, 13, 14, 17, 26, 36, 57, 157
Kennedy, Robert, 9, 10, 157
Kent State University, 87, 130
Kerr-McGee, 83
Khomeini, Ayatollah, 9, 20
Killer app, 217–18
King, Billie Jean, 112
King, Martin Luther, Jr., 9, 10, 23, 67, 167
King, Martin Luther, Sr., 16
Klute, 143
Kotto, Yaphet, 92–93
Kristel, Sylvia, 135
Ku Klux Klan, 65
Kwanzaa, 55

Labor, 183
    activists, 82, 83
    attitudes toward, 77–78
    civil rights link with, 95, 97–98
    organized, 75–84, 89–90, 92–93
    and people of color, 54, 64
    productivity, 3
    and race, 82
    and South, 82
    struggles, history of, 102
    and *Work in America* study, 81
    working conditions of, 78, 80–81
Labor unrest, 75–76, 78–84, 102
    in film, 91–93
    flight attendants, 83–84
    General Electric, 75
    General Motors, 76, 79–81
    J.P. Stevens, 82, 91–92, 98
    PATCO, 101
    postal workers, 75, 78–79
    and race, 92–93
    Teamsters' trucking strike, 75–76

UAW, 76, 79–80
UFW, 82–83
Labor-Management group, 99
LaGuardia, Fiorello, 134
Lasch, Christopher, 7, 159, 168, 173, 182, 188, 197
Last Tango in Paris, 138
Late Great Planet Earth, The, 1, 24
Laugh-In, 16
Laverne and Shirley, 90
"Law and order," 41, 65, 139
Leadership
    Christian 22–25
    crisis of, 9–14
    presidential, 10, 15, 17, 20, 22, 25
League of Revolutionary Black Workers, 80
Lear, Norman, 69
Lear, William P., 211
Led Zeppelin, 194
Lee, Bruce, 63, 171
Lee, Leigh, 142
Levison, Andrew, 88, 95
Lewis, Anthony, 20
Lewis, John L., 81
Liberal consensus, 26
Liberalism, 10, 24, 54, 55, 65, 96
    divisions within, 89, 90
    and working class, 77, 85
Liberation, 110, 111–12, 123
    computer, 212–13, 214, 215, 217, 218, 220, 221–22, 224
    self, 189
    sexual, 135–36, 138
Liberation News Service, 110
Liberty Baptist College, 24
Lichtenstein, Nelson, 96
Liepe–Levinson, Katherine, 151
Lifton, Robert, 173
Lindsay, Hal, 1, 24
Lindsay, John, 130
Looking for Mr. Goodbar, 117–19, 146
Lordstown, Ohio, 80, 92–93
Lorna Doom. *See* Ryan, Terri

❖ 238 ❖